Mexico: A History

Plaza of the Three Cultures, Tlatelolco.

Mexico: A History

by
Robert Ryal Miller

UNIVERSITY OF OKLAHOMA PRESS : NORMAN

BY ROBERT RYAL MILLER

For Science and National Glory: The Spanish Scientific Expedition to America, 1862-1866 (Norman, 1968)
Arms Across the Border: United States Aid to Juárez During the French Intervention in Mexico (Philadelphia, 1973)
Chronicle of Colonial Lima: The Diary of Josephe and Francisco Mugaburu, 1640-1697 (Norman, 1975)
Latin America (co-author with John Francis Bannon and Peter M. Dunne) (Encino, 1977, and Minneapolis, 1982)
Mexico: A History (Norman, 1985)

Library of Congress Cataloging in Publication Data

Miller, Robert Ryal.
  Mexico: a history.

  Bibliography: p. 381.
  Includes index.
  1. Mexico—History. I. Title.
F1226.M64 1985   972   84-28105
ISBN 0-8061-1932-2 (alk. paper)

The paper in this book meets the guidelines for permanence and durability of the Committee on Production Guidelines for Book Longevity of the Council on Library Resources, Inc.

Contents

Illustrations

Unless otherwise credited, all photographs were made by the author.

Maps and Tables

MAPS

All maps drawn by Robert E. Winter

TABLES

Preface

IT IS DIFFICULT to compress the complex and colorful history of Mexico into a single book. Few countries have had such an interesting past: several remarkable Indian civilizations; the dramatic Spanish conquest; three colonial centuries during which there was a blending of Old World and New World cultures; a decade of wars for independence heralded by a firebrand priest; the struggle of the young republic; its wars with the United States and France; confrontation between the Indian president, Juárez, and the Austrian-born emperor, Maximilian; a long dictatorship under Díaz; the Great Revolution that destroyed debt peonage, confiscated Church property, and reduced foreign economic power; and Mexico's recent drive to modernize through industrialization. These are conspicuous highlights, but they do not illuminate aspects of social history such as the daily life of peasants and urban workers, the important role of women, or the genius of many creative artists, writers and thinkers.

The writing of this book grew out of the need for a synthesis of Mexican history that would incorporate the traditional narrative with social and cultural life, recent historical findings, and representative primary sources. As a unique feature each chapter contains excerpts from books, letters, reports, decrees, or poems that were written during the period being described. In choosing the readings an attempt was made to select observations about daily life, dramatic events, or descriptions of principal historical figures. These firsthand reports lend authenticity and historical flavor to the eras discussed; at the same time, they expose readers to some of the vast literature and bibliography of Mexican history.

This book is the product of thirty years of professional

interest in Mexican history. It reflects the author's graduate studies at the Universities of California and Mexico, more than two decades of teaching university classes in Mexican history, continual reading and research, and recurrent visits to various regions of Mexico. The text relies heavily on the research of many scholars whose monographs are listed in the bibliography. Since there is scholarly controversy about many points of Mexican history, some readers may disagree with facts or interpretations presented here—a reaction that is inevitable in a survey that touches on many disciplines and spans many centuries.

It is not feasible to acknowledge individually the many persons who have helped shape this book, but generally they include colleagues, librarians, writers, and friends on both sides of the Rio Grande (*Río Bravo del Norte*). Most of all I am indebted to my former students, who over the years asked provocative questions, argued cogently, or contributed information and impressions. I hope this work will be useful to students as well as aficionados and general readers who wish to become acquainted with the principal characters, events, and trends of Mexico's exciting history.

                                                                            R. R. M.
Berkeley, California

Mexico: A History

CHAPTER 1

Early Indian Cultures

MEXICO'S HUMAN HISTORY BEGAN with the aboriginal people we call Indians—American Indians or Amerinds, to distinguish them from East Indians. Their archaeological records go back at least ten thousand years, and circumstantial evidence doubles that figure. Excavated sites reveal the presence of primitive men and women who used fire, had chipped-stone tools, and lived by hunting game and gathering wild plants. Over the centuries, hundreds of native tribes developed their own cultures, but only a few perfected an advanced civilization. Who were these "first Mexicans," and where did they come from? The records are meager; we must rely on scant archaeological evidence, oral traditions, comparison of artistic styles, and informed conjecture.

When Columbus landed in the Caribbean islands, he thought he was near India and called the natives "Indians." Ever since that time the aboriginal people of the New World have been considered to be of Asian or Mongoloid stock. A few writers or investigators proposed other hypotheses that are not generally accepted today: that the natives were emigrants from the mythical continents of Atlantis or Mu, descendants of Phoenicians or Egyptians, or remnants of lost tribes of Israel. According to one theory, man originated in the Americas, but that is highly improbable, because no remains of pre-Homo sapiens men have ever been found here, although they have been uncovered in Africa, Europe, and Asia.

Virtually all scholars believe that the primitive people of the Western Hemisphere originated in Asia. The most commonly held theory is that bands of hunters came to Alaska from northeastern Asia, using a land or ice bridge across

the Bering Strait. This gradual movement from Siberia probably occurred thirty to forty thousand years ago during the
Pleistocene Epoch (Ice Age), when the level of the oceans
was much lower than today. Successive waves of Mongoloids,
in pursuit of game or fleeing from danger, penetrated ever
deeper into the New World, pushing earlier groups south
and east. Assuming that the great majority of the first Americans came to this continent via the Bering Strait does not
preclude the possibility of other arrivals by sea along the
Aleutian Island chain, or transpacific crossings from Poly-
nesia or Asia. And over the centuries there may have been
a few people who crossed the Atlantic Ocean from Europe
or Africa, sailing west on purpose or carried that direction
by winds and currents. But the red men that the white men
encountered in America in 1492 certainly were neither Ne-
groid nor Caucasian—instead they were akin to Orientals.

There are a number of suggestive links between the peoples
and cultures of Asia and those of aboriginal America. Native
Americans do have physical body similarities to Asians—
brownish complexions, straight black hair, dark eyes, high
cheekbones set in a broad face, prominent teeth, and scant
body hair. Many Oriental and some Amerind babies, especially Maya, are born with the blue "Mongolian spot" at the
base of their spine. Philologists have pointed out linguistic
parallels: Chinese is monosyllabic and tonal, so are the Oto-
mían languages spoken in Mexico; and there are similarities
in their origin legends and fairy tales. The ancient Hindu
board game of pachisi (the modern Parcheesi) is almost identical to *patolli*, a game played by the Toltec and Aztec Indians. Art historians have noted common designs, such as
the lotus motif, in Asian and American Indian architecture
and pottery, along with the prizing of jade over all other
materials—an Oriental and Amerind phenomenon. Aboriginal burial sites containing jade associated with human skeletons have been unearthed in various parts of Mexico.

The scattered groups of nomadic hunters who first came to
what is now called Mexico were in the Paleolithic (Stone
Age) stage of development. Using traps, slings, throwing

sticks (*atlatls*), and stone-tipped spears they slaughtered the now extinct species of mammoth, camel, and wild horse, as well as bison, bear, deer, and smaller mammals. A veritable zoo of these animal bones has been found near Puebla, where archaeologists have unearthed associated stone and bone artifacts and remains of 20,000-year-old campfires, but no human skeletal remains. In 1947 they did find fossilized human bones near Tepexpán, northeast of Mexico City, and nearby in the same geological stratum were skeletons of two mammoths with chipped-stone points imbedded in their ribs. These fossils, and other artifacts found not far away, are estimated to be about ten thousand years old.

As food gatherers and hunters, these earliest Mexicans wandered in bands or family groups, foraging for fruits, seeds, or roots of wild plants. They collected various berries, mesquite beans, onion bulbs, piñon nuts, sunflower seeds, and prickly pear cactus fruit (tunas). After the big game became extinct about 7000 B.C.—probably because of the dramatic shift to a desert-like climate that affected northern and central Mexico at that time—they hunted deer, peccary, and smaller game, fished in lakes or streams, and trapped armadillos, birds, gophers, iguanas, rabbits, serpents, and turtles. Over the millennia, the bands were incorporated into tribes that grew in numbers, developed distinct languages, and elaborated more complex cultures. In domestic arts the Indians fabricated nets for snaring fish and animals; made baskets; fashioned clothing from fur, feathers, or hides; and wove fibers of cotton, yucca, sisal, and maguey.

About 7000 B.C. some ancestral Mexicans discovered agriculture—that is, that seeds and roots could be planted to produce more of the same kind. Very gradually they domesticated several plants: beans, squash, and eventually maize or Indian corn. Maize cultivation was a crucial step toward agriculture and an advanced civilization. They planted the corn along with squash and bean seeds in holes made with a fire-hardened digging stick. Their first ears of maize were less than three centimeters (about an inch) long and bore about fifty small kernels, but as time went on, the cobs grew larger because of seed selection and careful cultivation. Eventually, the hybrid would not reproduce without man's intervention. Indian women discovered several ways to prepare maize for eating. They roasted or boiled the ears, or hulled the corn and ground the dry kernels on a flat stone metate quern. Parched, ground corn, sometimes mixed with spices, was added to water for a nutritious drink, pinole; corn flour dough was used for tamales or in a porridge called atole; but most often the dough was patted out as tortillas, the thin unleavened cakes widely used as bread (even today), which they cooked on stone slabs heated by charcoal fires.

Ultimately, the practice of agriculture liberated some of the nomadic tribes from a constant search for food and permitted them to settle down. They acquired additional land for cultivation by burning undergrowth or jungle, by terracing the slopes, and by draining or filling suitable plots. This development was accompanied by an increase in population. The combination of an agricultural basis and village life gave the people more leisure time, made possible vast public projects, and led to chiefdoms, or hierarchical social systems wherein certain groups, such as the chief and his relatives, were supported by the rest of the population. It also became necessary to develop more elaborate rules or laws for land and water usage and to regulate societal behavior.

By 2000 b.c., many of the former hunter-gatherers had become farmers, dependent on agriculture and living in villages. Enjoying a regular food supply and sedentary life, they constructed thatch-roofed houses of poles or wattle daubed with mud. About this time they began to make fired clay cult objects and ceramic vessels used for dishes and to store foodstuffs and liquids. In some areas farmers irrigated their fields using crude dams and ditches, an innovation that increased their food supply. Eventually, their dams were impressive masonry structures. The American Indians never did invent the plow or make practical use of the wheel, except for some wheeled toys or cult objects; nor did the Middle American natives have any draft animals to help work their fields or carry their loads—human beings performed all the labor.

Through experiments in utilization of wild plants—their seeds, leaves, fruit, roots, bark, fiber, or resin—and the domestication of various wild vegetables, the more advanced Indian groups gradually acquired a sizable pharmacopoeia as well as additional foodstuffs to complement the trinity of maize, beans, and squash. The dozens of edible plants they tamed or used included avocados, chile peppers, tomatoes, mushrooms, amaranth, sunflowers, papaya, vanilla and cacao (chocolate). They supplemented their vegetarian diet with occasional game as well as eggs, fish, turtles and meat from domesticated dogs, ducks, and turkeys. For pleasure they smoked the rolled-up leaves of a native plant called *tabaco*, drank a fermented beer made from a species of agave, and some of them chewed chicle gum from the chicozapote tree.

As their society became more complex, so did their religion. To regulate planting and harvesting, shaman priests made astronomical observations and developed a calendar that involved mathematical calculations and some kind of record keeping. Priests organized celebrations related to fertility, rainmaking, and harvesting, and they presided over ceremonies connected with human birth, death, illness, and with civic affairs. Indian priests directed the construction of sacred mounds, usually built in the form of flat-topped pyramids, as centers for religious observances. At the pyramids and in their homes, Indians had idols made of wood, fired clay, bone, or stone to honor their deities or to serve as cult amulets. Evidence of human sacrifices shows an early concern with appeasing the forces of nature, and items associated with burials suggest that they had the concept of an afterlife.

Civilizations—generally defined as a relatively high level of human cultural and technological development—evolved in several parts of Mexico. Prominent features of these advanced cultures included: social stratification, labor specialization, monumental architecture, elaborate religious hierarchies closely integrated with the political structure, intensive agriculture, efficient methods for the distribution of food and other products, and a system of writing or record keeping. The evolution of civilized society was the culmination of millennia of cultural developments and ecological adaptation.

Many archaeologists and historians divide pre-Columbian cultures into three distinct phases of development. The first, called the Formative or pre-Classic, dates from 2500 B.C. to A.D. 1; next is the Classic period, which embraced the first nine centuries of the Christian era; and finally the post-Classic from A.D. 900 to 1520. This scheme is useful for classifying artifacts and making cross-cultural comparisons, but since some of the civilizations span more than one period, it will be more convenient here to narrate the history of the principal advanced cultures, identifying them by their tribal names. Actually, we do not know what some of the people called themselves; for them we use names applied much later.

The term Mesoamerica, or Middle America, refers to the region from central Mexico southward through Guatemala, western Honduras and Nicaragua, to the Gulf of Nicoya in Costa Rica, where similar higher Amerind civilizations flourished. (It runs from about 22° to 10° North Latitude.) Except for a few small river valleys, the desert-like lands north of the "civilized frontier" were unsuitable for agriculture and were inhabited by the Chichimecs and other semi-nomadic barbarian tribes. By contrast, the high plateaus of Mesoamerica, where fertile valleys and plains lie between higher mountains, were ecologically favorable for planting and for supporting a dense population. So were some lowland regions of Mesoamerica that had good soil and adequate rainfall. Here various Indian groups developed advanced cultures. They did not rise and thrive at the same time; indeed, some were long gone when others flowered, but the later ones often borrowed ideas, techniques, and sometimes even gods from the earlier ones.

Each Middle American Indian civilization had distinctive traits, but all had several things in common. They depended on maize as a staple food, as Mexicans still do; they cultivated maguey (agave) plants for fiber and for a beer-like beverage (*octli* or *pulque*); their polytheism was based on worshiping the forces of nature; they built truncated pyramids which served as platforms for their temples and in at least one case also served as a burial place for a dignitary; they had dual calendars, ceremonial and solar; and their crafts had reached a high level of artistic style and technical competence. Most of the advanced Indian societies had outdoor ball courts where games were played for the amusement of the upper class. A typical ball court had two stone rings or goals, one set vertically on each sidewall. Players were not permitted to use their hands—they maneuvered the rubber ball with feet, legs, hips, shoulders, and head. Sometimes they played a ball game to determine a question of state. Native leaders believed that the gods would show their preference by aiding one side or the other.

Ironically, one of the oldest pre-Columbian civilizations, the Olmec, is also the newest; that is, it was "discovered" and studied only since the late 1930s. This pre-Classic culture, which gradually emerged in the swampy lowlands of the Veracruz-Tabasco coast, flourished for hundreds of years in the first millennium B.C.; the most frequently cited dates are 1200 to 400 B.C. We do not know what these early people called themselves, but later dwellers in their homeland were called Olmecs (People of the Rubber Country). That area was long known for the latex extracted from native rubber trees (*guayule*) which was used for rubber balls and for waterproofing baskets and cloth. Olmecs ate seafood, aquatic birds, and toads, and they cultivated maize as well as harvested cacao trees. Their rise to civilization was related to an extensive trade network that may have been responsible for the emergence of a wealthy elite and the stratification of society.

The Olmecs did not build great cities, but they embellished their splendid, well-planned ceremonial centers with massive basalt monoliths. Three principal Olmec sites are called La Venta, San Lorenzo, and Tres Zapotes. At the first place, located on a small, swampy island in the Tonolá River, these founders built a complex of temples, mounds, and ceremon-

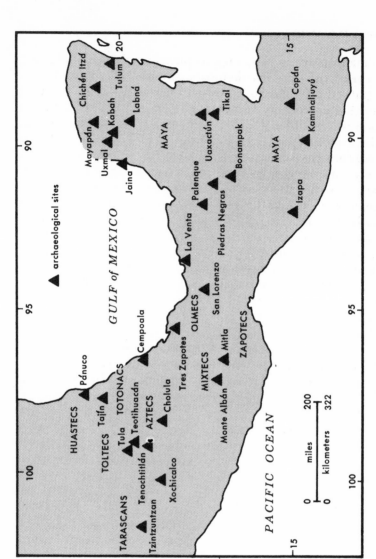

Pre-Columbian Indian Cultures and Sites

ial markers around rectangular plazas neatly oriented along a north-south axis. The dominant cone-shaped pyramid, built of packed clay and rising over thirty meters (one hundred feet) high, probably represented a volcano. The principal plaza was enclosed by rows of naturally shaped hexagonal pillars of basalt placed side by side to form a solid wall; these columns were quarried almost one hundred kilometers (sixty miles) away, as were the six enormous stone altars. Carved on the altars are scenes depicting important personages wearing elaborate headdresses, and on one altar the central figure, undoubtedly a priest, is shown emerging from a niche with a baby in arms. A motif of squalling babies carved on other altars hints at infant sacrifice, and the image of a man with Semitic features and a triangular beard suggests the possibility of a visitor from the Near East. Olmec ruins also have burial tombs, serpentine mosaic floors, hematite mirrors, and exquisitely carved jade figurines.

Colossal stone heads, some measuring three meters (nine feet) high and weighing eighteen metric tons, are the most spectacular feature of Olmec art. Archaeologists have found more than a dozen of these enormous ovoid monuments, which are believed to be portraits of actual Olmec leaders. The carved heads are topped by helmet-like caps that may have been worn in ritualistic ball games, and the faces have broad nostrils and thick lips like some Totonac Indians who still live in the general area. The question of how these monoliths were transported can only be answered with a guess that the ancients used rafts on artificial canals or waterways that have since disappeared.

The distinctive Olmec art style is recognized by figures with pear-shaped heads, wide noses, baby faces, large lips, drooping mouths, and sometimes with jaguar fangs. Pathological beings—dwarfs, hunchbacks, club-footed individuals—were often the subject matter, along with nude males and jaguar-man figures. The latter have been identified with the rain god. Olmec-style artifacts also have been found in the high plateaus of Mesoamerica. They are seen in clay figurines at Tlatilco in the Valley of Mexico, on the contorted life-sized

Olmec colossal head at La Venta. Photograph by Constantino Reyes-Valerio.

figures carved on large slabs at Monte Albán in Oaxaca, in southwestern Mexico, and on objects as far south as Guatemala and El Salvador. The objects or the style itself may have been diffused by traders, missionaries, or warriors. In addition to their artistic accomplishments, the Olmecs pioneered in astronomy, mathematics, and glyph writing. They also had Mesoamerica's earliest-known ball court.

We know little about the daily life of the Olmecs, their political organization, or reasons for the collapse of their civilization. San Lorenzo was violently destroyed about 900 B.C., and five centuries later La Venta suffered a similar catastrophe. The deliberate mutilation of stone monuments at these sites suggests internal rebellion or external invasion. Olmec cultural achievements did not disappear with the loss of these centers; they remained viable in the homeland for several hundred years and were passed on to other Mesoamerican peoples. Izapa, a temple and trading center near the Mexican-Guatemalan border, seems to have been a transition point where Olmec ideas moved on to highland Maya Indian settlements, especially to the early site of Kaminaljuyú in the outskirts of the present Guatemala City. Some archaeologists are convinced that the Olmecs were a northern branch of the early Maya culture; other scholars believe that the two were not closely related.

The ancient Maya Indians created a spectacular civilization in southern Mesoamerica. In many ways their achievements surpass all other native American groups — certainly their superb monumental remains are more numerous. Some historians have compared the Maya to the ancient Greeks, noting that both made great intellectual advances, designed aesthetically pleasing works of art and passed their civilization on to other peoples. Millions of their descendants still inhabit parts of southeastern Mexico, Guatemala, Belize, Honduras, and El Salvador, where they cultivate indigenous plants, produce traditional folk art, and speak various dialects of the Maya language.

Their history in the early Formative era is obscure, but for more than a thousand years before A.D. 300 the Maya per-

fected their agriculture, religion, and arts. By the first century B.C. they lived in small agricultural villages and cultivated maize, beans, squash, and in some places harvested cacao, vanilla, sisal, and cotton. From the last two plants they
made rope, mats, hammocks, and clothing. They also traded
extensively by land and sea with people far to the north and
south. Ecological adaptation, institutional order, and an understanding of higher mathematics were bases upon which
the Maya civilization was built.

Within the vast Maya area archaeologists distinguish three
geographical regions where different cultures evolved. The
highlands of central Guatemala, adjacent El Salvador, and
Honduras provided fertile land, a benign climate, and other
resources to support a large population, then and now. Many
early settlement sites, such as Kaminaljuyú, have been uncovered in the high inter-mountain valleys. The low-lying
Yucatán peninsula was a second ecological zone settled by
the Maya. It is a tropical plain, virtually treeless, with shallow soil deposits and very little rainfall; nevertheless, an
adequate supply of sub-surface water and natural wells (ce-
notes) along with man-made cisterns makes cultivation possible. Settled by humans long ago, this northern lowland
region still has a high population. Between Yucatán and the
highlands is a third Maya region that is scarcely inhabited
today, the central lowlands with its Petén jungle core and
adjacent uplands in Chiapas, Belize, and Honduras. Mostly
covered by dense tropical forests interspersed by rivers and
swamps, and with heavy rainfall and humidity that make
even slash and burn agriculture difficult, this region seems
least suitable for human settlement; yet it was here that the
Maya civilization flowered early and reached its highest peak.

The golden age of the Maya occurred from A.D. 300 to 900,
when their culture flourished in the central lowlands. During this Classic period they built the great ceremonial centers
known today as Bonampak, Copán, Palenque, Piedras Negras,
Tikal, Uaxactún, and a dozen others. A remarkable system of
causeways (sacbeob) connected some of these places, facili-
tating collection of tribute and exchange of trade items. These

The Palace, Maya temple at Palenque. Photograph by Dianne Weiss.

"cities" were not typical urban communities; instead they were civic-religious centers that had some elite dwellings, and dispersed in the surrounding area were scattered hamlets where the bulk of the peasants lived.

The genius of the Maya is revealed in their extant monuments at the Classic era sites. Here are handsome limestone temples with mansard-type roofs topped with decorative combs; stone-faced pyramids that usually served as a base for temples; cut-stone buildings that seem to have been used as government headquarters and official residences; ball courts, gateways, plazas, carved stone pillars (stelae); and water-reservoirs—all constructed without metal tools. The Maya, who invented and utilized the corbeled vault or arch that is the hallmark of their Classic architecture, were the only pre-Columbian Indians who used any form of the arch. Unlike the public buildings, houses of the ordinary men and women who toiled in these centers have long since disappeared, because they were made of wood, mud, and thatch.

15

Mural of warriors and captives, Maya temple at Bonampak. Courtesy Instituto Nacional de Antropología e Historia.

Maya clay figurine of a dignitary, Island of Jaina.
Courtesy Instituto Nacional de Antropología e His-
toria.

Yet, in many places, vestiges of the raised earth floors of these houses can be located.

Vivid colors were characteristic of Maya architecture and art. Their important buildings were decorated with friezes, frescoes, and stucco ornamentation. Traces of red and blue paint indicate that stelae and structures—even the limestone pyramids—were painted, and fragments of their textiles show the same proclivity for bright colors. Aside from their considerable aesthetic and technical merit, the realistic frescoed wall paintings, especially those at Bonampak, reveal much about life in their golden age. They show musicians with their instruments (drums, trumpets, flutes, whistles, rattles), nobles being served a banquet, dancers and entertainers, warrior chiefs in their elaborate costumes, and captured slaves who had been mutilated or tortured. Additional daily life data can be gleaned from pictures on the superb polychrome pottery and from many clay figurines such as those found on the island of Jaina. Maya artists often incorporated numbers and dates into their works.

The Maya numerical system was a brilliant achievement that paved the way for their advancements in astronomy, engineering, and calendrical calculations. With only three symbols—a dot for one, a bar for five, and a shell-like figure for zero—they made complicated computations by using a positional mode that increased by twenties from bottom to top (unlike our decimal system, which increases by tens from right to left of the decimal point). The bottom, or units, position recorded numbers from 0 through 19; the second position sub-total was multiplied by twenty; the third position multiplied by 400 (20x20); and so on, as shown in Table 1.

The Maya concept of zero antedated by many centuries its use in Europe, where it was introduced about A.D. 1200 by Arabs who had acquired the idea earlier from the Hindu culture in India. Maya priests combined mathematics and astronomy to develop a solar calendar that was more accurate than the contemporary Julian calendar used in Europe. Their Long Count dating system reckoned days from a mythical beginning correlated to 3,113 B.C.

Maya numerals also had an alternative form, a glyph that

TABLE 1. *Maya Counting System*

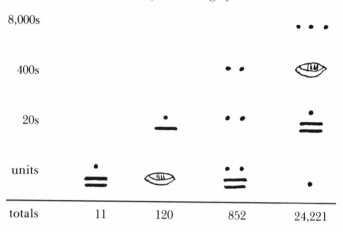

8,000s				● ● ●
400s			● ●	⬗
20s		●	● ●	●
units	●	⬗	● ●	●
totals	11	120	852	24,221

was the head of an animal, a bird, or a mythological creature. Numerical symbols were only part of the written communication pattern.

Maya hieroglyphic writing was the most sophisticated of all the American Indian inscription systems. More than four hundred glyphs, representing numbers, dates, colors, and more complicated matters, were chiseled in stone, painted in wet plaster and on pottery, and drawn in primitive books made from paper derived from the inner bark of the wild fig tree. These paper records, or codices, were folded accordian-fashion. Only three of them survive today, one each in Madrid, Paris, and Dresden. (There is also an unauthenticated fragment known as the Grolier Codex.) The glyphs, only partly deciphered today, recorded data and abstract knowledge related to chronology, astronomy, religion, and highlights of the rule of certain leaders.

Classic Maya society was stratified. At the top was an elite hereditary nobility composed of priests and ranking officials and their families; the middle sectors were the majority, the families of craftsmen and specialists, commoners, and peasant farmers; and at the bottom was a large component of slaves who were convicted criminals, or prisoners of war, or those who sold themselves or were sold by their families into

A Maya codex, or primitive book. Courtesy Instituto Nacional de Antropología e Historia.

servitude. Children of slaves were born free. Many scholars believe that the Classic Maya political organization was theocratic; others maintain there was a secular ruler and a high priest. Certainly there was a hierarchy of priests who were carried on litters and whose functions included prophesy, medicine, education of candidates for the priesthood, and religious rituals.

The Maya were polytheistic. Two chief gods in their pantheon were Itzamná, benevolent friend of man and inventor of writing, and Ix Chel, the moon goddess who was patroness of healing and pregnancy. Other important deities were patrons of rain (Chac), wind, maize, hunting, music, war, death, and a special goddess of suicides. Maya iconography is difficult to decipher because the supernatural beings had multiple manifestations, attributes, and symbols.

After six hundred years of splendor in the central lowlands, development suddenly ceased and the Maya centers were abandoned. No inscriptions dated later than A.D. 950 have been found there. Although there is some evidence of foreign intruders at the end of the Classic period, it is not believed that military conquest caused the collapse. Scholars have suggested several possible reasons: a maize virus, soil exhaustion, prolonged drought, epidemic disease, hurricanes, or supernatural visions perceived by leaders who were told to move elsewhere. But the best evidence points to peasant insurrections. Apparently the workers, oppressed by an increasing tax and work load to support the nobles and priests, retreated into the jungle, whereupon the whole society collapsed. The demographic and vital center of lowland civilization then shifted to northern Yucatán. The Maya highland petty states and chiefdoms, which had lagged far behind Classic era lowland developments, continued to exist.

A Maya renaissance occurred in northern Yucatán beginning in the tenth century. During this post-Classic period old centers in Yucatán were rebuilt and new ones were established near natural wells, the only reliable source of fresh water. Culture, techniques, and traditions from the south were transplanted in the north, perhaps carried there by priests or refugees. But the striking feature of this period

Maya-Toltec pyramid-temple of Kukulcan (or the Castillo), Chichén Itzá.

Maya-Toltec astronomical observatory, Chichén Itzá.

was the influence from central Mexico that came with an actual invasion by Nahuatl-speaking Toltecs who settled down and fused their culture with the Maya. The architecture of this renascent Maya-Toltec period is not as refined as the Classic period, but it has a grandeur based on magnitude coupled with a simplicity of decoration.

Both Maya and Toltec traditions confirm the merging of their cultures. A Toltec legend tells how one of their leaders, Quetzalcoatl ("Feathered Serpent" in Nahuatl), expelled from their chief city of Tula (then called Tollan) after a factional dispute, made his way to the Gulf Coast with a group of partisans. A parallel Maya historical tradition recalls that about the year 1000 the Toltec warrior Kukulcán ("Feathered Serpent" in Mayan) led followers to Yucatán where they seized the city of Chichén Itzá and rebuilt it. At this time, Toltec features first appeared in Yucatecan architecture: stone columns to support temple roofs, friezes of skulls, Chac-mools (statues of reclining figures with flexed knees), and

Chacmool figure, Chichén Itzá. Photograph by Robert Yaryan.

especially the feathered serpent motif. The warlike Toltecs also introduced human sacrifice on a large scale.

Maya-Toltec culture flourished for a few hundred years in Yucatán before it disintegrated. Oral traditions suggest that political stability was first maintained through a confederation or league of three cities: Chichén Itzá, Mayapán (a walled city), and Uxmal. Then about A.D. 1200 Mayapán destroyed Chichén Itzá and dominated the area until it was annihilated in a revolt in the mid-fifteenth century. Thereafter, small independent chiefdoms were established, but their intermittent civil wars hastened the cultural decline. The final blow to Maya civilization came from the Spanish, who first overran the highland Maya chiefdoms and then invaded the northern lowlands.

When Spanish conquistadors came to Yucatán in the second decade of the sixteenth century, they found destroyed cities and a disunited Maya-speaking people who could not read their ancient hieroglyphic writing. Although their political structure had waned and their culture and technology had declined, the Yucatecan self-sufficient economic base continued. Because of the native demographic dispersal and fierce guerrilla warfare tactics, the Spaniards had a difficult time subduing the region. The conquest lasted from 1527 to 1546, and one last group, the Itzá, who had retreated south to Lake Petén, maintained an isolated independence until 1697. Thus the first advanced Indian civilization seen by the Europeans—Columbus encountered a Maya trading canoe in 1502—was the last to be conquered.

Spanish conquistadors and missionary priests are responsible for the destruction of evidence about the Maya as well as for the preservation of it. In their zeal to abolish old religious practices, they destroyed temples, idols, stelae, and dozens of hieroglyphic books. The dismantled native shrines provided excellent building materials for erecting their colonial churches, homes, and public buildings. At the same time, a few literate Spaniards were interested in recording native oral traditions; their reports and journals reflect European impressions of the Maya culture as they encountered it in the sixteenth century.

Diego de Landa, a missionary who later became the first bishop of Yucatán, destroyed many of the codices, yet he also compiled a long report that is a principal source of our information about the Maya. In the following excerpts from his account he describes marriage customs of the Yucatecan Maya:

In olden times they married when they were twenty years old; but now they marry when they are twelve or fourteen. And on this account repudiation takes place more easily, since they marry without love and ignorant of married life and of the duties of married people. . . .
They never took a wife who bore their own name on the father's side . . . and if any married their sisters-in-law, wives of their broth-

ers, it was considered wicked. . . . They married all their other relations on their mother's side even though they were their own first
cousins. The fathers take great care to seek wives in good time of
good quality and position for their sons, and if possible of the same
place as themselves. It was considered mean-spirited for men to
seek wives for themselves, or for the fathers to seek marriage for
their daughters, and for arranging the matter, they employed
match-makers to take charge of this business. These affairs being
discussed and arranged, they settled on the ceremony and the
dowry, which was very small, and the father of the youth gave it
to the father-in-law and besides the dowry, the mother-in-law made
clothes for the daughter-in-law and for her son. And when the day
arrived, they assembled in the house of the bride's father and a
repast being prepared there, the guests and the priest came and
after the couple to be married and the fathers-in-law had gathered,
the priest arranged to do what they wished, since the fathers-in-law
had considered the matter thoroughly and were agreeable to it.
And so they gave his wife to the young man that night, if he was
ready for it. At once they had a feast and banquet, and from this
time forward the son-in-law stayed in the house of his father-in-
law for five or six years.*

  After the Spanish conquest some erudite natives used the
Maya language and Spanish script to record their oral traditions, mythology, and history in three important works known
in English as: the *Books of Chilam Balam*, the *Annals of the
Cakchiquels*, and *Popol Vuh: The Sacred Book of the Ancient
Quiché Maya*. Much of this lore was once recorded in hieroglyphic codices.
  Between Maya territory and the highland Valley of Mexico is the cultural crossroads of Oaxaca, home of the distinctive
Zapotec and Mixtec Indians. Both of these groups developed
advanced cultures that were as complex as any Mesoamerican
civilization. The origins of each society are clouded—a felici-
tous word since both called themselves "Cloud People."
  The Zapotec heydey occurred during the Classic era (A.D.

*Alfred M. Tozzer, ed. and trans., *Landa's Relaciòn de las Cosas de Yuca-
tán*, Papers of the Peabody Museum, 18:100–101 (Cambridge, 1941). Copyright by the President and Fellows of Harvard College.

200–900), when their principal center was at the hilltop of
Monte Albán. This crest, which overlooks the city of Oaxaca,
is located at the junction of three valleys; it had been a ceremonial center for hundreds of years before the Zapotecs shaped
it into an urban complex. The top of the hill was leveled to
form a gigantic plaza more than three hundred meters (330
yards) long, surrounded by pyramids, palaces, a ball court,
elaborately decorated tombs, and an observatory. The slopes
and adjacent hills were residential zones. Artifacts found
here show influences from the Gulf Coast, Yucatán, and the
central highlands. Like other advanced cultures, the Zapotecs
had a vigesimal counting system using bar and dot number
glyphs, and they had dual calendars, a ceremonial one of 260
days and another one based on the solar year.

About A.D. 900 the empire radiating from Monte Albán collapsed, and the hilltop complex was abandoned. Perhaps the
cause of this disintegration was related to the rise of militaristic societies and the contemporary turmoil throughout
Mesoamerica. In the succeeding post-Classic era rival Zapotec groups remained in the Oaxaca valleys—their political
chiefs sometimes at Zaachila and their priests at Mitla (Place
of the Dead), an old sacred site and necropolis forty-five
kilometers (twenty-seven miles) southeast of Monte Albán.
Mitla's temple architecture is unique, with handsome fitted
stone mosaic friezes in forty geometric designs, including
step frets, scrolls, and squared spirals. At the end of the
thirteenth century a few Mixtecs moved south into the Valley
of Oaxaca, where some of their elite intermarried with Zapotecs. Then, in the following century, the Mixtecs conquered
Zaachila and forced the principal Zapotec ruler to seek refuge in Tehuantepec. Subsequently, the Mixtecs expanded
their control over the region from their political center of
Cuilapan (also called Sayacu).

The Mixtecs, whose cultural crucible seems to have been
in the mountains between the Valley of Oaxaca and southern
Puebla (or perhaps farther north), reached their zenith in
the post-Classic era. Eight extant codices, painted in bright
colors on deerskin, trace their dynastic history from the late

View of Monté Albán, Zapotec site near Oaxaca.

Detail of stone work on Zapotec temple at Mitla.

seventh century to the coming of the Spaniards. These pictographs contain data on genealogies of various officials, plants
and animals utilized, gods and temples, human sacrifice, and
the conquest of towns. It is clear that the Mixtecs created
several militaristic states or princedoms based on subjuga-
tion of peoples in order to exact tribute.

After they displaced the Zapotec rulers in Oaxaca, the
Mixtecs settled in that region and superimposed their culture
on the area. There are mural paintings and artifacts at Mitla
that reflect the Mixtec style, and a few Mixtec dignitaries
were buried in Zapotec tombs at Monte Albán. In 1932, Mexican archaeologists, headed by Alfonso Caso, excavated a
tomb where they discovered more than five hundred pieces
of Mixtec jewelry—jade collars and earrings, gold and silver
bracelets, turquoise mosaic brooches, strings of pearls, small
gold bells, obsidian and rock crystal items, jet and amber
pieces, and a splendid golden diadem. Most intriguing were

Mixtec gold and turquoise brooch. Courtesy Instituto Nacional de Antropología e Historia.

thirty-five jaguar bones with delicate carvings and glyphs resembling the writing on Mixtec codices.

Sometime in the second half of the fifteenth century Aztec (Mexica) armies marched into Oaxaca, where, after much resistance, they subdued Cuilapan, Zaachila, and other cities. During this period there were various battles between combinations of Aztecs, Mixtecs, and Zapotecs. Finally, the region was politically unified by the Spaniards, who conquered it in the 1520s.

Northwest of the Mixtec-Zapotec country is the beautiful Valley of Mexico, a vast oval basin where several pre-Columbian civilizations developed and where Mexico City was eventually built. On the valley floor were five interconnected lakes (now reduced to one), and ringing it were snow-covered volcanos, notably Popocatépetl and Iztaccíhuatl. Although it is in the tropics, this large valley has a temperate climate because of its elevation of about 2,200 meters (7,200 feet). There were Formative era settlements at several valley sites such as Tlatilco and Cuicuilco, the latter abandoned after a volcanic eruption, but the earliest advanced civilization flowered in the Classic period in the northeast part of the valley. We do not know what the inhabitants called the place, but the Aztecs later named the abandoned urban site Teotihuacán (Place of the Gods), and the Spaniards renamed it San Juan de Teotihuacán.

The ruins of the vast complex of Teotihuacán, called simply "the Pyramids" by modern tourists, lie about forty kilometers (twenty-five miles) northeast of the present capital of Mexico. This site was occupied by a sedentary agricultural society for a thousand years before its rise as a Classic era city. From the beginning of the Christian era it grew rapidly until its peak about six centuries later, when it covered an area of twenty square kilometers (7.7 square miles) and had a population of at least 100,000—perhaps double that figure. Besides being the most highly urbanized place of its time in the New World it was also a preeminent temple center, seat of a powerful state, and focus of a far-reaching trade network. Except for some glyphs, there are no written records to document the rise and fall of the city, nor are there oral traditions. We have to rely on the abundant archaeological evidence. Objects excavated from more than four thousand buildings have made it possible to reconstruct many aspects of the center's history.

Dominating the landscape at Teotihuacán are monumental pyramids, which undoubtedly served as foci for religious ceremonies. Built of earth, adobe bricks, and rubble, these man-made mountains were erected along an axial thorough-

Avenue of the Dead, Teotihuacán. Photograph by Robert Yaryan.

Detail on the Temple of Quetzalcoatl, Teotihuacán.

fare later dubbed the "Avenue of the Dead," with the Pyramid
of the Moon on the north and the Citadel with its temple of
Quetzalcoatl (Feathered Serpent) on the south. Between these
two structures is the gigantic Pyramid of the Sun, which
measures 220 by 232 meters (241 by 253 yards) at its base and
rises to a flat-topped summit 66 meters (217 feet) above the
valley floor. These pyramids are terraced and truncated;
they have steps to the top, and they are faced with stone that
was stuccoed and originally painted in bright colors. Many
of the pyramids here and at other Mexican sites were enlarged
from time to time and thus are really a series of superimposed
structures.

Laid out in a grid pattern, the city was divided into four
quadrants, each containing apartments built around enclosed
patios or courtyards. Most of the residents probably lived
from the cultivation of adjacent lands. Evidence of irrigation
channels for those fields suggests competence in hydraulic

engineering as well as advanced agronomical technology. Special areas of the city were set aside for priests, traders, and craftsmen. There were more than five hundred workshops for objects of wood, ceramics, and obsidian, and knives, spear points, and arrowheads abound in the ruins. One of the area's strategic resources was a supply of obsidian.

A distinctive Teotihuacán art style is evident in the extant mural paintings and artifacts: three-legged ceramic pots, molded clay figurines, stone masks, jewelry, and other items produced there in its heyday. Several of the frescoes depict deities—Tlaloc (Rain God) and Quetzalcoatl (Feathered Serpent), for example—other murals show priests casting seeds and water from their hands, jaguars, butterflies, flowers, and humans in an underworld or afterworld. One of the monumental sculptural pieces from this culture is the 250-ton monolithic representation of Tlaloc that now stands in front of the National Museum of Anthropology in Mexico City. Inside the museum is an enormous statue of the Goddess of Waters (Chalchihuitlicue), considered the finest sculpture from Teotihuacán.

Teotihuacán's immense influence spread eastward to the Gulf and south to Guatemala. Hegemony over various regions was the result of a combination of trade, military campaigns, and religious power. The city's location along a principal route between the valleys of Puebla and Mexico gave it a commercial advantage, and it seems to have been linked culturally with Cholula, in the adjacent Puebla valley where the New World's largest pyramid was built. That secondary center continued to flourish long after the fall of Teotihuacán.

Mystery surrounds the downfall of Teotihuacán, which seems to have occurred in the eighth century. Many of the buildings show traces of burning and destruction—was the city plundered and put to the torch by invaders? Or was there an internal struggle between religious and military or secular forces? Clearly, the city was abandoned, but what happened to the former inhabitants after the catastrophe? So far, archaeologists have found insufficient evidence to answer these questions. After the fall of Teotihuacán another Indian civilization, the Toltec, began to use the deserted city for ceremonies and as a burial place for its leaders.

In many ways the Toltec empire, which flourished in the post-Classic period, spans the gap between the fall of Teotihuacán and the rise of Aztec predominance in central highland Mexico. In addition to archaeological data, we have legendary historical information about Toltec sites, events, and even the names of some rulers. To our consternation, the legends are intertwined with myths and give conflicting accounts, some of which were borrowed from other cultures. Furthermore, several Toltec leaders bore identical names, then as priest-kings they adopted the names of gods whose attributes they assumed, and later some of these rulers were deified. Thus, it is often difficult to distinguish between the terrestrial and celestial beings who have the same name.

The Toltecs were composed of two distinct ethnic groups: the Nonoalcas, who came to central highland Mexico from the Gulf Coast, and the Tolteca-Chichimecas, who moved southeast into settled areas in and around the Valley of Mexico. Their primary base was at Tula (Tollan in Nahuatl), about eighty kilometers (forty-eight miles) north of the present capital of Mexico and not far from the abandoned city of Teotihuacán. Here, where the junction of two rivers made irrigated agriculture possible, beginning about A.D. 800 the Toltecs developed a prosperous urban center with a peak size three centuries later of perhaps 65,000 inhabitants plus a sizeable rural population. Tula had a large ball court, various temples with friezes depicting jaguars and eagles eating human hearts, and those intriguing Chacmool statues of reclining figures with their elbows on the ground and knees raised. Most impressive of all is an extant truncated pyramid topped by giant stone Atlantean columns that once supported a temple roof. These pillars, carved to resemble warriors, are appropriate symbols for the militaristic state.

From their base at Tula the Toltecs created a tributary empire that extended south through the Valley of Mexico to Cuernavaca and Xochicalco, east to Tulancingo and Huachinango (halfway to the Gulf Coast), and west perhaps as far

Toltec Pyramid of the Warriors, Tula.

as Toluca. They seemed to have had an alliance with two
city-states, Otumba and Culhuacán, the latter located near
the southern shore of Lake Texcoco. There were also some
Toltec colonies, probably on the Gulf Coast, but certainly
at Chichén Itzá, Yucatán.

In the twelfth century, Tula suffered a series of crises
and disasters that led to the dispersal of many inhabitants
and the collapse of Toltec imperial power. Bands of semi-
nomadic Chichimecs invaded from the northwest; the ceremonial center of the city was damaged and burned; and later,
Huastecas from the Gulf Coast attacked the city. An internal
schism culminated about A.D. 1125 with the departure of a certain faction that ultimately took possession of Cholula.

At this time other Chichimecs under the leadership of
Mixcoatl moved into the Valley of Mexico, where they intermarried with Toltecs and established a new Toltec dynasty
based at Culhuacán. About A.D. 1150, Mixcoatl was assassinated and his position usurped, but his son (Ce Acatl) Topiltzin avenged the murder, regained his father's throne, and
moved the capital back to Tula. There was a short revival
marred by discord between Topiltzin, who assumed the name
and role of Quetzalcoatl—associated with the planet Venus
and the Wind god—and his co-ruler or deputy, Huemac, who
was a high priest of Tezcatlipoca—god of Night and the Underworld. This internal stress was accompanied by continued
pressure from outside militant forces until finally Topiltzin
and his followers were driven out and sought exile, and
Huemac, too, left Tula. Tradition holds that Topiltzin-
Quetzalcoatl went to the east, but he may have gone elsewhere. In the resulting chaos a major portion of the population left Tula, and Toltec power collapsed. There followed
an extended period of conflict between various groups in the
central highlands. No single state dominated the area until
the Aztecs created a confederation in the fifteenth century.

The Aztecs, who will be discussed in the next chapter,
revered the Toltecs as ancestors who had established many
of their cultural forms, religious concepts, and imperial pat-

terns. An Aztec chant glorifying these earlier people has
been translated into English:

> The Toltecs were a skillful people,
> all of their works were good, all were exact,
> all well made and admirable.
> Their houses were beautiful, with turquoise mosaics,
> the walls finished with plaster,
> clean and marvelous houses, which is to say
> Toltec houses, beautifully made,
> beautiful in everything. . . .
>
> Painters, sculptors, carvers of precious stones,
> feather artists, potters, spinners, weavers,
> skillful in all they made, they discovered
> the precious green stones, the turquoise,
> they knew the turquoise and its mines, they found
> its mines and they found the mountains hiding
> silver and gold, copper and tin
> and the metal of the moon.
>
> The Toltecs were truly wise,
> they conversed with their own hearts . . .
> They played their drums and rattles,
> They were singers, they composed songs
> and sang them among the people,
> they guarded the songs in their memories,
> they sanctified them in their hearts . . . .*

*Miguel León-Portilla, "A Náhuatl Concept of Art," *Evergreen Review* 2,
no. 7 (Winter 1959): 159–60.

CHAPTER 2

The Aztec Civilization

THE ULTIMATE Mesoamerican Indian civilization was created by the Aztecs, a determined and aggressive people who eventually imposed their hegemony over dozens of other tribes and chiefdoms. Because their advanced culture was in full bloom at the time of the Spanish conquest, we have historical records to document many aspects of their society as viewed by European conquistadors and priests. But the early history of these fascinating people is shrouded in conflicting legends, pictographs, and oral traditions. The Aztec practice of creatively reconstructing their history by eliminating some aspects and fabricating others—a practice not unknown in other times and places—compounds the difficulty of separating myth from fact.

Two and a half centuries of civil wars and chaos span the era between the collapse of the Toltec empire in the twelfth century and the rise of the Aztecs to power in central Mexico. During this period successive waves of wandering bands from the north invaded Tula and the Valley of Mexico, where these semi-nomadic groups came into conflict with the resident sedentary farmers. The newcomers were called Chichimecs, a general term roughly equivalent to barbarians, even though some of them practiced agriculture, wore clothing, and were familiar with the Mesoamerican calendar. According to their own traditions, the Aztecs had a Chichimec ancestry.

The Aztecs were composed of several related tribes, a principal one of which was the Mexica. Because the Mexica, or Mexicans, eventually dominated the others, and because they left the most abundant records, their story has formed the basis for all Aztec history. The name Aztec recalls their

Aztec migration pictograph (Codex Azcatitlán). Courtesy Bibliothéque Nationale, Paris.

legendary homeland of Aztlán, "Places of the Herons," or "Place of the Seven Caves," which was northwest of the Valley of Mexico, perhaps somewhere in the modern states of Jalisco, Nayarit, or Sinaloa. Since the Aztecs spoke the Nahuatl language they were sometimes referred to as Nahuas; another label was Tenochcas, derived from one of their chiefs named Tenoch. After some of their leaders married Toltec descendants at Culhuacán they referred to themselves as Culhua-Mexica. Thus they claimed a dual heritage, Toltec and Chichimec, the former suggesting a legacy of arts and culture, and the latter recalling their dynamic yet primitive origin.

When the Aztecs entered the Valley of Mexico, probably via Tula in the mid-thirteenth century or before, they had to compete with peoples already established there. More than two dozen villages and city-states studded the shores of the five interconnected lakes that covered much of the valley floor in those years. Xaltocan, a small town of Otomí Indians, controlled the north; Texcoco, populated by acculturated Chichimecs, was the chief power on the eastern shores; Culhuacán, whose leaders were descended from the Toltecs, ruled the south; and the Tepanec Indians of Azcapotzalco dominated the west. From the latter the Aztecs got permission to settle at Chapultepec (Grasshopper Hill) in return for military service as mercenaries. Fifty years later, after a military defeat the Aztec leader was captured and sacrificed, remnants of the tribe were scattered, and a large group under Tenoch was carried off to Culhuacán where the survivors were forced into serfdom.

At the end of twenty years of oppression by Culhuacán, the Aztecs were expelled or broke away and established themselves on a small, uninhabited island in the marshlands near the western shore of Lake Texcoco. They claimed that they had been guided there by a priest of their principal tribal deity, Huitzilopochtli (Hummingbird-on-the-left), who instructed them to settle where they would find an eagle with a serpent in its beak perched on a prickly pear cactus growing out of a rock. (This legendary symbol has become the modern national emblem that appears on official seals and on the Mexican flag.) According to Aztec lore this omen occurred in 1325, but recently discovered archaeological evidence points to a much earlier date for establishment of the Aztec capital, Tenochtitlán, which later became Mexico City.

In subsequent years, as rival groups fought with each other for supremacy, Tenochtitlán's strategic location kept it free from enemy attacks and permitted its inhabitants to trade by canoe with all the cities around the lakes. To overcome their lack of cultivable land, the Aztecs built *chinampas,* ingenious

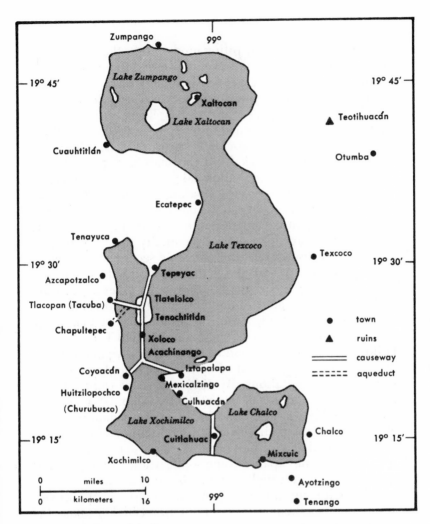

Lakes and Cities of Anáhuac

artificial islands made by piling mud on rafts that were stabilized with stakes until roots eventually tied them to the lake bottom. These "floating gardens" (some still in use) served as fertile fields capable of growing several crops a year.

Gradually the Aztecs transformed Tenochtitlán from a miserable village of thatched huts to a grand city with adobe houses and stone temples. Their hydraulic technology was unsurpassed — using rock from the mainland topped with mud dredged from the shallow lake, they greatly enlarged the small islets. Between the floating gardens and sections of the city a network of canals, bordered by footpaths and occasionally spanned by portable bridges for foot traffic, formed waterways for canoes. Eventually they constructed three stone causeways, with removable sections for defense, to connect the city with the mainland, and with significant help from neighboring people they built dikes to separate salty from sweet waters of the lakes and to control flooding. After a brief war in 1473, the sister island city of Tlatelolco, founded by a dissident faction, was annexed to Tenochtitlán. Following a disastrous flood in 1499, the principal buildings of the capital were rebuilt of volcanic *tezontle* stone by conscripted labor battalions. By 1520, the Aztec capital had a population of about 360,000 (60,000 households), making it one of the three largest cities in the world. Combined with other cities around the lakes, the population of the valley may have totaled a million or more.

Paralleling the expansion and sophistication of their island city, the Aztecs created a monarchy and a ruling class to govern their emerging empire. Acamapichtli, son of a Mexica father and a Culhua mother, was the first Chief Speaker (*Uei tlatoani*) who ruled from Tenochtitlán. The tradition is that his wife, also of Culhua descent, was sterile, so the Aztec chieftains gave him their daughters, by whom he had many children. These offspring and their descendants constituted a new noble class that boasted of its royal blood "stemming from Quetzalcoatl of Tula." Members of this nobility formed an elite from which Aztec leaders were chosen.

Itzcóatl, the fourth Chief Speaker, who ruled from 1427 to

Central area of Tenochtitlán (reconstruction), Courtesy American Museum of Natural History.

1440, secured independence for his people and put the Aztecs on the road to empire. He negotiated arrangements for the Triple Alliance with Texcoco and Tlacopan that resulted in the defeat of Azcapotzalco, which had been the dominant power. From that time forward, the league of the three cities, which lasted until the coming of the Spaniards almost a century later, was used to further Aztec imperial ambitions. Victory in battle brought about distribution of the spoils of war—jewels, tribute, slaves, and land—with Tenochtitlán and Texcoco each receiving two-fifths of the booty and Tlacopán one-fifth. The Aztecs dominated the Triple Alliance; they possessed superior military and economic power and even influenced domestic political decisions of their allies.

The allied city-state of Texcoco enjoyed a reputation as the cultural and intellectual capital of the region. Here poetry and oratory were cherished, archives of painted codices were accumulated, and artists and musicians had many privileges. Here also was located a high court where legal disputes between city-states or individuals were appealed. Nezahualcóyotl (whose name means Hungry Coyote) ruled Texcoco for forty years, beginning in 1430.

Nezahualcóyotl was a philosopher-king who visualized an "unknown god" reigning supreme over the universe. This talented ruler of Texcoco was also a poet whose verses have a timeless quality, as demonstrated in the following examples:

> The obscurity of the night
> Reveals the brilliancy of the stars.
> No one has power
> To alter these heavenly lights,
> For they serve to display
> The greatness of their Creator.
> And as our eyes see them now,
> So saw them our earliest ancestors,
> And so will see them
> Our latest posterity.
>
> The grandeurs of life
> Are like the flowers in color and in fate;
> The beauty of these remain

So long as their chaste buds gather and store
The rich pearls of the dawn,
And saving it, drop it in liquid dew;
But scarcely has the Cause of All
directed upon them the full rays of the sun,
When their beauty and glory fail,
and the brilliant gay colors
Which decked forth their pride
*Wither and fade.**

Nezahualcóyotl supported the beautification of Texcoco with new temples, observatories, gardens, and public baths as well as enhancement of his grandiose palace. He had a number of wives, the principal one being a sister of the Aztec ruler, and tradition says that he fathered 118 children. Before his death he appointed his seven-year-old son Nezahualpilli as his successor.

In neighboring Tenochtitlán, succession to the Aztec throne was not always from father to son—the highest office could pass to a brother, cousin, nephew, or grandson—but it stayed in the same family. It was an elective position, which kept incompetents from inheriting the office. At first, when the city was small, all heads of families had a voice in the decision, but when the empire grew, the "electoral college" was reduced to about a hundred persons who represented the highest level of civil, military, and religious officials. Thus Aztec government changed over the years from a democratic tribal organization to rule by an elite oligarchy. Since the Aztec ruler combined military with religious duties, his government may be characterized as a militaristic theocracy. When a new Chief Speaker was chosen, the great dignitaries, many of them his close relatives, received specific titles and positions in the government. Some had military functions, others judicial or religious duties.

Moctezuma I, surnamed Ilhuicamina, who reigned from 1440 to 1468, is reckoned the greatest of all Aztec rulers.

*Daniel G. Brinton, *Ancient Náhuatl Poetry* (Published by the author, Philadelphia, 1887), 45–46.

Coronation of Moctezuma I (Codex Durán). Courtesy The Bancroft Library.

He embellished Tenochtitlán with public works, including an aqueduct to bring fresh water from a spring at Chapultepec, and in the heart of the city he enlarged the great pyramid topped with dual temples to Tlaloc, the rain god, and Huitzilopochtli, god of war and of the sun. In a tropical valley south of the capital Moctezuma created a botanical garden with plants brought there from various parts of his realm. Like most Mexicans to this day, he loved flowers and plants.

Under Moctezuma I and his aggressive half-brother and deputy, Tlacaélel, the empire expanded out of the Valley of Mexico eastward to the Gulf and southward through Oaxaca to the Pacific. These conquests yielded a tremendous amount of tribute in maize and other foodstuffs as well as tobacco, incense, rubber, feathers, cotton cloth, copper, and weapons. The victors also brought prisoners of war to Tenochtitlán, where they were sacrificed. The Aztecs referred to the central part of their realm as Anáhuac (which means "on the edge of the water"); at first this designated the Valley of Mexico, but later it seems to have included lands outside the valley.

Imperialist expansion continued under the three succeeding rulers: Axayácatl (1469–1481), Tízoc (1481–1486), and Ahuítzotl (1486–1502), until most of central and southern Mexico came under Aztec control. In certain ways the relationship between the Aztecs and their thirty-eight tributary provinces was more of a confederacy than an empire. Each defeated tribe or area was permitted to retain its own local government, language, and religion, but it had to recognize Aztec sovereignty, worship Huitzilopochtli, pay annual tribute in goods, provide a levy of sacrificial victims, and surrender some land to Aztec nobles. Occasionally an Aztec governor and military contingent would be stationed in recently conquered areas; some daughters of Aztec nobles were pledged in marriage to subject tribal lords; and many idols worshipped in outlying regions were taken to Tenochtitlán to be placed in a special "temple of captive gods."

Although they lived relatively close to the Aztec capital,

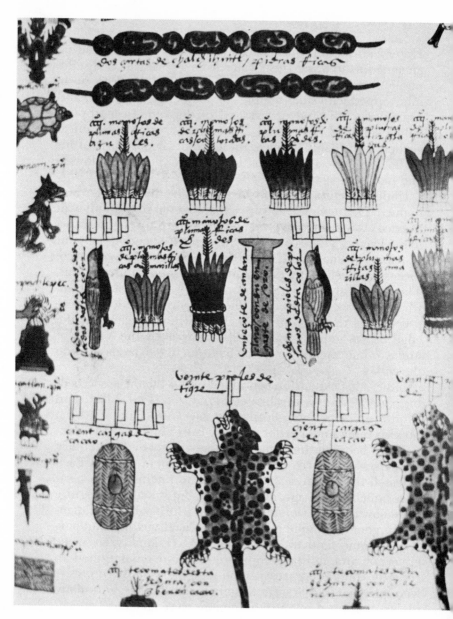

Aztec tribute list (Codex Mendoza). Courtesy Bòdleian Library, Oxford.

two Indian groups successfully resisted conquest, the Tarascans to the west and the Tlaxcala enclave to the east. In
1478 the Tarascans soundly defeated an invading Aztec army;
thereafter no further attempt was made by the valley cities
to subdue them. The relationship between the Triple Alliance
and Tlaxcala was governed by an arrangement for periodic
warfare, the Flower Wars (Xochiyaoyotl). These engagements,
sometimes called military fairs, were designed to test young
men in battle and to serve the gods through bloodshed on
the battlefield and sacrifice of captives.

The Aztec practice of human sacrifice was an indispensable part of their religion. Through the terror that it generated it also helped them consolidate their power and prevent subject people from rebelling. Besides war captives the
victims included convicted criminals whose offenses called
for capital punishment. Sacrificial techniques varied: rain
rituals involved slaying of children with the hope that their
tears would assure plentiful rainfall; the rite of spring was
celebrated by priests who donned the skins of flayed victims;
and other ceremonies were associated with shooting arrows
into captives who were lashed to a scaffold. All military prisoners were sacrificed. Some of them had a gladiatorial role in
which they were tied to a gigantic stone and forced to defend
themselves with a wooden club against an Aztec warrior
armed with an obsidian-edged sword. But by far the most
common method of sacrifice was to march or drag male captives up the steps to the summit of a pyramid, where each
man was stretched across a sacrificial stone while four priests
held his limbs and another priest plunged an obsidian knife
into his chest and tore out the palpitating heart, which he
offered to the appropriate god.

The rationale for all this bloodshed was that human blood
was the proper nourishment for gods. To assure plentiful
crops the rain god and earth goddess had to be appeased or
regularly presented with divine food, and if there was a
drought or flood, additional sacrifices were made. It was
believed that the sun, especially, needed human blood in
order to assure its continuance. The fact that it rose pale

each morning after cosmic battle during the night was proof of its frailty, according to Aztec priests. Huitzilopochtli, the Mexica tribal god imposed on the Aztec world, had several manifestations—sometimes he was Tonatiuh, the Sun God; at other times he was a war god or patron of war. In either guise he demanded human hearts and human blood.

Aztecs perceived an intimate relationship between religion and war. Huitzilopochtli, who spoke to them through oracles, insisted that only continuous warfare and human sacrifice could maintain the sun in the sky. The Aztecs believed that there had been four previous worlds, or suns, each of which had suffered a cataclysmic end. The current Fifth Sun was doomed to destruction in a great earthquake, but that final day could be postponed by human sacrifice. Thus war was a sacred duty, and all able-bodied males received military training to become soldiers in time of war. There was no standing army, but the frequency of military campaigns gave ample opportunity for youths to prove themselves in battle. Warriors, whether they brought prisoners to the sacrificial stone, were themselves killed in battle, or were captured and sacrificed by the enemy, performed the highest service to church and state. These "men with hearts of stone"were idealized by the Aztecs; their final reward was an elevated place in the hereafter, a warrior's paradise.

Three groups dominated Aztec society: the warrior elite (*teteuctin*), the hereditary nobility (*pipiltin*), and the high priests. The warrior elite, or knights, were those of noble birth who had proved themselves in battle by capturing prisoners. They were eligible for membership in the military lodges: Eagle Knights, Jaguar Knights, and Knights of the Arrow. A *teuctli* warrior had a number of privileges—he could wear an elaborate costume, participate in war councils, acquire former enemy property and slaves, have a harem, and eat human flesh. Portions of sacrificial victims, cooked with squash and flowers, were served to warriors. This was "divine food," for it was believed that the victim had become a demigod once sacrificed. The knights were not allowed to keep the victim's heads; these were skewered on public skull racks. There were several of these racks in Tenochtitlán, each with many thousands of skulls accumulated over the years.

Because the Aztecs had so many religious festivals and more than two hundred deities, there was a need for many priests. By the sixteenth century, some five thousand officiated in Tenochtitlán alone. These religious leaders, virtually all of whom practiced celibacy, were organized into a hierarchy and were supported by their own properties as well as by tribute. Their functions varied—some were in charge of temples, sacrifices, or festivals; others were soothsayers or custodians of tribal lore. By learning to read and write pictographic codices priests preserved and extended knowledge in various fields, including astronomy, mathematics, theology, medicine, law, history, and oral literature. Many priests served the state as government advisors, medicine men, or as teachers in the schools for noble youths.

Aztec nobles (*pipiltin*) were part of the ruling class and as such enjoyed specific prerogatives. They wore distinctive clothing, had their own courts, were permitted polygamous marriages that were advantageous in politico-economic terms through family alliances, and their children could attend the *cálmecac* school that was a prerequisite for obtaining the highest positions in church and state. Nobles had hereditary lands from which they received tribute. Although the nobles had contempt for the commoners, a few of the latter who performed outstanding service, usually in war, were rewarded with non-inheritable noble status.

Commoners (*macehualtin*) were the largest segment of the empire's population. Their basic socio-economic unit was the *calpulli,* something akin to a clan or a ward, which owned the agricultural land, assigned the use of the land to its members, and paid tribute or taxes as a unit. Each *calpulli* had its own elected officers who regulated local affairs, supervised communal storehouses, kept tribute records, controlled the armory, and in wartime commanded the unit's military forces. They also maintained for teen-aged boys a barracks school, the *telpóchcalli,* which offered instruction in citizenship, military training, religion, and crafts.

Serfs (*mayeques*), who tilled landholdings that belonged to the nobility and clergy, composed almost one-third of the Aztec population. Tied to the land and dispersed throughout the empire, they were not organized into *calpulli* and thus did not have the advantages or tribute responsibilities of the commoners. Their status was fixed; they could not expect to move up in society.

Among the lowest members of the social scale were day laborers (*tlalmaitl*), who were not members of a *calpulli;* and at the very bottom were slaves (*tlacotin*) who constituted about 5 percent of the population. There were several categories of slaves, depending on the circumstances of enslavement. Male captives taken in warfare were usually sacrificed, but not the many enemy women and children who were enslaved through conquest. Contractual slaves were individuals who sold themselves into slavery when they could not pay their debts. Others sold their children into slavery. The punishment for many criminal offenses was slavery, and it was not uncommon for a condemned person to become a slave of his victim's family. Mitigating features of this servitude permitted slaves to own property, maintain families, and, for some, to regain their freedom after their debt or purchase price was repaid. All children born to slaves were free and enjoyed full citizenship rights.

Aztec women formed part of the various social ranks from nobility to slavery. Although they were not eligible for the highest offices of state, some women acted as regents for their minor sons, and of course marriages of a chief's daughters or sisters were important in cementing tribal alliances. For commoners, marriages were arranged through a marriage broker, usually an older woman, who followed tribal customs such as making certain that each partner came from a different clan. The great majority of women were wives and mothers with the usual household duties of food preparation and child rearing. But there were other female occupations: priestesses, temple virgins, midwives, weavers, herbalists, potters, musicians, dancers, prostitutes, and market vendors.

An Aztec woman had definite legal rights, such as those of holding property or entering into contracts in her own name. She could obtain a divorce from her husband if he deserted her, was cruel, or failed to support her or their children. If divorced, she could remarry. Widows could only marry within the clan of their deceased husband. Divorce and remarriage were relatively easy for Aztec males; grounds for legal dissolution included sterility, neglect of household duties, or declaration that a wife was habitually ill-tempered. Married women were expected to be faithful to their husbands, and girls were supposed to be chaste, but a man could have extramarital relations with unmarried females. Women's rights were definitely inferior to those of men, and females had a secondary role in the warrior-dominated and class-conscious society.

Long distance traders or merchants (*pochteca*) constituted a special hereditary class in the Aztec community. Not included in this category were the petty barterers who daily hawked wares in markets throughout the country. The large-scale merchants had their own patron gods, regulations, courts, ceremonies, and prerogatives. On their trading expeditions they took highland products to exchange for tropical goods. Outbound cargoes included obsidian weapons and tools, onyx, cinnabar, herbs, rabbit pelts, cloth, and rope; they returned with jaguar skins, quetzal feathers, shells, cotton, rubber, jade, gold, turquoise, vanilla, and cacao beans (which were used for chocolate and as money). Indian slaves accompanied trading caravans as human bearers and also were themselves an important article of commerce.

Traders performed a vital function in the imperialist Aztec state. They were intelligence gatherers and spies who reported on conditions along their route, with special attention to potential areas of conquest and trade. Occasionally they were accused of spying and were executed by local authorities. Such an event generally led to an invasion by Aztec military forces. In spite of their important role, traders were barred from membership in the military lodges, and they could not flaunt their wealth or else it would be confiscated by the great lords. The chief traders lived in Tlatelolco, site of the greatest Aztec marketplace.

In 1520, Hernán Cortés visited the market at Tlatelolco, which he described in a letter to the Spanish emperor:

> This city has many squares where trading is done and markets are held continuously. There is also one square twice as big as that of Salamanca, with arcades all around, where more than sixty thousand people come each day to buy and sell, and where every kind of merchandise produced in these lands is found, provisions as well as ornaments of gold and silver, lead, brass, copper, tin, stones, shells, bones, and feathers. They also sell lime, hewn and unhewn stone, adobe bricks, tiles, and cut and uncut woods of various kinds. There is a street where they sell game birds of every species found in this land. . . . They sell rabbits and hares, and stags and small gelded dogs which they breed for eating.
>
> There are streets of herbalists where all the medicinal herbs and roots found in the land are sold. There are shops like apothecaries', where they sell ready-made medicines as well as liquid ointments and plasters. There are shops like barbers' where they can have their hair washed and shaved, and shops where they sell food and drink. . . . There is every sort of vegetable . . . and there are many sorts of fruit. . . .
>
> They sell deerskins, with and without the hair, and some are dyed white or in various colors. They sell much earthenware, which for the most part is very good; there are both large and small pitchers, jugs, pots, tiles and many other sorts of vessel, all of good clay and most of them glazed and painted. They sell maize both as grain and as bread and it is better both in appearance and in taste than any found in the islands or on the mainland.*

The market was a news and social center as well as a place to buy and sell commodities, and Cortés also noted that the market was governed by a panel of judges who adjudicated disputes, regulated the size of measures used and sentenced offenders.

---

*Anthony R. Pagden, ed. and trans., *Hernán Cortés: Letters from Mexico* (New York: Grossman Publishers, 1971), 103–104.

When Cortés arrived in Mexico, Moctezuma II was ruling the Aztec confederation. His distinctive name, Moctezuma Xocoyotzín (the Cadet or the younger), set him apart from his great-grandfather, who had ruled earlier. His reign, beginning in 1503 when he was thirty-four years old, followed a distinguished career as a warrior, during which he had taken a number of captives in battle and performed exceptional and daring feats. He had four wives and dozens of concubines; the marriages were arranged to cement political alliances and reinforce his regal claims. In many ways Moctezuma's prerogatives resembled those of an Oriental potentate: he had more than a thousand personal servants; visiting lords had to come before him barefoot and poorly dressed; under pain of death, all subjects had to avoid looking at him directly; and more than any previous Aztec ruler, he demanded to be treated as semi-divine.

Moctezuma's rule was stern—his personality seems to have been a blend of military commander and religious fanatic. Upon assuming office he issued several decrees that reflected his attitudes about caste and discipline. Commoners were purged from all positions in the bureaucracy and were ordered to prostrate themselves face down when the emperor passed through the streets; illegitimate youths in the *cálmecac* school were expelled and none admitted thereafter; and instant death was ordered for young nobles who made blunders while serving at court. To control outlying provinces a hostage system was employed whereby great lords were required to spend part of each year in Tenochtitlán. From this contingent Moctezuma selected an honor guard. Thus the court was filled with nobles who were required to serve the emperor.

The splendor of Moctezuma's court was observed by Bernal Díaz del Castillo, a Spanish soldier who accompanied Cortés to Tenochtitlán. In his book about the conquest of the Aztecs, he described the palaces, armories, treasure rooms, aviary, and zoological garden. His account of the emperor's dining arrangements is most vivid:

His cooks prepared over thirty kinds of dishes for every meal, done the way he liked them, and they placed small pottery braziers under them so they wouldn't get cold. They prepared over three hundred plates of the food Montezuma was going to eat and more than a thousand plates for the guard. Every day they cooked chicken, turkey, pheasant, partridge, quail, tame and wild duck, venison, wild pig, reed birds, pigeons, hares, rabbits, and many varieties of birds and other things. . . .

When he began to eat, they placed in front of him a kind of screen of wood lavishly painted with gold, so he could not be seen eating. . . . They served him on pottery from Cholula, one kind red and another black. . . .

From time to time they served him in cups of pure gold a certain drink made from cacao. It was said that it gave one power over women, but this I never saw. . . .

While Montezuma was at table, as I have described, two other very lovely women would bring him tortillas made with eggs and other substantial things. . . . They also placed on the table three painted and decorated pipes filled with liquidambar and mixed with an herb they call tobacco. After he finished eating, after the dancing and singing and removal of the table, he would take a little smoke from one of these pipes, and with it fall asleep.*

Not surprisingly, this passage mentions several Aztec folk arts, for the Mexicans were highly skilled, and still are, in a variety of crafts. The Spaniards were amazed by the richness of the Indian cotton textiles, especially headdresses and cloaks that incorporated brightly colored feathers woven into the fabric, something never seen before in Europe. Metalworking was practiced, but only for ritual objects and ornaments. The metal craftsmen worked principally in gold, silver, and copper; they had not discovered the techniques of bronze or ironworking. Wood carving, inlaid mosaics, feather mosaics, basketry, and lacquering of gourds for utensils were other

*Albert Idell, ed. and trans., *The Bernal Díaz Chronicles* (Garden City: Doubleday, 1956), 149–51. Copyright © 1956 by Albert Idell. Reprinted by permission of Doubleday & Company, Inc.

Aztec Indian wearing a feather cloak. Watercolor by Christopher Weiditz, 1542. Courtesy Germanisches Nationalmuseum, Nürenburg.

outstanding skills. Aztec potters made ceramic items for ceremonial use, architectural ornamentation, household dishes, jewelry, and musical instruments.

Music and dance not only were found at the emperor's court, but these art forms permeated all strata of Aztec society. Besides their role as entertainers, musicians played an important part in ceremonies of church and state. Some of the dances were sacred, to be performed only on certain occasions such as when supplicating Tlaloc, the rain god. One function of songs was as a mnemonic device for recording and recalling tribal history and folklore. Aztec instruments included various types of drums, bells, rattles made from seed-filled gourds, ceramic flutes, notched-stick rasps, conch shell trumpets, and reed whistles. One can imagine the hypnotic effect of these instruments, played by elaborately costumed and masked professionals, at rituals adjacent to the imposing pyramid temples!

Pyramids exemplified Aztec achievements in architecture and engineering. These structures involved the quarrying of stone, transportation of massive blocks, sinking of pilings to stabilize them, and all the skills of construction, decoration, and landscaping. Ball courts, schools, palaces of the nobles, plazas, and waterways were also well built of stone and mortar, often highly decorated with frescoes and three-dimensional elements. Aztec artists excelled in stone sculpture, often massive in concept yet delicate in treatment. Besides granite they worked in obsidian, lava rock, onyx, and rock crystal. One of the most interesting of surviving Aztec sculptures is the so-called Calendar Stone (or Fifth Sun Stone), which weighs sixteen metric tons and is covered with carved glyphs representing the sun god (Tonatiuh), serpents, and names of the days.

Like other Mesoamerican cultures, the Aztecs had two interlocking calendars—one was based on the solar year of 365 days, the other was a sacred period of 260 days. The two calendars ran concurrently; the solar one (*xiuitl*) had eighteen twenty-day months followed by a five day unlucky or

Curly-haired coyote, Aztec sculpture. Courtesy Instituto Nacional de Antropología e Historia.

"useless" period, and the religious one (*tonalpohualli*) had twenty periods or "weeks" of thirteen days each. Each day was designated by a combination of a number from one through thirteen plus a name from a list of twenty day-names: One-Rabbit, Two-Water, Three-Dog, Four-Monkey, Five-Grass, Six-Reed, and so on. The solar years were named for the day on which they began, such as Two-Reed. Every fifty-two years, when the two calendars coincided and the cycle or "century" ended, the Aztecs, fearing that the world might come to a cataclysmic end, did penance, fasted, destroyed their cooking pottery, and extinguished their hearth fires. When the priest-astronomers had determined that another cycle was beginning, they kindled a new fire in the breast of a sacrificial victim, and runners carried torches to all parts of the realm.

Aztecs believed that the fate of individuals, towns, and even gods was determined by certain aspects of the calendar; thus priests and soothsayers analyzed the book of fates (*tonalámatl*) for good or bad omens. When a child was born on an unlucky day, its naming was postponed until a more propitious time. Merchants left with their caravans only on specific days; artisans offered flowers or burned incense to gods on their lucky days; wars were initiated or peace concluded only when calendar signs appeared to be proper. In addition to calendar divination, the ancient Mexicans paid special attention to extraordinary phenomena that could portend success or disaster.

Bad omens occurred throughout the reign of Moctezuma II. A severe drought in 1505–1506, which caused a shortage of maize and much suffering, was interpreted as a reflection of displeasure of the rain god. In 1506 lightning struck a temple in the heart of Tenochtitlán and set it afire—obviously another message from the gods. And in 1509 a "cone of light with a tongue of fire," perhaps a comet or zodiacal light, appeared in the eastern sky; for almost a year it was visible from midnight to daylight in all parts of Anáhuac. Because it came from the east it was associated with Quetzalcoatl,

Toltec god-ruler who had sailed away several centuries earlier, promising to return. Moctezuma assumed that the heavenly light was a sign of Quetzalcoatl's imminent arrival, but various sorcerers interpreted the omen as portending evil, so he held a conference with Nezahualpilli, the ruler of Texcoco who was famed as an astrologer. When Nezahualpilli foretold that "calamities would occur and kingdoms would be destroyed," the Aztec emperor decided to submit the matter to the gods for a decision. Accordingly, a sacred ball game was played, the outcome of which was an ominous defeat for Moctezuma, who was markedly affected by the prophesy of a violent end to the empire. During the last decade of his rule the emperor built several new temples and ordered others to be rebuilt. His reasons may have been to appease the gods or, perhaps, to divert public attention from the increasing problems of state.

During his seventeen-year reign, Moctezuma II had to use the army to put down rebellions in various parts of the empire; these uprisings were easily suppressed but indicated growing unrest on the part of subject peoples. A related problem involved the Triple Alliance, which was weakened after leaders in Tenochtitlán reduced their allies to a subservient position and interfered in elections in Tlacopan and Texcoco.

When Nezahualpilli of Texcoco died in 1515, a serious schism divided the city-state as his sons contended for succession to the throne. The two strongest and logical candidates were Cacama, who accepted domination by Tenochtitlán, and his brother Ixtlilxochitl, who wanted his city to regain equality with the Aztec capital. Because a consensus could not be reached, the electors designated a third candidate, but when he died suddenly, Moctezuma proclaimed Cacama to be the ruler of Texcoco. Meanwhile, the uncompromising Ixtlilxochitl fled with a force of followers to the northern highlands, vowing to return someday to take over the throne and expressing his hostility toward Tenochtitlán. Moctezuma's armies were not successful in suppressing this renegade, who had even dispatched agents to the Gulf Coast seeking supplies and moral support in his fight against the metropolis. This dynastic split in Texcoco weakened the unity of the Aztec empire. Later, when the Spaniards arrived and expressed a desire to overthrow Moctezuma, they found willing Indian allies on the Gulf Coast and in the person of Ixtlilxochitl.

In 1515, rumors that Quetzalcoatl had returned circulated throughout Anáhuac. Reports filtered up to the highland plateau about large watercraft, "temples in the sea," that had been sighted along Mexico's eastern littoral. Other stories told of strangers who had landed on the Tabasco coast, where their mysterious "fire-breathing" weapons killed many natives, perhaps in retribution for not having received them properly. The hearsay was substantiated in 1518 when a Gulf Coast local chief named Pinotl and four other witnesses hurried to Tenochtitlán, where they told Moctezuma that they had seen these strange ships, had communicated by sign language with the bearded men aboard them, and had received some green and yellow beads from the intruders. The Indian spokesman then gave the beads to Moctezuma who placed them in a sanctuary and ordered that other items taken from the strangers should be enshrined in the temple of Quetzalcoatl at Tula (Tollan).

The eyewitness report prompted Moctezuma to call the leaders of Tlacopan and Texcoco to a summit meeting of the highest officials. Moctezuma already had developed a schizoid view of the mysterious and powerful strangers. They could be potential enemies, thus they should be encouraged to go away; or they might be headed by Quetzalcoatl, in which case he should be invited to take over the kingdom he had come back to claim. Either way, gifts should be sent. After much discussion, the majority of the leaders, concluding that the intrusion was a return of the Feathered Serpent god-king or his disciples, appointed a welcoming committee headed by five nobles to take presents to the strangers. By the time the embassy reached the coast, the ships had sailed away, but coastal dwellers reported that the "gods" had promised to return the following year. The next year was 1519, or One-Reed, the year of Quetzalcoatl's prophesy. Indeed, the bearded strangers disembarked that fateful year and made plans to visit Tenochtitlán, thus initiating one of the most fascinating cultural confrontations in all of recorded history.

CHAPTER 3

The Spanish Conquest

SPAIN'S expansion to the Western Hemisphere came at the end of eight centuries of intermittent struggle between Christians and Moslems on the Iberian peninsula. This extended crusade had two important influences on the Spanish character — it fostered Christian fanaticism and it glorified military life. During those years, Catholic clergymen enjoyed special privileges through preaching and supporting the *reconquista* (reconquest), and Spanish soldiers found an avenue of upward mobility through warfare. Men who won battles or performed brave deeds were generally rewarded, sometimes with a promotion, a grant of newly-conquered land, perhaps a title of lesser nobility, or even an allotment of labor to be performed by the defeated enemy. Then in January of 1492 the last Moorish king of Granada surrendered to Ferdinand and Isabella, sovereigns of Aragon and Castile. After that date, when there were no longer lands to wrest from the infidel at home, many would-be knights sought glory and feudal rewards overseas, and many clergymen looked abroad for service.

During their reign the "Catholic Kings," Ferdinand and Isabella, adopted a number of measures designed to unify and strengthen Spain. They curtailed privileges of the nobility and the municipalities, reduced the power of the *Cortes* (parliament), restrained the might of the Spanish military orders, initiated a uniform system of weights and measures, established a civil militia (*Santa Hermandad*) to counter lawlessness, and promulgated reforms in taxation and the judicial system. To assure orthodoxy and primacy of Roman Catholicism, the state religion, they established the Inquisition, obtained concessions from the papacy that gave the crown control over Church government in Spain (the *patronato real*), and by royal decree they expelled half a million Jews and Moslems who refused to convert to Christianity. Historians have suggested that the deportees, many of whom were hard-working and possessed valuable skills and intellectual talents, might have contributed notably to Spain's future well-being. But the monarchs, especially Isabella, felt that these non-Christian subjects were an impediment to Spanish unity.

Aragon and Castile had different foci for their overseas expansion. Traditionally, the Aragonese directed their attention and energy toward the Mediterranean, where they opposed Turkish threats as well as French attempts to dominate the Italian peninsula. Meanwhile, Castilians, with a history of successful conquest and occupation of the Canary Islands and with the adjacent Atlantic ports of Cadiz and Seville (upriver), placed their overseas hopes on the western sea. A strong stimulus here was Portugal's steady exploration southward along Africa's west coast in search of an all-water route to the Indies of the East. This Portuguese thrust had resulted in their discovery of the Cape Verde Islands, establishment of enclaves on the Gold Coast, and profitable trade in gold, ivory, and black slaves.

Castile and its monarch were central to the creation of Spain's transatlantic empire. For six years Christopher Columbus directed appeals to Queen Isabella for support of his "Westward to the Orient" plan. At last, shortly after the fall of Granada, she signed the contract naming him Admiral of the Ocean Sea, Captain-General of any new lands discovered, and granting him a tenth part of all wealth that might be found, "whether it be pearls, precious stones, gold, silver, spices, and other things whatsoever." In August, 1492, Columbus, already over forty and gray-haired, set sail with ninety men aboard three small ships; in October they made landfall in the Bahamas. Believing that he had reached some islands off the coast of India, Columbus called the people he encountered "Indians" and the region, "the Indies." After reconnoitering the coasts of several Caribbean islands, the discoverer left thirty-nine men on an island the natives called

Haiti and returned to Spain, taking with him as proof of his discoveries gold jewelry, forty parrots, tobacco leaves, an iguana, and ten native Americans. In Spain the newly-discovered lands (the Indies) were considered the exclusive possession of the crown of Castile; they were not colonies of the Castilian kingdom, nor were they, strictly speaking, Spanish.

To confirm possession of the islands, Queen Isabella appealed to Pope Alexander VI, an Aragonese, who responded with the Line of Demarcation (1493) drawn one hundred leagues west of the Azores and Cape Verde Islands. Pagan lands east of the line would belong to the Portuguese; those to the west would be under Castilian royal control; both monarchs had the obligation of Christianizing the inhabitants. One year later, by the Treaty of Tordesillas, the Portuguese, who earlier had discovered and occupied the Azores and Madeira, persuaded the Spanish to shift the line westward to a point three hundred and seventy leagues beyond the Cape Verdes.

Columbus's epic voyage of 1492 was soon followed by other Spanish expeditions that transported thousands of conquistadors, missionaries, and colonists to the West Indies. Columbus himself took fifteen hundred on his second voyage in 1494, and Nicolás Ovando carried two thousand in 1502. The island of Haiti, called Española by Spaniards and Hispaniola in its Anglicized form, became the first center of Spanish settlement in the New World. This island was a crucible where Spanish colonial institutions and Indian policies developed. Here the newcomers took formal possession of the land; founded towns, ranches, and sugar plantations; introduced European plants and animals; and mined for gold (Columbus took thirty thousand ducats of gold to Spain after his second expedition). They also forced the Indians to work for them, Christianized them, decimated their numbers through overwork and transmission of diseases, and imported black slaves from Africa. When the supply of gold, estates, and Indians diminished, many Spaniards, especially late arrivals or those who preferred adventure to farming, used the island as a springboard to further exploration.

From Española the conquistadors sailed to other Caribbean islands or to the mainland of the Americas. Juan Ponce de León began the conquest of Puerto Rico in 1508, after which he discovered Florida in 1513. Jamaica was conquered by Juan de Esquivel in 1509, the year in which Alonso de Ojeda and Diego de Nicuesa headed expeditions to the Isthmus of Panama, where their followers suffered appalling disasters as they fought with each other and against hostile Indians armed with poison arrows. Finally they made a permanent settlement at Darién. From there Vasco Núñez de Balboa crossed the Isthmus in 1513 to look upon the South Sea, later called the Pacific Ocean. Meanwhile, the conquest of Cuba was undertaken in 1511 by a force of three hundred men out of Española led by Diego de Velásquez, who became governor of the new territory. Cuba was the stepping-stone to Mexico—the island is separated from Yucatán by a channel only 217 kilometers (135 miles) wide.

By the time the Spanish conquerers first came to Mexico their compatriots had already occupied parts of the Caribbean for a quarter of a century, and they had cruised along the mainland coast from Honduras to Argentina, occasionally going ashore. Nowhere had they found well-clothed Indians, stone buildings, or great cities. Mexico proved to be different. On the eve of the conquest of Mexico, the crown of Spain passed to Ferdinand and Isabella's Hapsburg grandson Charles I, who arrived in Spain in 1517 to begin a reign that lasted for four decades. When he was elected Holy Roman Emperor in 1519 his title changed to Emperor Charles V. It was under his rule that Mexico was unveiled, conquered, and colonized by Spaniards.

Governor Velásquez of Cuba sponsored three expeditions that led to the discovery of the high civilizations of Mexico. The first party of 110 adventurers set out from Cuba in February, 1517, under the leadership of Francisco Hernández de Córdoba, owner of two of the ships used. Antón de Alaminos, who had sailed as a cabin boy with Columbus, went along as chief pilot; another member was Bernal Díaz del Castillo, who later wrote a voluminous history known in translation as *The Discovery and Conquest of Mexico.* After three weeks in uncharted and stormy waters they made landfall at the northeastern extremity of the Yucatán peninsula. (The name Yucatán is believed to be a Spanish corruption of an Indian's answer, "I do not understand you," when asked the name of the land.) Ashore in some uninhabited buildings the Spaniards found a small amount of Indian booty, wooden chests containing textiles and a few gold and copper trinkets. But here and at other places along the coast they were ambushed by fierce Maya warriors wearing quilted cotton armor and equipped with bows and arrows, spears, slings, and wooden clubs edged with obsidian points. At Champotón, a port in the modern state of Campeche, hordes of natives attacked the Spaniards, most of whom had gone ashore for food and water, killing half of them and wounding most of the others, including Hernández de Córdoba. After this loss the commander was obliged to return to Cuba, where he died of his wounds, but not before informing the governor that to the west lay a fabulous and rich land inhabited by aborigines with a notably higher civilization than had yet been encountered.

In April, 1518, Governor Velásquez fitted out a second expedition, recruited 240 men, and appointed his nephew Juan de Grijalva as captain-general of the four ships. Aboard were two translators—Maya youths who had been taken prisoner by Hernández de Córdoba. Crossing the channel in eight days, the ships first anchored at the island of Cozumel off the eastern shore of the Yucatán peninsula. The explorers then moved on around Cape Catoche and put in at Champotón to avenge the defeat of the previous year. After three days of hard fighting the Indians retreated into the swamps, having lost about two hundred men. Seven Spaniards were killed and sixty injured, including Grijalva, who had three arrow wounds.

Grijalva's ships then continued to explore and chart the Gulf Coast. At the mouth of a river in Tabasco, which the Spaniards named Río Grijalva, they encountered friendly Maya-speaking Indians who traded food and gold ornaments for blue beads and told them that farther on, "in the direction of the sunset," there was plenty of gold. They repeated "Colúa, Colúa, Méjico, Méjico," but the Spaniards did not know what those words meant or that they had reached the outer edge of the Aztec empire.

When the expedition moved north and anchored at the mouth of the Río Jamapa (site of modern Veracruz), they came to Nahuatl-speaking territory. Moctezuma II, having received reports of the various landings, had ordered his vassals on the coast to be on the lookout for bearded white strangers whom they were to entertain, interrogate, then implore to leave the country. Although Grijalva's men could not communicate with the natives, they understood the friendly signs of white banners and gestures inviting them to land. Once ashore they were astonished at the grand feast prepared for them as well as the gifts of jewels and gold valued at sixteen thousand pesos. Offsetting this bonanza the Spaniards found evidence of human sacrifice in blood-drenched temples on offshore islands.

On June 24, the feast day of Saint John the Baptist, the Spaniards visited a small island that they named San Juan de Ulúa. From there Grijalva ordered Pedro de Alvarado, captain of one of the ships, to return to Cuba with the good tidings and some of the loot. The other three ships continued exploring northward along the Gulf of Mexico as far as the Pánuco River where they turned back and headed homeward. By the time Grijalva returned, he had been gone from Cuba for more than six months. Meanwhile, the news brought by Alvarado spurred Governor Velásquez to authorize a third voyage, this one to be commanded by Hernán Cortés.

Cortés was an *hidalgo* (an untitled nobleman) from Extremadura, a western province of Spain that produced a number of New World conquistadors. As a young man he had studied Latin and served an apprenticeship to a notary before deciding to seek fame and fortune overseas. He wavered between joining the armies fighting in Italy or attaching himself to an expedition bound for the West Indies; finally he opted for the latter. In 1502, when he was scheduled to leave

Hernán Cortés. Watercolor by Christopher Weiditz, 1542. Courtesy Germanisches Nationalmuseum, Nürenberg.

with Ovando, he missed the boat because of an amorous escapade, but two years later, at age nineteen, he sailed for Española. Bernal Díaz later wrote, "I heard it said that when he was a young man in Española he was a little wild about women." At first Cortés tried mining on the island; then, after helping to subdue an Indian rebellion, he received an *encomienda* of Indians, a trusteeship whereby he could collect tribute or labor from natives in return for protecting and Christianizing them. Cortés also was appointed notary of the town of Azúa.

In 1511 when Diego Velásquez went to conquer Cuba and become its Spanish governor, Cortés accompanied him as his secretary. By distinguishing himself in combat, Cortés acquired land and Indians to work for him panning for gold, planting sugar cane, and taking care of livestock. During the succeeding seven years in Cuba he amassed a fortune of three thousand *castellanos;* courted and eventually married Doña Catalina Xuárez (sister-in-law of Governor Velásquez); became *alcalde* (mayor) of Santiago, the principal town; and quarreled bitterly with Velásquez and then became friendly again. Proof of the governor's amity was his commissioning of Cortés as commander of the projected armada. His official instructions, dated October 23, 1518, dealt with Indian treatment, treasure that might be found, and trade; but they were ambiguous enough to give the commander a free hand in conquering any areas he chose.

Cortés, who had agreed to contribute two-thirds of the cost of the expedition, immediately began to assemble ships, supplies and men. Nearly all the veterans of Grijalva's voyage enlisted again, even though they had to furnish their own equipment and would receive no pay until booty or profits might be distributed. Moreover, all the men were asked to invest money in the adventure. The pilot, Alaminos, and chronicler, Díaz, both of whom had been with Hernández de Córdoba and Grijalva, signed up, as did two veteran captains of the second expedition, Pedro de Alvarado and Francisco de Montejo, who later would gain fame as conquerors of Guatemala and Yucatán respectively. Names of two priests were on the roster—Father Juan Díaz and the chaplain, Fray Bartolomé de Olmedo. Juan Sedeño was one of the richest men in the fleet; he furnished a ship, a store of cassava bread and salt pork, and came aboard with his own horse and a black slave. After leaving Santiago in late December, the squadron spent about six weeks along the Cuban coast loading provisions and recruiting additional men.

While preparations were underway, some of Cortés's enemies convinced Velásquez that his choice of a leader was a mistake. They persuaded him to send orders withdrawing the commission; but Cortés, who had invested his fortune in the scheme and who was filled with high ambition and quixotic pride, chose to disobey the governor. The stakes were high—failure could lead to his execution for acting contrary to royal orders, but success would permit him to override any legal irregularities. Bernal Díaz noted that upon receipt of his recall orders, "Cortés wrote Velásquez in the agreeable and complimentary terms which he knew so well how to use, and told him that he would set sail the next day and that he remained his humble servant."

In mid-February, 1519, the flotillà of eleven ships weighed anchor and sailed west. According to Díaz, the force totaled 508 soldiers, a hundred seamen, ten brass cannons, four falconets, two greyhounds, and sixteen horses—increased by one when Sedeño's mare foaled on the voyage. There were thirty-two cross-bowmen and thirteen musketeers; the great majority of the soldiers were armed with Toledo swords, their principal weapon. The men were a tough lot. Some had fought against Moors in Spain, others had been in combat in Italy, and all had battled Indians in various parts of the Caribbean. A few were partisans of Velásquez, but most were loyal to Cortés, who continued to hold their affection by his talent of combining firmness with tact and graciousness. In spite of his limited military experience, he proved to be a courageous and resourceful commander.

Landfall was at the Island of Cozumel off the east shore of the Yucatán peninsula. When Cortés heard rumors that two Spaniards were kept as captives by Indians on the mainland, he sent messengers with ransom beads to find them. One of the rescued men was Jerónimo de Aguilar who had been a slave of the Maya for eight years. Delighted to join his compatriots on Cozumel, he told how he was one of a dozen Spanish shipwreck survivors who had been cast upon the shore in Yucatán, where some of his companions had been sacrificed and only two were still alive. The other castaway, Gonzalo de Guerrero, refused to join the Spaniards because he had "gone native," with skin tattooed, ears and lips pierced, and he had an Indian wife and three children, the first known *mestizos* (offspring of European and Indian parents) in Mexican history. Cortés was fortunate to find Aguilar, whose bilingualism gave the Spaniards a valuable key to the Maya tongue.

From Cozumel the Spaniards sailed around the tip of Yucatán and along the Gulf Coast. At the mouth of the Grijalva River, where the previous expedition had received gold from the natives, the situation had changed; this time thousands of warriors opposed their landing. Aguilar later found out that their attitude had altered because they had been called cowards by the warlike people of Champotón. He also learned that one of the Indian translators brought from Yucatán by Hernández had run away and encouraged these Tabascans to fight against the Spaniards. It was here that Cortés first realized the value of horses in fighting against Indians — having never seen such animals, the natives feared them and fled. A few mounted men, swinging their battle clubs, could overwhelm a numerically superior foe. After the battle Cortés took formal possession of the land in the name of His Majesty, Charles V.

The Tabascan *caciques,* or chiefs, then came to make peace, bearing many gifts including, in the custom of the country, twenty Indian maidens for the principal officers. Because the young women were pagans, the Spaniards did not want to cohabit with them — until they were baptized by the chaplain. One of the damsels, whose native name was Malinche and Christian name Marina, was the daughter of an Aztec *cacique* from the Coatzacoalcos region. Some years earlier she had been traded into servitude to the Tabascan tribe; thus she could speak both Nahuatl and Maya, and in the early days of the conquest, before she learned Spanish, she translated Aztec speech into Maya which Aguilar then rendered into Spanish. Moreover, she became a loyal friend and advisor of the conquistadors, saving them from several embarrassing or threatening situations. At first Marina was given to Alonso Hernández Puertocarrero, but when, a short time later, Cortés sent him to Spain, Don Hernán took Doña Marina as his mistress. Eventually she bore him a son named Martín, and later she married another conquistador, Juan Jaramillo. Some historians consider Marina the heroine of the conquest; others view her as a traitor who sold out her Indian compatriots to foreign conquerors. In any case she was a remarkable woman, who formed a part of the "Indian conquest of Mexico."

Marina's bilingualism proved useful when Cortés's fleet anchored near the small offshore island of San Juan de Ulúa. The next day, Good Friday, April 22, 1519, the captain disembarked his troops and established temporary headquarters on sand dunes near the future site of Veracruz. Here Cortés's men first came into direct contact with Aztecs when the native governor and tax collector welcomed them, gave them gifts, and said they had been expecting the strangers. For the next several months the Spanish commander and agents of Moctezuma conducted a complicated series of interviews, negotiations, and exchanges of gifts while each leader attempted to find out as much as he could about the other. From the beginning, Cortés insisted that he would visit Tenochtitlán but Moctezuma, who was unsure about the "divinity" of the visitors, adopted a policy of delay and appeasement.

To impress Moctezuma's ambassadors, the Spaniards put on a show for them. First the chaplain chanted mass, during which the Spanish soldiers demonstrated their humility and religious devotion. Then there was a banquet followed by a long speech in which the commander, through his interpreters Aguilar and Marina, explained that they were Christians and vassals of Emperor Charles V, "the greatest lord on earth," who had many great princes as his vassals and who

Cortés and La Malinche (Lienzo de Tlaxcala). Courtesy Organization of American States.

wanted to be a friend of Moctezuma. Later, cannons were fired and cavalrymen galloped their snorting horses to impress the Aztec agents. All the while, native artists painted pictures on cotton cloth depicting the men, horses, guns, swords, cross, and crossbows. Runners carried these pictographs to the Mexican emperor's palace along with Cortés's presents: twisted glass beads, Dutch linen shirts, a crimson cap with a gold medal of Saint George, and an inlaid armchair for Moctezuma "so that he could be seated in it when he, Cortés, came to see and speak with him."

Moctezuma's generous gifts dazzled and pleased the Spaniards. One embassy of five nobles, accompanied by a hundred Indian bearers, brought thirty loads of cotton cloth woven with colored feathers, fans, gold ornaments shaped like animals, necklaces, a helmet full of gold nuggets, and the regalia of Quetzalcoatl that his high priest would don on special occasions. This outfit included a turquoise mask topped by a headdress of quetzal feathers and a breastplate covered with jewels. Accoutrements for two other gods, Tlaloc and Tezcatlipoca, were also presented. To the Spaniards, the most important articles were two great discs the size of cart-wheels. One was of gold and represented the sun; the other was solid silver and imitated the moon. Both were finely wrought and handsomely tooled. With these presents the ambassadors entreated the "gods" to return to the east from whence they came. Instead of appeasing the visitors, the gifts whetted their appetites and suggested the opulence awaiting them in the Aztec capital.

Before Cortés could march to Tenochtitlán he had to deal with dissidence within his company. Some partisans of Velásquez thought that Cortés was exceeding his orders; others, who were ill, homesick, or cowardly, wanted to return to Cuba. Already thirty men had died from fevers or wounds received in previous battles. As a way of unifying his troops and gaining independent control of the expedition, the commander decided on a legal expedient—he would found a town to be called La Villa Rica de la Vera Cruz (the rich town of the True Cross), later simplified to Vera Cruz and generally spelled as one word today. When a *cabildo* or town council was elected, it demanded to see Cortés's instructions from Velásquez, and having examined them found that the armada captain no longer had any authority. Thereupon the *cabildo* elected Cortés to serve His Majesty as "Chief Justice, *Alcalde,* and Captain of Your Royal Armies," and it authorized him a fifth—in addition to the king's fifth—of all booty that might be obtained. By these legal maneuvers Cortés claimed that he was no longer an agent of the Cuban governor but a loyal captain directly responsible to the Spanish monarch.

The arrival of Francisco de Salcedo's caravel, which had been delayed in leaving Cuba, brought news that Velásquez had been granted rights of settlement on the mainland. Such potential competition prompted the *cabildo* of Veracruz to send two agents, Francisco de Montejo and Alonso Hernández Puertocarrero, to Spain with treasure and letters of explanation requesting royal approval of Cortés's embryo colony. Wishing to make the best impression possible, the two men asked their companions to assemble the treasure they had thus far acquired and "give it all voluntarily to His Majesty, so that he may bestow favors on us."

Meanwhile, Cortés and his men had been exploring the neighborhood, especially Cempoala, a settlement of Totonac Indians north of Veracruz. Here the local *cacique*, dubbed "Gordo" ("Fatty") by the Spaniards, complained that his people and other tribes subject to the Aztecs were being oppressed by constant demands for tribute and young men to be slain as sacrificial victims. When five Mexican tax collectors (*calpixques*) suddenly appeared. Cortés advised Gordo to have them arrested. That night the Spaniards secretly released the agents and sent them back to Moctezuma. Gordo's action against the Aztecs forced him to ally with the Spaniards. The Europeans then set about destroying idols in Cempoala and Christianizing the people of that village. In place of blood-spattered stone images the Europeans erected a whitewashed altar to the Virgin, and they ordered four Totonac priests to wash themselves, cut their hair, change their garments from black to white, and take charge of the shrine. To celebrate the new alliance, eight Indian maidens, newly baptized, were presented to the Spanish officers; Cortés being the senior officer was obliged to take Gordo's niece, Catalina, acknowledged to be the ugliest of the group.

Two dramatic events occurred before the Spaniards began their march inland. When he learned that several men planned to desert and sail back to Cuba, Cortés ordered the execution of two instigators of the plot. Bernal Díaz remembered his captain saying, "Would that I did not know how to write, so as not to have to sign away men's lives!" To prevent similar defections Cortés ordered all the ships scuttled after removal of anchors, cables, sails, and other useful items. This was a clever move; it not only cut off easy retreat, it reinforced his army with about a hundred masters, pilots, and sailors, many of whom proved to be good soldiers. Before leaving the coast, Cortés detailed a small party of men under Juan de Escalante to garrison the fort at Veracruz.

On August 16, 1519, the expeditionary force of four hundred Spaniards moved toward the highlands, destination Tenochtitlán, by way of the independent nation of Tlaxcala. Two hundred Totonac bearers, fifty Indian warriors, and several Cempoalan nobles were in the entourage. Two weeks later the invaders crossed the rock wall into Tlaxcalan territory where they fought and narrowly won three battles. Then the Tlaxcalan chief, Xicoténcatl, invited them into the city of Tlaxcala where he housed the Spanish officers in his palace. The natives seemed friendly to the visitors, and there was much fraternization. When noble maidens of Tlaxcala were offered to the Spanish officers as concubines, Cortés refused, but his lieutenant, Pedro de Alvarado, accepted Xicoténcatl's daughter, a handsome young woman baptized as Luisa. In Tlaxcala the Spaniards erected a Christian altar, and they released several Indian captives from cages where they had been awaiting sacrifice. After some discussion the Tlaxcalans allied themselves with the Spaniards and agreed to provide a large military escort for them, a move disliked by Moctezuma's envoys, who had come bearing more gifts for the bearded strangers.

In the second week of October, Cortés continued his march to the Aztec capital, taking the route by way of Cholula. This ancient city, about a day's march from Tlaxcala, was devoted to the god Quetzalcoatl, whose temple was atop the huge pyramid that still dominates the area. Indian priests and leaders welcomed the Spaniards at the outskirts of Cholula, but they insisted that the five thousand Tlaxcalan war-

riors camp outside their city. During the first three days
that the Spaniards, their Cempoalan allies, and a few Tlaxcalan bearers spent in Cholula, their hosts' attitude cooled,
and it became apparent that an ambush was being prepared.
Some of the streets were barricaded; others had cleverly-
concealed holes full of pointed sticks to injure the horses;
piles of stones were observed on many of the flat rooftops;
many women and children had left the city; twenty thousand
Aztec warriors from the capital were reported to be hidden
in ravines a league and a half away; and the Cholulans
(Cholotecas) had sacrificed seven persons to their god of war,
a customary ceremony before a battle. Doña Marina corrobo-
rated this intelligence when she cajoled a native woman into
revealing some of the plans.

Cortés turned the planned ambush into the tragic "Cholula
Massacre." After ordering all his men and allies to be on the
alert, he summoned as many Cholulan leaders as he could
gather and locked them in a room. Outside, he mounted his
horse and led most of his soldiers to a plaza where a great
number of Cholulan warriors had assembled, and on a pre-
arranged signal the Spaniards attacked the leaderless Indians.
It was a blood bath! Reporting to the Spanish king, Cortés
said, "We fought so hard that in two hours more than three
thousand men were killed." The Tlaxcalan warriors had
rushed into the city where they ran amok, killing, looting,
and taking prisoners. Later Cortés ordered the Tlaxcalans
to free their captives and return to their camp. When he
reprimanded the confined Cholulan leaders for their duplic-
ity, they said they had followed orders from Tenochtitlán,
a claim later repudiated by Moctezuma. The defeated leaders
asked for and received clemency after swearing loyalty to the
Spanish king and agreeing to reestablish friendly relations
with Tlaxcala.

The Spaniards remained in Cholula for the next two weeks,
pacifying the region and reconnoitering the road to the
Aztec capital. To demonstrate the supremacy of their religion they replaced the Quetzalcoatl temple with a huge cross
on the great pyramid; it was visible for miles around. Curi-

ous about the smoking volcano, Popocatépetl, which straddles the ridge between Cholula and the Valley of Mexico, a squad of men under Diego de Ordáz decided to climb it. It is not clear whether they reached the crater at 5,452 meters (17,890 feet) above the sea, but from the snowy mountain they saw the Valley of Mexico with its lagoons and cities. More important, they discovered a good road that led rather directly to the capital. Before the invaders set out along this road, most of the Cempoalan allies returned to their coastal homeland. About four thousand Tlaxcalan Indians accompanied the four hundred European soldiers—a relatively small force to invade the heartland of the Aztec empire.

The march from Cholula to Tenochtitlán occupied the first week of November, 1519. Along the way the visitors received assurances of friendship and gifts from local leaders as well as from embassies sent by Moctezuma; presents included food, gold, cloth, and female slaves. When several *caciques* complained privately to Cortés about the harsh treatment and oppressive taxes imposed by the central government, he realized that the empire had internal weaknesses, even in the region close to the capital. Two Aztec ambassadors were members of the royal family: Cacama, who ruled Texcoco, and Cuitláhuac, Moctezuma's brother, whose seat of power was Iztapalapa. At the latter place the visitors were lodged in spacious and well-built palaces "of beautiful stone work and cedar wood . . . with great rooms and courts." From that city, a stone causeway eight paces wide led directly to the island capital. Moctezuma, carried on a gold-encrusted litter and surrounded by great nobles, came out to meet the visitors. Bernal Díaz, who witnessed the confrontation of the Aztec emperor and the Spanish captain, described the meeting of November 8, 1519:

When we came close to Mexico [Tenochtitlán], where there were other smaller towers, Montezuma descended from his litter while these great chiefs supported him with their arms beneath a marvelously rich canopy of green feathers, worked with gold and silver, pearls and *chalchiuis* [jades or turquoises], which hung from a kind of border that was wonderful to see. He was richly dressed and wore shoes like sandals, with soles of gold covered with precious stones. The four chiefs who supported him were also richly dressed, in clothes that had apparently been held ready for them on the road, for they had not worn them when they received us. . . .

When Cortés saw the great Montezuma approaching, he jumped from his horse and they showed great respect toward each other. Montezuma welcomed him; and through Doña Marina, Cortés replied that he hoped that Montezuma was in good health. . . .

Then Cortés gave him a necklace he had ready at hand, made of the glass stones that I have already called margaritas, which have in them many designs and a variety of colors. They were strung on a golden cord and sweetly scented with musk. He placed it around Montezuma's neck and was going to embrace him when the princes accompanying him caught Cortés by the arm so that he could not do so, for they thought it an indignity.

Through Doña Marina, Cortés said he rejoiced at meeting so great a prince, and Montezuma answered politely and commanded his nephews to show us to our quarters.*

In Tenochtitlán the Spaniards were lodged in the old imperial palace which had belonged to Moctezuma's father, Axayácatl; it was on the west side of the principal plaza near the new royal residence and adjacent to the temple compound. During the next few days Cortés and Moctezuma exchanged formal visits, during which Doña Marina acted as interpreter. At each visit the Aztec emperor gave the Spanish officers clothing, gold chains, and many gifts, including one of his own daughters to Cortés. He also conducted them on a tour of the great pyramid of Tlatelolco where Cortés, repelled by the bloody idols, human skulls, and burning hearts, unsuccessfully tried to preach Christianity to his host. Although Moctezuma was not ready to abandon his gods, he did declare that the prophesy of his ancestors had been fulfilled, and he acknowledged as his overlord the king to whom Cortés owed allegiance.

*Albert Idell, ed. and trans., *The Bernal Díaz Chronicles* (Garden City: Doubleday, 1956), 142. Copyright ©1956 by Albert Idell. Reprinted by permission of Doubleday & Company, Inc.

Moctezuma's acquiescence to the "Men from the East" made it easy for them to imprison him. Only a week after their arrival they persuaded the Aztec chief to move into their quarters — Doña Marina cautioned him that the alternative was death. In his palace-prison he was permitted the customary retinue of personal service, and he carried on government business with several high officials in attendance at all times. But in reality he had become a puppet, issuing orders that Cortés dictated.

About the time the Aztec leader was confined, his captors received news that Indians on the Gulf Coast had killed Juan de Escalante, commander of the garrison at Veracruz, and six of his men. Suspecting that Moctezuma had ordered the attack, Cortés confronted him with the issue and demanded that those responsible be brought to Tenochtitlán. Some days later Qualpopoca, leader of the attack, and sixteen other Indians appeared before Cortés, who interrogated them. At first the men denied Moctezuma's connection, then later, perhaps in a desperate attempt to save their own lives, they said they were obeying the command of their emperor. In any event, Cortés ordered them to be burned alive in public, and while that sentence was carried out, the implicated Moctezuma was put in chains, a humiliating experience for a great chief.

During the next five months the Spanish officers tried to determine the extent of the Aztec empire, locate its sources of wealth, and devise ways to subjugate the entire region. In their own palace-quarters they discovered a plastered-over doorway which they secretly opened to reveal a treasure chamber filled with slabs of gold, jewels, idols, and magnificent featherwork. Bernal Díaz said, "When I saw it I marvelled, and as at that time I was a youth and had never seen such riches as those in my life before, I took it for certain that there could not be another such store of wealth in the whole world." Much later the treasure, six hundred thousand pesos of it in gold, was melted into ingots; after setting aside the *quinto real* (king's fifth, a legal requirement), it was divided among the Spaniards according to rank. As might be expected, there were quarrels over the uneven distribution of spoils. When asked about the original source of the precious metals, Moctezuma sent guides with two Spaniards to each of the four principal mining regions. These men returned with nuggets as well as descriptions of the provinces they passed through. Spanish supremacy was consolidated when all of Moctezuma's tributary *caciques* and lords were summoned to Tenochtitlán, where he told them that henceforth they were to pay tribute and fealty to the Spanish emperor.

Although Moctezuma had been won over and seemed resigned to his fate, several of his princely relatives plotted an uprising to expel or kill the invaders. Cacama, Moctezuma's nephew and the ruler of Texcoco, led the movement, which was supported by the emperor's brother Cuitláhuac, chief of Iztapalapa, and the lords of Tlacopan (Tacuba) and Coyoacán. Emissaries from Texcoco made it clear that Cacama intended to seize power. To prevent this coup d'etat and possible civil war, Moctezuma arranged for the arrest of Cacama and his fellow conspirators, who were all imprisoned in the Aztec capital.

Having subdued the Aztec political leaders, Cortés next turned his attention to religious matters. He himself mounted the principal pyramid, entered the shrines atop it, cast blood-encrusted idols down the steps, and ordered the temples cleansed before a cross and images of the Virgin and Catholic saints were installed there. He also lectured to the native high priests, urging them to abandon human sacrifice since it was abhorrent to God and contrary to laws of the Spanish empire. Desecration of their shrines and idols shocked the religious leaders and Moctezuma. In their outrage they demanded that the Spaniards return to their own land. Cortés finally agreed to leave, but said that first he would have to build ships.

In this strained situation the Spanish commander received word in April, 1520, that an armada of eighteen ships bearing some eight hundred men and eighty horses had landed on the Gulf Coast. They were not an auxiliary from Spain—on the contrary, they had been sent out by Governor Velásquez, who gave the leader, Pánfilo de Narváez, orders to arrest Cortés and return him to Cuba for judgment. Furthermore, Indian messengers had advised Moctezuma about the purpose of the new invasion. Cortés met this threat to his position in a characteristic way; he sent Narváez a formal letter welcoming him to the mainland "because he knew that he had come to serve His Majesty." The best way to do that, he maintained, was through cooperation with his countrymen who already had established Spanish authority by founding towns and pacifying Indian settlements including the rich capital of Tenochtitlán.

In addition to diplomacy Cortés employed bribery and arms to win over the interlopers from Cuba. He sent Fray Bartolomé de Olmedo and other agents to Narváez's camp near Cempoala; they carried bags of gold to embellish their arguments. Leaving Pedro de Alvarado in command of about 120 men at the capital, Cortés took the remaining soldiers and moved slowly toward the coast for the expected showdown. Although outnumbered almost three to one, the "old-timers" won by using superior tactics. They attacked at night, seized the cannons, and took the rival leader prisoner. Narváez lost the battle, his liberty, and one eye in the skirmish. Cortés gained confidence and an important reinforcement of munitions, horses, and men, with which he headed back toward the Valley of Anáhuac.

Meanwhile, relations between Spaniards and Indians in the capital had greatly deteriorated. The temporary commander, golden-haired Pedro de Alvarado, called "Sunlight" (Tonatiuh) by the natives, was brave but impetuous, and he lacked the tact and wisdom of his captain. When he learned that Aztec priests, warriors, and dancers had gathered in the temple enclosure to celebrate the spring festival, and when he heard that they were preparing to sacrifice human victims, perhaps as a prelude to an uprising, he ordered his men to attack the worshippers. Hundreds of defenseless Mexicans were butchered in this massacre. The native popu-

Narváez and a black soldier arrive at Cempoala (Codex Durán). Courtesy The Bancroft Library.

lation then rose against the foreigners and besieged them in the palace where Moctezuma was still held prisoner.

At this critical moment the Aztecs permitted Cortés and his men, along with three thousand Tlaxcalan allies, to enter the capital city, where they joined Alvarado on June 24, 1520. Doubtless the native strategy was to destroy the united forces by isolating them on the island where they could be cut off from foodstuffs and reinforcements. During the last week in June the Aztecs launched a series of attacks on the palace, even setting fire to a part of it; they removed the causeway bridges to prevent escape; they cut off provisions to the foreigners; and they beat back Spanish sallies out of the fortress. Moctezuma himself was powerless; prodded by the Spaniards, he went to the palace roof to implore his subjects to call off the attack, but they refused to heed him, and he was struck on the head by a stone. Bernal Díaz says that he died from the injury a few days later, but another source states that he was stabbed five times with a Spanish dagger. In any event, he had already been deposed as Chief Speaker— replaced by his brother Cuitláhuac, who was determined to expel or kill the outlanders. Rather than face starvation or certain defeat in the city, the Spaniards chose to withdraw temporarily.

The retreat was planned in secrecy with the night of June 30 set for the escape. Preparations in the palace included construction of a portable wooden bridge to span the causeway gaps. Soldiers carefully loaded Aztec treasure on horses and mules; Cortés later wrote to the Spanish emperor, "I took all Your Majesty's gold and jewels which we could carry . . . and distributed the remainder among the Spaniards." The total force to be evacuated was considerable: about a thousand Spaniards and four thousand Tlaxcalans. Among those who received special consideration were Doña Marina; Alvarado's mistress, Doña Luisa; a son and two daughters of Moctezuma; and several Aztec chiefs who had been held as prisoners.

As the retreating army moved out along the Tlacopan (Tacuba) causeway, the alarm was given, and Aztec warriors attacked from hundreds of canoes while others hurled arrows, darts, and stones. Hand-to-hand fighting was continuous along the causeway, which stretched for more than five kilometers (three miles) to the mainland. In a short while the bridge was unnecessary because the water openings were choked with horses, dead bodies, boxes, and baggage. Casualties were high. More than half of the Spaniards were killed; some drowned, weighed down with gold; others were captured, later to be sacrificed. Dead Indian allies totaled at least a thousand, all of the cannon were lost, most of the treasure was abandoned or fell into the canals, and only twenty-three horses survived. A number of the foot soldiers were injured, "nor was there a horseman who could raise his arm." The captain himself was wounded in the head and lost the use of two fingers; after mustering the survivors near Tacuba, he sat down and wept. Ever since then, the Spanish rout has been known in Mexican history as *la noche triste,* the sad night.

After the *noche triste,* the retiring forces headed for the security of Tlaxcala, where they planned to recuperate before attempting the reconquest of Anáhuac. An Aztec army harassed the Spaniards on their way out of the valley, but at the battle of Otumba the Europeans won a decisive victory after slaying the enemy chieftain and dispersing his plumed followers.

During the autumn of 1520, Cortés and his men carried out raids and used diplomacy to gain adherents in the area to the east of the Valley of Mexico. They defeated the Indians at Tepeaca, where they founded a garrison town named Segura de la Frontera. It was located at a strategic point on the Veracruz road and controlled access to the south. Here two hundred additional Spanish recruits joined them, bringing their horses and weapons. Some of the men were from Jamaica, others had arrived from Cuba, intended as reinforcements for Narváez. Late in December, when preparations were completed, the combined Spanish-Tlaxcalan army crossed the mountains westward into the heartland of Anáhuac.

Strategy for the final conquest of the Aztecs involved

reducing the outlying towns before laying siege to Tenochtitlán. From their headquarters in Texcoco, where they had
the support of rebel chief Ixtlilxochitl, the Spaniards subdued settlements around Lake Texcoco from Xaltocan on the
north to Xochimilco and Iztapalapa on the south. Fierce battles were fought at the last two places, but leaders and residents of Chalco, who felt harassed under Tenochca rule,
readily allied themselves with the foreigners. By May, 1521,
when the island capital had been isolated and blockaded,
Cortés initiated an amphibious attack using a secret weapon,
thirteen brigantines, which were launched on Lake Texcoco.
These vessels had been constructed by a force of Tlaxcalans
under the supervision of a Spanish shipwright, then they
were dismantled and carried over the mountains to Lake
Texcoco, where they were bolted together and fitted out with
sails, oars, and swivel cannons. Each brigantine was thirteen
meters (forty-two feet) long and carried a crew of twenty-
five, including oarsmen, archers, and gunners. The brigantines were a key factor in the campaign—they could out-
maneuver the frail Aztec canoes, ram them, or destroy them
by gunfire.

The Spanish attacking army totaled about nine hundred
men, formed into three columns commanded by Alvarado,
Olid, and Sandoval. Cortés managed overall operations and
dispatched the brigantines. Each of the three land units,
supported by cavalrymen and thousands of Indian allies,
approached the capital from a different causeway. Because
the Mexicans defended their chief city with a fanatical tenac-
ity, the bloody siege lasted for almost eighty days. The courageous and determined Aztec chief, subsequently revered as
a great hero, was Cuauhtémoc a young nephew of Moctezuma
who had been elected to succeed Cuitláhuac when the latter
died in a smallpox epidemic. Unwittingly introduced into
Mexico by Narváez's men, this disease proved to be another
deadly weapon as it decimated Indians during the conquest.
In addition to that plague, the defenders of the capital suffered from famine and were reduced to eating reptiles,
weeds, tree bark, corn cobs, and scum from the lake. Their

potable water was scarce after Spaniards severed the Chapultepec aqueduct, yet they refused to surrender.

Day by day the attackers made sallies into the island city, filling in causeway gaps with rubble, tearing down barricades, engaging the enemy, then at sunset retreating to the mainland. In retaliation the city's defenders opened up the breaches and continually harassed the Spaniards with frontal attacks supported by canoe landings all along the causeways. Contemporary accounts reveal that cannibalism was practiced on both sides. After an ambush in which more than five hundred Aztecs were killed, Cortés wrote "That night our allies dined sumptuously, for all those they had killed were sliced up and eaten." At the end of June the Aztec defenders won a great victory when they killed a number of besiegers and captured alive sixty-six Spaniards. Close to the action, a contingent of Alvarado's soldiers watched as their erstwhile companions were marched naked to the top of a pyramid where they were sacrificed to Huitzilopochtli. This Spanish reverse caused thousands of Indian allies to desert and return home.

Cortés then determined to demolish all the buildings as his troops advanced into the city, filling up not only causeways but also most of the canals, thereby converting water into firm land. In a dispatch to Spain the captain expressed regret for the destruction of "the most beautiful city in the world." Even after seven-eighths of the metropolis had been ruined, temples on top of pyramids set to the torch, palaces razed to the ground, and corpses piled high in the streets, the indomitable Cuauhtémoc held on. Prophetically, his name meant "Falling Eagle."

An anonymous survivor composed in Nahuatl the following epic description of the besieged city:

> *Broken spears lie in the roads;*
> *we have torn our hair in our grief.*
> *The houses are roofless now, and their walls*
> *are red with blood.*

Worms are swarming in the streets and plazas,
and the walls are splattered with gore.
The water has turned red, as if it were dyed,
and when we drink it,
it has the taste of brine.

We have pounded our hands in despair
against the adobe walls,
for our inheritance, our city, is lost and dead.
The shields of our warriors were its defense,
but they could not save it.

We have chewed dry twigs and salt grasses . . .
we have eaten lizards, rats and worms. . . .
Gold, jade, rich cloths, quetzal feathers —
everything that once was precious
*was now considered worthless.**

Finally, after tens of thousands of his followers had died or been killed, the last Aztec emperor was apprehended aboard the royal canoe as he attempted to slip away from the capital. Taken to Cortés, he is reported to have pointed to the victor's dagger and demanded death. He lived as a prisoner for three additional years, but Cuauhtémoc's empire ceased with his capture on August 13, 1521.

How do we explain the victory of those few hundred Spaniards against an Aztec confederation of millions? A major factor was the compared military technology: steel swords versus obsidian-edged clubs; muskets and cannon against arrows and spears; metal helmets and bucklers in contrast to feathered headdresses and shields. In addition, the Europeans had horses, war dogs, armed brigantines, and the services of thousands of Indian allies. While the Aztecs tried to capture enemy soldiers rather than kill them, the Spaniards concentrated on killing the easily identifiable Indian commanders, a tactic that demoralized and confused the Aztec defenders. The invaders' accumulated experience battling

---

*Miguel León-Portilla, ed., *The Broken Spears; The Aztec Account of the Conquest of Mexico* (Boston: The Beacon Press, 1962), 137–38.

Moors and Caribbean Indians undoubtedly gave them valuable skills as well as confidence in their prowess.

Although superseded by the culture of the Spanish conquistadors, many elements of the great Aztec civilization persisted throughout the Spanish colonial era and still exist today. Nahuatl is spoken by hundreds of thousands of Mexicans; cultivation of maize, maguey, tomatoes, henequin, cacao, and other indigenous crops dominates the agricultural sector; enchiladas, tacos, and tamales are served in most homes and restaurants; pre-Columbian folkways, folk medicine, and folk arts continue; and "Aztec blood" courses through the veins of millions of descendants of that proud race.

CHAPTER 4

New Spain Established

ON THE RUINS of the Aztec empire the conquistadors established a colony they called *Nueva España*, or New Spain, a name suggested by Cortés himself. This Spanish colony endured for three hundred years—three times as long as the Aztecs had controlled central Mexico—and at its zenith its geographical extent (not counting the Caribbean or Philippine Islands that were under New Spain's jurisdiction) was more than forty-five times that of Cuauhtémoc's empire, fourteen times larger than Spain, and three and a half times the size of modern Mexico. The colony of New Spain, like its Caribbean antecedants, was transformed over the years into a series of provinces with Iberian institutions, culture, and technology superimposed on the indigenous American society.

The society that emerged was openly racist, with white Europeans dominating red Indians. An exception was the remnant of Aztec nobility whose members were respected and whose daughters married without prejudice into Spanish families; through assimilation this anomaly disappeared in a few decades. Generally the races lived apart, but there soon arose a hybrid population of *mestizos,* offspring of Spanish-Indian unions. This was a result of the Spanish "sexual conquest of Mexico" carried out by conquistadors and later male immigrants, many of whom acquired native concubines or wives. As related in the previous chapter, miscegenation began in earnest with Hernán Cortés, who had at least eight Mexican Indian mistresses. But not all his energies were expended in matters of love.

After the fall of Tenochtitlán, Cortés established his temporary headquarters in nearby Coyoacán while the old Aztec metropolis was rebuilt as a splendid capital that was renamed Mexico (City). Indian *caciques* directed native laborers in the work of demolition and construction of new buildings, many built of the handsome *tezontle*, a brown lava stone. The cathedral, *cabildo* (city hall), and Cortés's palace were built on the *zócalo*, or central plaza, where once stood the great pyramid with twin temples dedicated to Huitzilopochtli and Tlaloc. (Archaeological excavation begun in 1978 uncovered the base of the pyramid and many Aztec artifacts.) By 1524, more than thirty thousand people lived in Mexico City, and the markets were functioning again, but it would be many years longer before the city reached its pre-Columbian population. In addition to civic buildings the forced labor battalions erected town houses for the conquistadors. Spanish soldiers received land and Indian labor as a reward for their services; this bonus proved to be more valuable than their share of Aztec booty.

Much of the Aztec treasure was either lost during the *noche triste* or hidden by Indian chiefs before the final Spanish conquest. According to an official report the gold booty amounted to 130,000 pesos. When the royal fifth and the captain's fifth had been set aside, the treasurer divided the remainder "by rank and merit." Bernal Díaz said that horsemen received eighty pesos, about the cost of a horse, and infantrymen only fifty. Dissatisfied soldiers and the royal treasurer then persuaded Cortés to torture Cuauhtémoc and Tetlepanquetzatl (the former ruler of Tacuba), hoping that they would reveal the location of more Aztec treasure. Their feet were daubed with oil and then set over a charcoal fire, but this coercion produced no disclosures; instead the ordeal brightened the reputation of the stoic native chiefs while it smudged that of Cortés.

Besides a limited amount of gold and their town lots, many conquistadors acquired rural land, which was a principal source of prestige, wealth, and political power in Spanish society. According to Castilian law and custom, as new lands were conquered they automatically passed to the crown, which then, through its agents, made grants of the tillable

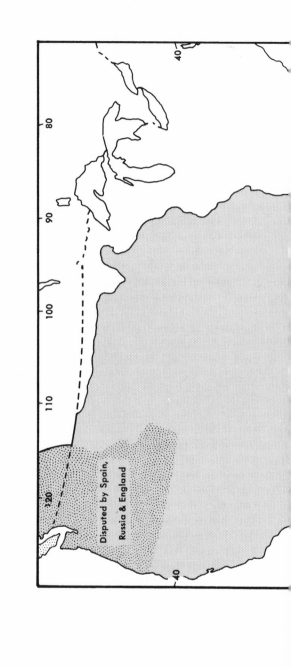

Disputed by Spain,
Russia & England

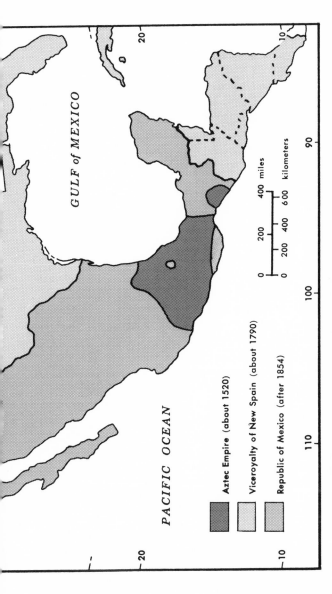

Extent of Aztec Empire, Viceroyalty, and Republic

surface, reserving the subsoil or mineral rights for royal ownership. Most Indians had little concept of private land ownership in the European sense. Their fields were held in common by a clan, village, or tribe, and vast areas were unoccupied or uncultivated. After the conquest most villages were permitted to retain their traditional lands, but encroachment by Spaniards was a continuing problem. Scattered Indian families and small communities were forced to live together in *congregaciones* or concentrated towns; this rule made control of them easier, and it freed additional lands for the conquerors. Although many Spaniards became great landowners, they preferred to live in a town or city and have a major-domo or overseer manage their rural estates.

The granting of Indian tribute to principal conquistadors followed a pattern established earlier in the Caribbean Islands. Under this practice, known as the *encomienda,* a village or group of Indians was commended to a deserving Spaniard who had the obligation to protect, Christianize, and civilize the natives. In return he could collect and keep the tribute or tax that the village customarily paid and that otherwise would go to the crown. (The *encomienda* was not a land grant.) When the Indians could not pay the tribute in goods, as frequently happened, the *encomendero* (grantee) commuted the obligation into personal service or labor. In New Spain the towns of Tlaxcalans and other loyal Indian allies were exempt from this assessment. Villages not encompassed by an *encomienda* became crown towns and were obliged to pay the crown the same annual tribute formerly rendered to Indian overlords. Aztec tribute lists in picture writing identified over four hundred subject towns and showed types and amounts of tribute paid.

Cortés's awarding of *encomiendas* involved him in a dispute with the crown. A generation of experience with the system in the Caribbean had proved disastrous to the natives—they were overworked, physically abused, and often cheated. A bitter controversy over the institution arose in Spain, and in 1520 Charles V enjoined Cortés from granting *encomiendas;* the Mexican Indians were supposed to become vassals of the crown. Nevertheless, Cortés ignored the royal ban and gave grants to his subordinate officers, arguing that the Indians needed to be protected from their own *caciques,* that it was the only way to assure Hispanization and Christianization of the natives, and that his men deserved and demanded them. The monarch reluctantly agreed to the *fait accompli,* but for the rest of the century the crown maneuvered to suppress approximately three hundred *encomiendas* granted to individuals in New Spain. There were also church and government *encomiendas.*

When New Spain was first established, Cortés attempted to secure royal approval of his actions and confirmation of his authority over the colony. To Charles V he sent long letters justifying each stage of the conquest, describing the potential wealth of various Indian regions, complaining about Spanish rivals, requesting religious missionaries to convert the natives, and listing Aztec treasures that were being forwarded to the crown. Not all the booty reached Spain. In 1523 a French corsair, Jean Fleury, captured two ships loaded with royal treasure and turned over part of the loot to King Francis I, a bitter foe of the Spanish monarch. This treasure trove was evidence to other Europeans that the Spaniards had hit upon a rich American civilization, and it encouraged them to challenge Iberian monopoly of the New World. And within the Spanish empire there were ambitious bureaucrats who wished to supplant Cortés.

All during the 1520s, Cortés's opponents in Spain and the Indies attempted to wrest the government of New Spain from him. At the end of 1521, Cristóbal de Tapia arrived in Veracruz with a royal mandate to take charge of the colony. His sponsor was Juan Rodríguez de Fonseca, bishop of Seville and "quasi-colonial minister" of Spain, who was also a patron of Governor Velásquez of Cuba. Tapia withdrew from New Spain after Cortés's supporters convinced him that it was in the royal interest not to upset the status quo. A year later Cortés was confirmed as governor and captain-general of

New Spain, but he was advised that a quartet of royal officials would soon arrive to assist him in the management of affairs.

Meanwhile, lieutenants of Cortés were expanding Spanish control beyond the Aztec heartland. In 1522 forces under Cristóbal de Olid marched northwestward into the land of the Tarascan Indians of Michoacán; then they moved on to the Pacific Coast where, at the mouth of the Balsas River, they founded a settlement at Zacatula. Here, a few years later, ships were built with which Cortés hoped to explore the Pacific and reach the East Indian islands recently discovered by Magellan. Along the Gulf of Mexico, Gonzalo de Sandoval reduced several areas to Spanish authority and founded towns south of Veracruz. In the Oaxaca Valley of southern Mexico an army under Francisco de Orozco subdued the Zapotecs, but their mountain-dwelling neighbors the Mixtecs proved more difficult until Pedro de Alvarado led a successful campaign against them. Alvarado's main column of four hundred Spaniards and twenty thousand Indian allies then moved south through the Isthmus of Tehuantepec, and in 1523–24 they conquered the highland Maya-speaking tribes of Guatemala and El Salvador. Later the Spanish king appointed Alvarado as governor and captain-general of Guatemala, a position he held until his death.

While Cortés's men were bringing more Indians under the Spanish colonial yoke, the spiritual conquest of Mexico also was under way. Systematic conversion of the natives to Christianity began with the arrival of Fray Pedro de Gante and two other Franciscan missionaries in 1523. The following year, Martín de Valencia headed a dozen members of that order who walked barefoot from Veracruz to Mexico City, where Cortés knelt before them and kissed their coarse gowns, an obeisance that greatly impressed the Indian witnesses. Soon members of the Dominican, Mercedarian, and Augustinian religious orders came to preach, baptize, establish schools and orphanages, and minister to the natives. Their new churches often were built at or near aboriginal sacred sites. Secular clergy, or parish priests under the control

Spanish church on Zapotec pyramid base, Mitla.

of a bishop, also began their labors early. They served the religious needs of the Spaniards and took over from the missionaries when their work of converting the natives was accomplished. Convents of nuns were established beginning in 1547, and members of other religious orders, including the Society of Jesus (Jesuits), arrived in the sixteenth century. In many ways the compassion and good works of the clerics countervailed the rapacity of the soldiers toward the Indians, but the priests could do little about feuding among the conquistadors.

More than once, Cortés encountered competition from fellow Spaniards who wanted to carve out their own empires in areas he claimed. In 1523, Francisco de Garay, governor of Jamaica, set out with a party to found a colony in the Huasteca Indian country at the mouth of the Pánuco River (near modern Tampico). He had obtained a royal grant for a vast territory that extended along the Gulf of Mexico from Florida well down the Mexican coast. Cortés had been in the Pánuco area the previous year and had set up a small post. When he heard of Garay's landing, he sent troops under Alvarado to enforce his claim. The crown ultimately decided in favor of Cortés, but a consequence of the conflict was a serious Indian rebellion, which was finally quelled. A few years later many Huasteca Indians were enslaved and sent as laborers to the Caribbean islands by another rival, Nuño de Guzmán, a noble who had been appointed governor of the region.

One of the most serious challenges to Cortés's authority took place in Honduras, where there was a clash between the men of New Spain and those sent north by the governor of Panama. In 1524 when Cortés sent Cristóbal de Olid by sea to enforce his claim to the area, Olid stopped in Cuba, conspired with Governor Velásquez, then sailed on to proclaim himself *adelantado* (frontier governor) of Honduras, renouncing his allegiance to the "Captain from Castile." But Olid's success was short-lived and he was beheaded by rivals.

In the meantime, Cortés, who was worried about the outcome, decided to march overland to Honduras on a hazardous and daring expedition. After appointing royal treasury officials to govern in his absence, in October, 1524, he set off with a force of about 140 Spaniards and 3,000 Indians, among them Cuauhtémoc and Doña Marina. For six months they hacked their way through dense forests, forded or bridged dozens of rivers, and crossed swamps and marshlands until they finally reached Honduras. Along the way, Cuauhtémoc and the former chief of Tacuba were hanged; they were accused of conspiring to organize an Indian rebellion against all Spaniards. Many Mexicans today, proud of their Indian heritage and heroes, assert that the charges were trumped-up, and they consider this act the most infamous of all of Cortés's deeds. Whether or not there was a conspiracy, the executions marked a radical change from the earlier treatment of Indian nobles by the conquistadors. When he arrived in Honduras and discovered that Olid was dead, Cortés began a systematic conquest of the region, but within a year he had to return to Mexico, where there was serious trouble.

Quarrels between government officials as well as their general misrule had resulted in virtual civil war in Mexico City. Partisanship of the leaders split the Spanish population, and the royal officials' greed led to wholesale exploitation and enslavement of Indians, some of whom rebelled against the Europeans. Alonzo de Estrada, one of the treasury officials Cortés had designated as his temporary replacement, was ousted by the royal *factor* (business agent) Gonzalo de Salazar and his associate Pedro Almíndez Cherino. This duo then conspired to unseat the captain-general. They sent reports to Spain accusing Cortés of defrauding the royal treasury, of plotting to set up an independent kingdom, and of murdering his wife, Catalina, who had died within a few months after her arrival in Mexico in 1522. When rumors spread that Cortés had perished on the trip to Honduras, the treasury officials held funeral services for him, confiscated his property, and persecuted his friends.

After Cortés heard of the rapacity of the royal agents, he sent his army back to Mexico via Guatemala while he returned by sea. Learning that Governor Velásquez had died, he stopped briefly in Cuba, where he was welcomed by old friends.

Cortés's return to Mexico in May, 1526, caused a sensation, even though he was so emaciated some of his companions did not immediately recognize him. When it was verified that the captain-general was still alive, his followers seized Salazar and Chirino and put them in cages in the plaza, where they were taunted by ruffians and townspeople. A fiesta was held to celebrate the return of Cortés, under whose leadership order was soon restored. Cortés also attempted to remedy the injuries suffered during the tyranny of the treasury officials, but his rule was cut short by the arrival of various officials from Spain.

Charles V and his Council of the Indies, an agency that had been established in 1524 to oversee New World affairs, alarmed by stories they heard about misgovernment in New Spain, decided to check the power of Cortés. This was a familiar pattern—Columbus, Balboa, and other discoverers had been replaced by professional bureaucrats sent to the Indies from the Iberian Peninsula. In 1526 the licentiate Luis Ponce de León came to Mexico as *visitador* (royal visitor or inspector), with orders to administer a *residencia* (review of an official's conduct) for Cortés and relieve him of administrative and judicial (but not military) duties. The *visitador's* untimely death from a fever within a few weeks of his arrival, followed by the demise of his aged and infirm deputy, started rumors that they had been poisoned. When Estrada, the treasury official whose ineptness had already been demonstrated, succeeded to the position, he listened to advice from the captain-general's enemies and banished Cortés from Mexico City in the autumn of 1527. Cortés then determined to visit Spain in order to plead his case before the emperor and counter accusations made by his opponents.

Cortés arrived in Spain in 1528—he was forty-three years old and had spent more than half of his life in the Indies. During his two-year stay in the country of his birth, he visited various parts of the kingdom, traveling in the style of a great lord. Accompanying him were Andrés de Tapia, Gonzalo de

Sandoval, and several other conquistadors; forty Indian *principales* (nobles), including sons and daughters of Moctezuma and Maxixca (of Tlaxcala); eight Indian acrobats; native dwarfs and albinos; and a veritable zoo made up of native American animals including armadillos, jaguars, and opossums. He also carried thirty thousand pesos in gold, fifteen hundred marks of silver, many rich jewels, and gifts of feathered shields, fans, textiles, and inlaid stone items. In the city of Toledo the emperor received Cortés, listened to his account of affairs in New Spain, and considered his petition for governorship of the colony as well as his request for "suitable rewards" and a title of nobility.

In recognition of service to the crown, Cortés was named Marqués del Valle (Marquis of the Valley of Oaxaca) and given jurisdiction over a vast area in which he could collect Indian tribute. His *encomiendas* embraced twenty-two towns, including Coyoacán, Tacubaya, Toluca, Cuernavaca, Tepoztlán, Tepeaca, Oaxaca, and San Andrés Tuxtla. Although the grant specified twenty-three thousand Indian vassals living in this region, there must have been at least four times that many. Cortés's title as captain-general of New Spain was reconfirmed; however, it was mostly an honorific military rank and conveyed no power of government. In spite of the honors received, the conquistador was piqued—he had hoped to become a duke and be named governor of New Spain.

Another reason for Cortés's trip to Spain was to acquire a wife of noble birth who might provide him with heirs. After the death of his first wife in Mexico, Cortés had sent a power-of-attorney to his father, who arranged betrothal of the conquistador to Doña Juana de Zúñiga, daughter of a count and niece of a duke, both of whom were supporters of Cortés at the royal court. The marriage was consummated and successful; Doña Juana was young and beautiful and eventually bore the only legitimate children of the captain-general, a son and three daughters.

While Cortés was in Spain, an *audiencia* (administrative court) was appointed to take over the government of New Spain and to continue the *residencia* of Cortés. The court consisted of four *oidores* (judges) and a president. Named to the latter post was Nuño de Guzmán whose excesses as governor of Pánuco were unknown to policy makers in Spain. This first *audiencia* (1529–30) was a fiasco; Guzmán proved to be a tyrant, and the judges—two of whom died before taking office—were inept and corrupt. They persecuted the absent Cortés, auctioning off his goods; they assailed the captain-general's supporters, even imprisoning Pedro de Alvarado who had just returned from Spain with the title of governor of Guatemala; they mistreated Indians and sold them into slavery; and they established censorship at the seaports to prevent any negative reports from reaching Spain. When missionaries protested, they were harassed, one being dragged from the pulpit during a sermon in which he spoke out against Guzmán. The first bishop of Mexico, Juan de Zumárraga, who had been named "Protector of the Indians," tirelessly denounced the *audiencia* and barely escaped assassination, presumably by ruffians in the employ of the judges. He excommunicated the judges, but they paid little attention to that censure. Finally, he succeeded in smuggling to Spain a letter detailing many abuses. That letter caused the emperor's advisors to recommend a new form of government for the Indies.

The remedy for misgovernment in New Spain was to elevate the region to a viceroyalty headed by a viceroy, a surrogate king, who would be a personal representative of the monarch, exercising virtually absolute power in his overseas realm. Pending appointment of a suitable viceroy, with prestige and administrative experience, and the drawing-up of his orders, a second *audiencia* was established in Mexico under the presidency of Sebastián Ramírez Fuenleal, bishop of Santo Domingo. This board (1531–36) proved to be one of the ablest in the history of the colony. One of the judges was Vasco de Quiroga, who later founded Indian schools, hospitals, and model towns among the Tarascans of Michoacán.

Suspecting that he might be replaced, the president of the first *audiencia,* Nuño de Guzmán, left Mexico City in December, 1529, with a large army, hoping to secure fame and fortune by conquering a vast area to the northwest later called New Galicia. Here, from Michoacán to Sinaloa the self-appointed governor pillaged the land, burned villages, enslaved thousands of Indians, and forced others into hiding. One of his techniques was to goad friendly Indians into rebellion, thereby giving the Spaniards a legal pretext for enslaving them (the "Just War" concept). Guzmán eventually founded the towns of Tepic, Culiacán, and Guadalajara, the latter named for his birthplace in Spain. In 1536 he was replaced as governor of New Galicia and, after a year of imprisonment in Mexico, was ordered back to Spain, where he faced charges of misgovernment and served many years as a "royal court prisoner."

At the same time that Nuño de Guzmán was ravaging the northwest, Francisco de Montejo, a former lieutenant of Cortés, attempted to subjugate the Maya Indians of Yucatán. The region and its people proved difficult to subdue—the tropical terrain precluded cavalry assaults, supply lines and adequate provisions were hard to maintain, the Maya waged bitter guerrilla warfare, and Montejo was a poor leader of men. In 1539, after nine years of intermittent battles, he left the command to his son and to a nephew, both also named Francisco Montejo. By 1542, when the city of Mérida was founded, much of the northern region was under Spanish control, but five years later there was a serious native uprising that led to much bloodshed before it was quelled. During two decades of warfare in Yucatán some five hundred Spaniards lost their lives; countless Maya were killed, and their chiefs who refused to submit were burnt alive; many male captives had their arms cut off; and women collaborators were drowned or hanged. In many ways the conquest of the Maya and their cultural assimilation proved to be more prolonged and arduous than that of the Aztecs.

Meanwhile, the conqueror of the Aztecs, Hernán Cortés, returned to New Spain with his wife. In 1530 they settled in Cuernavaca, where he built a handsome stone palace (now a regional museum), organized plantations and sugar mills, and made plans for further conquests in the Pacific. His

Cortés's palace, Cuernavaca.

shipyards at Zacatula, Acapulco, and Tehuantepec turned out a number of sailing ships that were dispatched to find new islands or the legendary Strait of Anian, which was supposed to connect the Atlantic and Pacific. Although the captain-general spent more than 275,000 pesos on Pacific explorations, none of his explorers found a new Tenochtitlán; worse, many of the vessels were lost at sea and others were seized by Guzman's forces on the west coast. After some pearls were discovered by one of his men near La Paz, Baja California, Cortés spent six months there in 1535 in an abortive attempt to establish a colony, but the land was barren, the natives did not practice agriculture, and there was no mineral wealth to exploit. He also feuded with Guzmán and with the first viceroy, Antonio de Mendoza, over rights of exploration and discovery. Faced with failure on the Pacific, and lacking any real power in New Spain, the "Captain from Castile" returned home in 1540.

Cortés's last years in Spain were plagued by frustration and ill health. His reception at the royal court was cool, his lawsuit with Nuño de Guzmán was not settled, his advice in military strategy was ignored, on a disastrous military expedition to Algiers he lost five precious emeralds worth one hundred thousand ducats, and his daughter María's arranged marriage to a titled nobleman was not consummated. Finally, in 1547, he decided to return to New Spain, but he fell ill and died near Seville in his sixty-third year. Some years later, according to a provision in his will, his bones were interred in the Hospital de Jesús, which he had founded in Mexico City. Mexico has never honored Cortés with an official statue; instead, his monument is the Spanish colony he founded, which lasted for three hundred years.

Spanish control of the Mexican colony was consolidated and strengthened in 1535 with the arrival of the first viceroy, Don Antonio de Mendoza, the Count of Tendilla. Born to an aristocratic family of Granada, he had served as a diplomat in Flanders, Hungary, and Italy before his appointment to New Spain. Mendoza proved to be an excellent administrator during his fifteen years as the ranking royal official in the Indies. He supervised the execution of royal decrees and laws, issued ordinances dealing with local administration, reformed the collection of tribute, founded the first mint, introduced merino sheep that led to weaving of woolen textiles, and sponsored a school for orphans. He fostered Indian justice by regularly hearing complaints of the natives and confirming their rights.

Two years after Mendoza's arrival, Pope Paul III issued a series of encyclicals designed to help the native Americans. Declaring that it was heresy to say that Indians were not human beings and thus incapable of conversion, the pope urged clergy and laymen to bring them to salvation "by preaching and by example." Furthermore, these bulls forbade any enslavement of Indians or seizure of their possessions; anyone who did so incurred automatic excommunication.

Antonio de Mendoza, first viceroy of New Spain. Courtesy The Bancroft Library.

The bulls were largely nullified in New Spain when the crown revoked them in 1538, claiming interference in the *patronato real.*

About the same time, a reform movement in Spain, led by the Dominican friar, Bartolomé de Las Casas, who was a former *encomendero* and long-time champion of the Indians, had resulted in the New Laws of 1542. These "Laws for the Government of the Indies and Good Treatment of the Indians" forbade all enslavement of Indians under any pretext, abolished all compulsory personal service by Indians, precluded the granting of any new *encomiendas,* ordered royal officials and churchmen to give up their grants of Indian tribute, and specified that existing private *encomiendas* would revert to the crown on the death of the holders. When a special *visitador,* Francisco Tello de Sandoval, came to New Spain to publish and enforce the New Laws, he found widespread opposition to them by the colonists and clerics. Fearing a general revolt if the laws were implemented, the special agent and the viceroy decided to suspend them, pending appeal. The crown later relaxed its position regarding inheritance of *encomiendas,* a change that mollified the *encomenderos* for the time being.

Mexican archives contain records of most if not all the *encomiendas.* Although tributes varied from one region to another and adjustments were made occasionally, the following excerpts from legal documents will give an idea of Indian village obligations about 1540.

VILLAGE OF TEQUEPILPA, commended to Pedro de Meneses, resident of Puebla.

First they are obliged to give each year one thousand *cargas* of maize, each *carga* to be half a *fanega* [2.5 bushels per *fanega*].

They must sow wheat to the extent of ten *fanegas* of seed.

Each eighty days they must supply one hundred blankets of the type called *zamaguatos,* fifty of henequen and the other fifty of cotton, each valued at one *tomín* [one-third of a peseta].

Each day they must furnish twenty-five Indians for work, five in the house and twenty for the grounds and livestock.

Each day they must furnish one chicken, one hundred and twenty grains [7.7 grams] of *ají* [red pepper], five tomatoes, half a cake of salt, twenty *tunas* [prickly pear cactus fruit], ten potatoes, two loads of firewood, a bundle of torch pine, two loads of fodder, and eight eggs.

VILLAGE OF TULAN, Crown grant overseen by Rodrigo de Albornoz, treasurer.

Each day they will furnish ten Indians as servants for his house; six chickens, and on fast days sixty eggs, forty fish and forty frogs; a small pail of fruit which they are accustomed to give; fifteen loads of firewood; and fifteen loads of fodder. And they will give the steward who is in the village one chicken daily and fifteen tortillas.

Each year they will plant maize near a palm tree at a place called Yezotitlán, which is a thousand yards long and six hundred wide, and which they declare is presently seeded. Also they will sow two fields of wheat: one near the river where the mill is located, which is four hundred yards long and is presently seeded; the other, which is in Ilaca, is one hundred and sixty yards long. And they must cultivate the vineyard which is in the village.*

In addition to providing tribute and labor for the elite *encomenderos,* natives also were conscripted to work under the *repartimiento* system. This levy or forced work allotment required each village to provide a weekly quota of Indians for work on projects involving "the public good." These workers, who were paid one *real* (one-eighth of a peso), erected government buildings and churches, built and maintained roads and irrigation ditches, and sometimes were assigned to produce foodstuffs or work in mines. As can be imagined, the *repartimiento* system led to widespread abuses; furthermore, it lasted for most of the colonial era.

The hope of securing Indian tribute, labor, and treasure continued to stimulate the imagination of Spanish adventurers in the sixteenth century, and it lured them as far north as the Kansas prairie. Rumors of fabulous kingdoms in the northern wilderness were intensified in 1536 when Alvar

---

El libro de las tasaciones de pueblos de la Nueva España, Siglo XVI (Mexico: Archivo General de la Nación, 1952), 420–21, 535.

Núñez Cabeza de Vaca, two Spanish companions, and a black man named Esteban appeared on the west coast of Mexico. Survivors of an unsuccessful attempt to occupy Florida, they had constructed boats and made their way along the Gulf Coast to Texas, then wandered southwestward—sometimes as medicine men, sometimes as slaves to the Indians—until they met up with fellow Spaniards. Although the newly-arrived men had not actually seen any great towns during their odyssey, they repeated Indian tales of a land called Cíbola, where there were supposedly seven rich cities. When Cabeza de Vaca's group reached Mexico City, the viceroy quizzed the men carefully, then he made plans for a conquest that he hoped might surpass that of Cortés.

Before sending out a large-scale expedition, Viceroy Mendoza commissioned a Franciscan friar, Marcos de Niza, to reconnoiter the north, guided by Esteban, who could also serve as interpreter. With a band of Indian guides the two men left Culiacán in March, 1539, but after Esteban pushed on ahead as an advance scout, Fray Marcos never saw him again. Finally, the friar met an Indian who was a lucky sur-vivor of the advance party—all but two of the rest had been killed at Cíbola (the Zuñi pueblo of Hawikuh). Fray Marcos later reported, "With . . . my own Indians and interpreters, I continued my journey until I came within sight of Cí-bola. . . . It appears to be a very beautiful city . . . the houses are of the type the Indians described to me, all of stone. . . . The town is bigger than the city of Mexico." Perhaps the friar was the victim of a desert mirage, or else his imagina-tion created what he was sent to find. In any case, his glowing report spurred the viceroy to organize a large expedition to conquer the cities of Cíbola.

Francisco Vásquez de Coronado, the thirty-year-old gov-ernor of New Galicia who had sailed to New Spain with Vice-roy Mendoza, headed the military expedition. With him were 225 cavalrymen, 62 foot soldiers, 1,000 Indian allies, and a contingent of Indian servants and Negro slaves who served as drovers for the thousands of head of livestock used for remounts and provisions. Coronado's men spent the years

1540–42 investigating parts of the present states of Sonora, Arizona, New Mexico, Texas, Oklahoma and Kansas. What they found was a great disappointment: the Seven Cities of Cíbola were poor adobe and rock Zuñi villages; the Hopi Indian towns were similar; the Pueblo settlements of the upper Rio Grande (Río Bravo) had fertile fields, but there was little in the way of booty; the inhospitable buffalo plains were traversed by nomadic Apache and Comanche warriors; and the legendary golden city of Quivira proved to be a Wichita Indian settlement of grass-covered huts.

Two of Coronado's auxiliary expeditions also were disappointing. A maritime expedition under Hernando de Alarcón sailed up the Gulf of California and explored the Colorado River for sixty leagues, while an overland party under García López de Cárdenas found the Grand Canyon but nothing promising in the way of mineral, vegetable, or human wealth. When the disillusioned Coronado returned to Mexico City, he was received coldly, but his journey had advanced geographical knowledge and disproved the existence of legendary cities in the north. His report had the effect of delaying for sixty years Spanish colonization of the region.

In the same years that Coronado was crossing from Arizona to Kansas, another group of about six hundred Spaniards explored the region from Florida to Arkansas. Captained by Hernando de Soto, a veteran of campaigns in Nicaragua and Peru, the men left Cuba in 1539. Landing on Florida's western shore, they wandered through some of the states of the future southeastern United States without finding any riches other than a few poor-grade pearls. After de Soto died on the Mississippi River in 1542, the rest of his party, led by Luis de Moscoso, built a brigantine in which they sailed down the river and along the Gulf shore to Pánuco, New Spain, where they sent the viceroy a report about the ill-fated expedition.

While Coronado and de Soto were looking for treasures or rich kingdoms in the "mysterious north," a serious native revolt known as the Mixtón War occurred in New Galicia.

Indians of the region, who had suffered from the depredations of Nuño de Guzmán and brutalities inflicted by *encomenderos*, took advantage of the weakened Spanish military situation and in 1541 launched a series of guerrilla raids that soon became a general insurrection extending from Guadalajara to Culiacán. Tenamaxtli, the Indian leader, urged his followers to kill all Spaniards and burn their churches as the first step toward a return to old ways and old gods. He soon had over a hundred thousand warriors, many concentrated in the fortified rocky hills (*peñoles*) of Nochistlán and Mixtón.

Unable to quell the uprising, Lieutenant Governor Cristóbal de Oñate appealed to Viceroy Mendoza, who took to the field at the head of a force of four hundred Spaniards and about thirty thousand Tlaxcalan and Aztec warriors. Because of the grave situation, Indian allies were given firearms for the first time. After many assaults the rebels were defeated, and the war ended. One battle fatality was Pedro de Alvarado, who was crushed when a companion's horse fell on him. Alvarado had come from Guatemala to the west coast of Mexico in preparation for a voyage to the Spice Islands when he was diverted by the viceroy. After Alvarado's death his ships were taken over by Mendoza.

Viceroy Mendoza hoped to uncover new kingdoms and expand his domain by backing voyages of discovery in the Pacific. If rich cities were not encountered, perhaps his lieutenants might find the Strait of Anian, that phantom waterway through the American continent. In 1542 he sent two of Alvarado's ships, captained by Juan Rodríguez Cabrillo with Bartolomé Ferrelo as chief pilot, to search the Pacific coast north from Baja California. They sailed to a point about 42 degrees north along the California-Oregon border, encountered Indian villages in the Santa Barbara (Channel) Islands, and put in at San Diego Bay, but they missed the bays later named Monterey and San Francisco. After a voyage of almost ten months the crews returned without their commander, who had died from a fall aboard ship. Because their report contained no sighting of a strait or mention of any rich settlements, Spanish colonization of Alta California would have to wait for many years. Meanwhile, exploration of the Pacific continued.

Ever since Magellan's voyage, Spaniards had hoped to establish a base in the East Indies, where Portuguese merchants were profitably exporting spices to Europe. In 1542, Viceroy Mendoza dispatched from Mexico's west coast six ships under Ruy López de Villalobos, with orders to search for the Spice Islands. In three months they reached the Philippines, but contrary winds prevented their return eastward across the Pacific, so the survivors eventually made their way around Africa to Spain. Although this expedition did not conquer any of the Philippine Islands, one sent out from New Spain twenty-two years later, under Miguel López de Legazpi, initiated Spanish colonization of the archipelago and founded the town of Manila. From that time until the early nineteenth century the Philippines were administered as part of the Viceroyalty of New Spain.

The Manila Galleon, or China Ship, as it was also called, was a feature of the colonial era. All Spanish governmental and Church personnel, mail, and cargo were transported between Acapulco and Manila on a government-chartered ship that was supposed to sail annually. Thus Manila became an entrepôt for Mexican silver, and Acapulco received goods from the Orient: spices, silks, tapestries, and items made of jade, ivory, gold, brass, porcelain, or rare woods. Pirates operating in the Pacific worried the Spaniards, especially after Thomas Cavendish captured a galleon off Baja California in 1586. To counteract this threat the Manila ships were heavily armed, and a search was begun for a suitable port in Alta California that could serve as a defense and supply station. That search and the continued hope of finding treasure focused attention toward the north.

During the sixteenth century there was a gradual overland movement of settlers to the northern regions of New Spain. The attractions were silver mines, various groups of Indians —some migratory, some settled—to convert and exploit, and free ranch land for the taking. In 1546 a scouting party under

Captain Juan de Tolosa discovered a rich lode of silver in Zacatecas; news of this find set off the first great mining rush in North American history. Within decades other prospectors found silver in the north central region at Guanajuato, Fresnillo, Durango, Santa Bárbara, San Luis Potosí, and other sites. The impact was tremendous: some individuals became wealthy overnight, mining camps grew into towns, livestock ranches were developed to supply the miners, mule trains were organized to haul supplies in and silver out, and a steady stream of silver began to flow to Mexico City and on to the mother country. Spain's silver bonanza from Mexico (and Peru) financed a series of European wars, caused an enormous inflation of prices in the Old World, and accelerated the growth of capitalism. In New Spain the increased demand for Indian labor to mine the ore and raise the crops occurred at a time when the native population was decreasing rapidly from disease and overwork and, coincidentally, at a time when the crown threatened to abolish *encomiendas* and other forced labor systems.

The struggle between the crown and *encomenderos* culminated in a conspiracy and reign of terror that shook the viceroyalty in the 1560s. Gradually the government had moved to curtail control of natives by conquistadors or their sons. "Protectors of Indians" were appointed for various districts, and more than four thousand Indian slaves were freed in the middle of the century. Personal service by Indians in lieu of tribute was forbidden; many *encomiendas* reverted to the crown; and rumors persisted that the grants would no longer be inheritable. By the 1560s most of the *encomenderos* were *criollos* (creoles), that is, they were Mexican-born Spaniards. That status made them "second-class citizens" and precluded their appointment to high positions of Church or state—those jobs were held by Spaniards born in Spain. Thus there was a growing disaffection by many sons of conquerors who thought they had a natural leader when Martín Cortés, the second Marqués del Valle, arrived in New Spain in 1563.

Martín Cortés, the only legitimate son of the conqueror,

was involved in a strange plot to take over the colony his father had founded. He had spent his first eight years in New Spain, then in 1540 he went to Spain, where he became a favorite at the royal court. When he was thirty-one, the rich nobleman returned to Mexico and established a palatial household in the capital. His *palacio* was often visited by two brothers, Alonso and Gil González de Ávila, and other *criollo encomenderos* who aired their grievances. What may have begun as loose talk by idle young men grew into a conspiracy to assassinate the highest officials and set up an independent monarchy with Martín Cortés as king of Mexico. Led by the Ávila brothers, the conspirators claimed to have more than a hundred trusted followers, but because of delays and compromises their plan was never carried out.

In July, 1566, the *audiencia* judges ordered the arrest of leaders of the plot. The Ávila brothers were tried for high treason and beheaded, the Marqués was sent back to Spain, and the following year a *visitador* imprisoned, tortured, and executed more suspects. One of those investigated and banished from the Indies was the young Marqués's half-brother, also named Martín Cortés; he was the *mestizo* son of Doña Marina and the conqueror. The severity with which the conspirators were punished astonished the colonists and kept other *criollos* from seriously challenging the system.

Meanwhile, Spanish government officials continued to support penetration and pacification of northern New Spain. They sent military units on punitive *entradas* or campaigns against savage Indians, they established *presidios* (forts) and defense towns such as San Miguel and San Felipe de los Reyes, and they created new political jurisdictions headed by military men with frontier experience. In the 1560s the province of Nueva Vizcaya, embracing the future states of Sinaloa, Sonora, Durango, and Chihuahua, was put under the control of Francisco de Ibarra. To the east, Francisco de Urdiñola headed the province which later became Coahuila; and in the northeast, Nuevo León was organized in 1579 by Governor Luis de Carvajal, who founded the town of Monterrey. Later, Carvajal was accused of being a crypto-Jew;

in his Inquisition trial he confessed and denounced five other members of his family, all of whom received the death penalty.

At the end of the sixteenth century, Spanish northern expansion reached New Mexico, a distance of three thousand kilometers (1,800 miles) from Mexico City. Motives for settling there were multiple: to convert the sedentary Pueblo Indians reported on by Coronado, to investigate rumors of turquoise and silver mines, and to establish a defensive outpost. Political leaders in Spain feared that the English privateer Francis Drake, after raiding Pacific ports from Peru to Panama and touching at California (1578–79), had found the Strait of Anian. Thus a colonizing expedition was authorized to occupy New Mexico, search for the Strait, and fortify the area against English penetration. In 1598, Don Juan de Oñate, scion of a wealthy Zacatecas mining family, at his own expense outfitted the pioneer party composed of 129 soldier-colonists with their families, 10 Franciscan friars, 83 wagons, and 7,000 head of livestock. New Mexico's capital, first established along the Rio Grande at San Juan, was moved south to Santa Fe in 1610.

Oñate and his men brought central New Mexico under Spanish control, searched unsuccessfully for mines, and cooperated with the friars in building mission churches in Indian *pueblos* (villages). For years internal conflicts plagued the isolated colony, weakening it at the same time that Indian resentment mounted. The outcome was the destructive Pueblo Revolt of 1680, during which some four hundred Spaniards were massacred and the survivors fled south to Chihuahua. A dozen years later the province was reconquered by military forces under Don Diego de Vargas. After that, New Mexico remained a salient defense bastion of New Spain.

The territory of Florida was another Spanish defensive outpost occupied in the sixteenth century. Early armed *entradas* by conquistadors Ponce de León, Narváez, and De Soto were followed by an unsuccessful missionary attempt by Dominicans, who sailed out of Veracruz in 1549. A decade later, Tristán de Luna left New Spain with an armada and

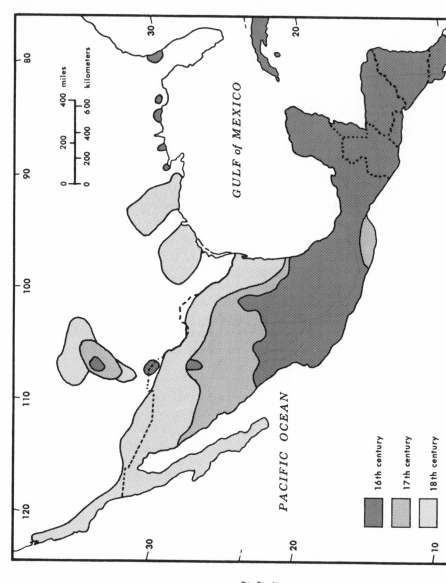

Colonial Settlement Frontiers

GULF of MEXICO

PACIFIC OCEAN

16th century
17th century
18th century

orders to found one or more bases in Florida, but hurricanes frustrated the enterprise. When King Philip II of Spain learned that French Huguenots had settled on the Florida coast, he appointed Don Pedro Menéndez de Avilés as governor of Florida, with orders to clear out the trespassers. In 1565, Menéndez left Cuba with eight hundred men, who defeated the Frenchmen and founded San Agustín (Saint Augustine), the first permanent European settlement in America north of the present Mexico. Missionaries arrived in Florida the next year to begin working with the Indians. Eventually a line of missions extended far up the Atlantic Coast toward the Carolinas and westward into the province of Apalache. Spanish military bases at San Agustín and Pensacola, founded later in the century, protected Spanish interests on the Florida peninsula and guarded the route of treasure ships bound from Veracruz to Cadiz.

After Columbus's discovery and the Treaty of Tordesillas, other nations challenged the Iberian monopoly of the New World. Monarchs of England and France sent out explorers and employed the services of maritime adventurers commissioned as privateers. In addition, freebooters, corsairs, or pirates captured Spanish treasure ships, raided port towns or held them for ransom, and smuggled goods and African slaves into the colonies. The Spanish government responded with new decrees prohibiting trade with foreigners, and they bolstered defense units, but it proved impossible to protect an entire hemisphere.

In 1568, the Englishman John Hawkins was attempting to trade in the Caribbean with a fleet of eight ships, two of them belonging to Queen Elizabeth, when a hurricane forced him to seek shelter and permission to refit in the harbor of Veracruz. Before he could clear port a Spanish fleet of thirteen vessels arrived, one of them bearing the newly appointed viceroy, Don Martín Enríquez de Almanza, who ordered his admiral to open fire on the interlopers. Hawkins escaped with only two ships, one captained by his kinsman Francis Drake, leaving more than a hundred English sailors on shore there and at Pánuco. Most of the marooned men were captured and sent on to Mexico City, where they were tried by the Inquisition as heretics; sixty-eight were sentenced to row in the galleys or do other hard labor for periods up to ten years, and three "unrepentant apostates" were burned at the stake.

During the next quarter of a century Francis Drake (*El Draque*) continued to harass Spain and Spanish America. He intercepted Peruvian silver in Panama, plundered Pacific ports of Peru and New Spain, sacked Santo Domingo, invaded Cartagena, burned San Agustín, and destroyed thirty-three ships in the harbor at Cadiz. These and other attacks hurt Spain, but at the end of the sixteenth century there were no other European colonies in the Americas. Spain and Portugal, united under one crown between 1580 and 1640, had maintained their exclusive hold on the Western Hemisphere for more than a century.

In view of the Spanish crown's policy of excluding foreigners from its New World colonies, it is surprising to learn that several Englishmen and Italians visited New Spain in the sixteenth century. Most of the visitors were merchants who had lived in Spain, where they married or made business connections. John Chilton spent eighteen years in Spain and Spanish America; he traded from Veracruz to Guadalajara and south to Guatemala between 1568 and 1572. Another merchant, Henry Hawks, spent five years in New Spain, after which he returned to England in 1572, where he wrote an account of his travels. The following excerpts, reproduced in the original Elizabethan English, give us his unique view of some parts of colonial New Spain.

Five leagues from [the island of] Saint John de Ullua is a faire river; it lieth Northwest from the port, and goeth to a little towne of the Spanyards called Vera Cruz.... This town is inclined to many kinde of diseases, by reason of the great heat, and a certeine gnat or flie which they call a mosquito, which biteth both men and women in their sleepe; and as soone as they are bitten, incontinently the flesh swelleth as though they had bene bitten with some venimouse worme ... many there are that die of this annoyance....

This hote or sicke countrey continueth five and forty miles towards the city of Mexico; and the five and forty miles being passed, then there is a temperate countrey, and full of tillage: but they water all their corne with rivers which they turne in upon it. And they gather their Wheat twise a yere. . . .

Mexico is a great city; it hath more than fifty thousand households, whereof there are not past five or sixe thousand houses of the Spanyards: all the other are the people of the countrey, which live under the Spanyards lawes. There are in this city stately buildings, and many monasteries of friers and nunnes, which the Spanyards have made. And the building of the Indians is somewhat beautiful outwardly, and within full of small chambers, with very small windowes, which is not so comly as the building of the Spanyards. This city standeth in the midst of a great lake, and the water goeth thorow all or the most part of the streets, and there come small boats, which they call canoas, and in them they bring all things necessary, as wood, and coales, and grasse for their horses, stones and lime to build, and corne.*

Hawks clearly indicates that New Spain was a hodgepodge of Old and New World ideas and goods. Metropolitan Spain was likewise influenced by American products; indeed there was a vast transatlantic interchange of flora, fauna, applied sciences, and even diseases. Technological transfers from Spain included the wheel, the plow, clocks, the foot-operated loom, and gunpowder, as well as the practice of ironworking, glassblowing, printing, and silk culture. These and other innovations revolutionized life in New Spain.

*Richard Hakluyt, ed., *The Principal Navigations, Voyages, Traffiques & Discoveries of the English Nation*, 10 vols. (London: J. M. Dent & Sons, Ltd., 1927), 6:280–81.

CHAPTER 5

Colonial Institutions and Life

LIFE in colonial New Spain was complex — the dominant institutions and cultural patterns were Spanish in origin, but they were modified in their New World setting. Society was not static; evolution marked the political and religious systems; and change was a feature of the economic, social, and intellectual life. These adaptations generally mirrored developments in Europe, the source of basic decisions and control. During its three centuries as a colony, New Spain was kept subservient to the mother country in a number of ways, beginning with an enforced loyalty to the crown.

The government of the Spanish empire functioned through a massive bureaucracy, with the Spanish monarch at the peak of the administrative pyramid. Claiming divine appointment and espousing the political philosophy of absolutism, the monarch was a supreme earthly master to all his subjects. The reigning king or queen was responsible to God alone, and disobedience of royal edicts was considered both treason and sacrilege. Since the Indies technically did not belong to Spain but were the personal patrimony of the crown of Castile, they were not administered by the *Cortes* (Spanish parliament) or traditional royal councils. Instead, two agencies were created in Spain to administer the overseas territories for the monarch.

Headquartered in Seville, the Council of the Indies was the principal governing body for Spain's crown colonies in the New World. First composed of seven members, the Council later added other officers including a cosmographer and historian. The personnel of the Council was composed of lawyers, clerics, treasurers, and high officials who had returned to Spain after service in the colonies. The councillors considered themselves to be advisors to the monarch, but in reality they regulated the Spanish Indies. They drafted royal laws, ordinances, and *cédulas* (decrees) and had the power of judicial review over local legislation enacted in the colonies. A codification of all the laws and regulations of the Council was compiled and published several times as the *Recopilación de Leyes de los Reynos de las Indias*. It was a humane and comprehensive code for colonial government. By 1681 there were 6,377 laws indexed under various titles such as Bishops of New Spain, Universities, Treatment of Pirates, Fabrication of Gunpowder, and The Mail Service.

In addition to legislative duties, the Council of the Indies had administrative, ecclesiastical, and judicial powers. It acted as a supreme court for cases appealed from overseas, it granted permission for new expeditions, it supervised the treatment of Indians, it provided for military defense, it was a censorship board for printed matter bound for the Indies, it supervised the colonial treasury, and it organized *visitas* (inspections) and *residencias* (reviews) of retiring officials. One of the most important functions was to nominate for royal approval appointees for all overseas positions—civil, military, and religious—except those few selected by the colonists themselves. The Council's authority began to decline in the eighteenth century, but it was not abolished until 1834.

The *Casa de Contratación* (Board of Colonial Trade) was an agency in Spain charged with regulating New World commerce and emigration. Besides serving as a kind of passport office, it registered goods shipped between Spain and the Indies, making certain that the royal taxes were paid. Located first at Seville and later at Cadiz, the *Casa* maintained metropolitan Spain's trade monopoly, served as a commercial court, and was a clearinghouse for all traffic with the colonies. Its power declined in the eighteenth century, and the *Casa* was abolished in 1790, after Spain had been forced to liberalize its trading policies.

In New Spain itself the viceroy was the ranking officer and agent of royal absolutism. As a personal representative of the king he was armed with considerable authority and enjoyed high honors and deference. He received a handsome salary (twenty thousand pesos in the seventeenth century, triple that amount in the eighteenth), lived in a splendid palace surrounded by liveried servants, and maintained a court like a petty European monarch. During the colonial era there were sixty-one viceroys. Most of them belonged to the titled nobility or at least were of high birth; eleven were from the Church hierarchy, and only three holders of this exalted office were *criollos*, two of them being sons of viceroys.

The viceroy functioned as chief executive, captain-general of military forces, governor, supervisor of the royal treasury (*real hacienda*), and president of the *audiencia* (administrative court) of Mexico. He enforced royal laws and decrees, issued ordinances dealing with local matters, nominated minor colonial officials, distributed land and titles, promoted colonization and settlement, and protected the Indians. He was vice-patron of most religious endeavors, and his ecclesiastical powers included the right to determine boundaries of bishoprics and to nominate some Church officers.

The mother country maintained several checks on the power of viceroys. Beginning in the seventeenth century their term of office was limited to three years; later it was raised to five. To keep them from favoring the colony over metropolitan Spain, viceroys were prohibited from marrying subjects, owning land, engaging in business, or borrowing or lending money within their jurisdiction. At the end of their term they (and other high royal officials) were subject to a *residencia* (when they were mere residents without authority); this public review of their administration and accounts normally was conducted by their successor. During their term they might be inspected by a special *visita* sent out by the Council of the Indies; if the affairs of the entire viceroyalty were being checked, a *visitador-general* arrived with extraordinary powers overlapping and sometimes superceding those of the viceroy. After service in New Spain some viceroys were promoted, a few were fined for violating regulations, and except for those who died in office or were transferred to Peru, virtually all returned home to Spain.

Because the Viceroyalty of New Spain was so vast, it was

divided into various kingdoms and provinces. In theory the viceroy ruled all the territory in his domain, but actually regional governments functioned under five *audiencias*, or administrative courts. The *audiencia* for the central Kingdom of New Spain was located in Mexico City; for the northern region called Nueva Galicia, it was at Guadalajara; for Central America, at Guatemala City; for the Caribbean Islands and Florida, at Havana; and one at Manila covered the Philippine Islands. The viceroy presided *ex-officio* over the *audiencia* in the capital. The others had presidents of their own, generally the captain-general of the region.

Audiencias were courts of appeal for both criminal and civil cases, and they also had political or administrative functions. The judges, called *oidores,* were usually Spanish-born lawyers who were appointed by the crown for unlimited terms. In the seventeenth century the *audiencia* of Mexico City had twelve judges plus two *fiscales* or attorneys for the crown. Lesser officials included a sheriff, chaplain, notaries, reporters, custodians of funds, and a lawyer for poor suitors. At first the *audiencias* heard cases involving the native Americans, but in 1573 a General Indian Court of New Spain was created. There were other special courts for merchants, for the *mesta* or livestock guild, a *proto-medicato* to regulate the medical profession, and the Church and army maintained separate courts for their own personnel.

As a council of state, the *audiencia* met with its president on certain days of the week in *acuerdo* sessions to discuss administrative or financial matters. During the first part of the colonial era if the viceroy died or was seriously ill, the *audiencia* at Mexico City governed until the arrival of a replacement. Later viceroys brought with them sealed orders naming their successor in case of emergency. *Oidores* and their children needed royal permission to marry in the colony; they could not own real estate in their jurisdiction; and they were forbidden to engage in business of any sort, borrow or lend money, or even attend weddings and funerals of *criollos* or *mestizos.* Such measures were an attempt to keep the judges free from local influences that might prejudice them in the administration of justice. The term *audiencia* was also used for the territory of the court's jurisdiction.

The *audiencias* or presidencies were subdivided into smaller jurisdictions governed from their chief towns by officials called variously governors, *corregidores,* or *alcaldes mayores.* Sparsely settled, large frontier provinces were headed by a governor; those with many Indian villages by a *corregidor;* and an *alcalde mayor* controlled the areas of Europeanized settlement. At first these regional officials were appointed by the viceroy, but gradually the crown took over the designation of important provincial officers. If a landowner or merchant of New Spain was appointed to one of those offices, he could not serve in the district where he maintained his principal residence. A governor's term of office was three or five years, depending on where he was at the time of appointment. Reappointment was permissible, but it was generally to another district. Before taking office the appointee had to furnish an inventory of his property and provide a bond to insure his presence for the *residencia* and to cover any fines that might be levied.

Although charged with safeguarding the property and people of their region, governors and *corregidores* were noted for their tyranny and exploitation of natives. They often forced Indians to render personal service, give excessive tribute, or sell them produce at prices below market value. *Corregidores* were also permitted to introduce into their district certain articles to be distributed to the natives at reasonable rates; often these items were forced on the Indians at exorbitant prices. Such abuses were difficult to remedy, given the distance from Spain and the slowness of communications.

Colonial cities, towns, and villages were governed by municipal councils known as *cabildos* (sometimes called *ayuntamientos*). The term *cabildo* also refers to the meeting place or building of the city council. In New Spain, as in the mother country, towns were important because Spaniards tended to live in them instead of on their farm, ranch, or plantation, and since Roman times Spanish political and social organization had been based on an urban pattern.

Each town, or *municipio,* was like a city-state; it included a large surrounding district, and in the settled areas its boundaries extended to those of its neighboring towns. Depending on a town's size, membership of each town council was composed of from five to fifteen *regidores* or councilmen, who annually elected a chief magistrate or mayor called the *alcalde ordinario.* The viceregal capital, Mexico City, had two *alcaldes.* Other officers attached to the *cabildo* were a constable, standard bearer, inspector of weights and measures, and collector of fines. *Criollos* often served on town councils.

Hernán Cortés and other frontier town founders appointed the officers of the communities they founded, but it soon became common for the crown to name *regidores* as life members. Later these offices, and others, were sold by the government, with the right of bequest, so that by the beginning of the seventeenth century most of the city positions had become proprietary and hereditary. Mexican historian Lucas Alamán described the *cabildo* of Mexico City at the end of the colonial period:

The fifteen permanent *regidores* held offices which were ancient entailed estates; in general the men were of little education and most were ruined in their fortune. [Each year] they chose the two *alcaldes* and [every two years] six honorary *regidores* from among the more notable merchants, landowners, and lawyers, and these honorary officials, by their superior abilities, exercised a preponderant influence in the municipal corporation.... The permanent *regidores* were almost all *criollos,* having inherited the offices from their ancestors who had purchased them to give luster to their families, but it was the custom to choose the *alcaldes* and honorary *regidores,* half from American, half from European residents.*

Areas where the natives had a long tradition of sedentary civilization were divided into *cabeceras,* or districts, which consisted of native villages with their outlying areas. Heading each *cabecera* was an Indian *juez gobernador* (judge-governor),

*Lucas Alamán, *Historia de Méjico,* 5 vols. (Mexico: Imp. J. M. Lara, 1849–52), 1:57–58.

and under him was a native municipal council. The officials were supposed to be elected annually, and there were restrictions on reelection, but generally the Indian officers served for many years, reflecting the pre-conquest tradition of lifetime election or appointment. Native office-holders typically came from families whose ancestors had been *caciques* (chieftains) or from the group the Spanish called *principales* (nobles). The Spanish government, through its colonial bureaucracy, dealt with Indian village officers and sometimes appointed or removed them.

The crown's economic policy was another aspect of peninsular control over New Spain. Even before political economists had formulated the philosophy of mercantilism, which among other tenets mandates that colonies exist for the benefit of the mother country, the Spanish crown had incorporated many of its principles into laws and regulations for the Indies. Under that economic system the value of exports was supposed to exceed that of imports so that bullion would be accumulated at home. Colonists were required to buy processed goods from Spanish merchants (although many of the items were from other countries) and ship raw materials to the homeland. Foreign traders and investors generally were excluded from the Indies for two reasons: so that Castilian merchants would enjoy the commercial monopoly and through taxes enrich the royal treasury, and to exclude religious heresies that foreign merchants might introduce into the colonies. Most of the original large mercantile companies that operated in New Spain were branches of concerns headquartered in Seville; there too was the *Consulado,* a merchants' guild that arranged the annual sailing of merchant ships.

Pirate raids and the threat of them forced the crown to regulate shipping to and from the Indies; merchant ships had to travel together, convoyed by warships of the royal navy. The *flota* (fleet) of ships that traded with New Spain carried the mail and government communications, all officials and religious personnel, all emigrants or returnees, and all trade merchandise to and from Veracruz, which was the only legal trading port on Mexico's Gulf Coast. In the seventeenth century there was a *flota* almost every year, with an average of six merchant ships each, but in the following century European wars or domestic crises disrupted the service, once for two decades (1736–56). Finally, in 1789, the fleet system was abolished and replaced by registration of individual ships. This change, coupled with the opening of all Spanish ports to colonial trade, produced a greater volume of shipping and tended to lower prices of goods in the Indies.

Throughout the colonial era, in spite of minute regulation and supervision, there was considerable contraband trade, especially with foreigners. This was occasioned by exhorbitant Spanish prices, delays of shipments, high taxes, and an inordinate amount of "red tape"—forms to fill out, official seals or stamps to purchase, and signatures to obtain. The cost of goods in the colonies was at least double and generally several times the price in Spain.

When European merchandise was unloaded at Veracruz, it was transported inland to the more salubrious town of Jalapa, where merchants congregated to select their goods. No doubt thieves, gamblers, and prostitutes also attended these trade fairs. Merchant *consulados* in Mexico City, Veracruz, and Guadalajara (the last two established late in the eighteenth century), controlled the distribution of goods to their members. Imported cargo items included clothing, textiles, lace, buttons, jewelry, furniture, dishes, utensils, silverware, glassware, books, hardware, iron and steel, paints, tools, weapons, religious goods, toys, musical instruments, candles, wine, brandy, olive oil, sweetmeats, fancy foods, seeds and plant cuttings, medicines, livestock, and mercury (used in mining).

Another item of cargo, black slaves, came on special ships, first from Seville and later directly from Africa or via slave marts in Lisbon or Caribbean ports. Formal contracts called *asientos,* which gave the holders an exclusive right to import black slaves, were awarded to individuals and companies, most of them foreign. For example, in the second half of the seventeenth century Dutch capitalists controlled the slave traffic; then the *asiento* passed to the French Royal Guinea Company; and between 1714 and 1750 the English South Sea Company held the exclusive privilege. Some illicit merchandise came into New Spain aboard slave ships.

Spanish officials carefully monitored the fleets returning from America because they carried silver and gold bullion. In addition to that precious cargo and some cowhides, principal items exported from New Spain were products not grown in the mother country: sugar, cacao (chocolate), tobacco, vanilla, cotton, dyewood, and indigo and cochineal dyes. In value of cargo exported, cochineal was second only to bullion. Oriental merchandise, which arrived at Acapulco on Manila galleons, was taken by mule trains to Mexico City, where some of it was sent on to Veracruz for transshipment to the Iberian Peninsula. Returning clergy and government officials, plus Spanish-bound mail, took the same route in the annual fleet of convoyed merchant vessels.

Besides its restrictive trade policies, the home government erected an elaborate tax structure that vexed the colonists. There was the *quinto,* or fifth (later lowered to a tenth), on gold, silver, pearls, gems, and the sale of slaves; the *alcabala* sales tax; the *avería,* which supported the naval escort for the *flota; almojarifazgo* taxes on imports and exports; an excise tax on liquors; the Indian tribute or head tax; the Church tithe; and other taxes. In addition, the government maintained monopolies on gunpowder, mercury, salt, playing cards, and stamped legal paper. Other sources of income included the sale of offices or titles; the *media anata* (half of the first year's salary) paid by an appointee to a public office or one promoted to a higher post; the *mesada* (a month's salary) collected from newly appointed lower clergy; plus gifts to the king, some actively solicited or forced in times of crisis. It should be pointed out that the rate of taxation in New Spain was much less than in metropolitan Spain, and there was no tax on income, except the tithe, and no taxes on land.

Mining for gold and silver was an important economic

activity that provided a rich source of wealth for both colony and mother country. The early treasure shipments came from booty and tribute, but soon rich veins were discovered that continued to produce throughout the colonial period. These bonanzas attracted many Spaniards to New Spain and the continued finding of additional lodes helped expand the colonial frontier. Because miners needed food, farms and ranches sprang up; the silver had to be transported, so mule trains were organized and roads improved; and along the roads came priests, peddlers, and colonists; soon towns developed at the mining sites or *reales*. The search for treasure was officially encouraged in many ways—by lowering the *quinto* tax to 10 percent, granting bonuses and honors to discoverers, furnishing military escorts for prospectors, and enacting regulations that assured a supply of laborers to work the mines.

Miners employed various techniques to extract precious metals from the mined ore. At first heat was used in a smelting process, but about 1554 the "patio method," which used mercury (quicksilver) as an amalgam, was introduced by the Spaniard Bartolomé de Medina. When that process was universally adopted, it created a demand for mercury, which came from mines in Spain or Peru. The crown's monopoly on mercury provided a check on production of precious metals; another control was the requirement that all gold and silver had to be taken to a royal mint where ingots were exchanged for minted coinage after payment of taxes and fees.

Although mining was important, the real basis for colonial life was agriculture and ranching, which also supported employment for the great majority of the population. The arrival of the Spanish conquistadors heralded an agricultural revolution, because the Europeans introduced draft animals, the plow, metal shovels and forks, wheeled carts, barrows, and a variety of useful plants and animals. Native American plants continued to be an important source of food and fiber, as they still are, but the output was greatly increased with the application of European agronomical technology.

There occurred in the sixteenth century a great transatlan-

TABLE 2.

NEW WORLD PLANTS	OLD WORLD PLANTS
maize	wheat
tomato	rye
squash	oats
pumpkin	alfalfa
red pepper	hops
kidney bean	flax
navy bean	rice
string bean	apple
pole bean	peach
wax bean	pear
white potato	plum
sweet potato	apricot
guava	cherry
avocado	orange
cacao (chocolate)	lemon
peanut	lime
pecan	almond
plantain	olive
pineapple	grape
papaya	lentil
strawberry	garbanza
persimmon	turnip
vanilla	lettuce
tobacco	radish
rubber	carrot
sarsaparilla	cabbage
mamey	onion
agave	garlic

tic interchange—what one author has felicitously termed
"The Columbian Exchange." Table 2 shows some of the hundreds of useful plants that were taken to and from New Spain.
The exchange was actually worldwide, since Spaniards transplanted various African plants—sugar cane, yam, globe arti-
choke, okra, watermelon, and coffee—to New Spain, and from
Asia and Oceania they brought coconut palm, mango, and
white mulberry trees.

Subsistence farming and commercial agriculture existed

side by side in New Spain. Indian village communal land-holdings, called *ejidos* by the Spanish, continued to be farmed in the traditional manner with pre-Columbian crops. The *ejidos* produced enough to feed their commune and some surplus to pay the tribute. Outside the Aztec area many Indian families engaged in subsistence farming by tilling their small plots using old methods and familiar domesticated plants. In the lowland tropical zone, Spanish and *criollo* entrepreneurs established plantations to grow the export products of sugar, tobacco, cacao, indigo, and henequen with labor performed by gangs of Indians or black slaves. Large commercial haciendas in the central part of the colony specialized in wheat, maize, or agave (for fermented *pulque*); their production was important because it sustained the urban population. Workers on these farms were unskilled day laborers called peons, who worked for wages.

Cultivation was radically changed by the introduction of European livestock. Pre-Columbian Indians of Middle America had no domesticated animals except the dog, turkey, duck, and bee; thus the imported draft animals — horses, burros, mules, and oxen — not only made it possible to cultivate more land, they altered the method, speed, and capacity of transport. Both the diet and the rural occupation of a great number of people were modified with the introduction of European animals raised for food: cattle, swine, sheep, goats, chickens, and geese. At the same time, sheep's wool gave colonial weavers a new textile fiber that, when made into garments, provided more warmth than the native cotton, and the abundant cowhides became the basis for a leather industry as well as an important export item. The specialized occupation of breeding fighting bulls for bullfights was another innovation. A negative impact of the new pastoralism was the destruction of native crops and watering patterns by the livestock.

Stock raising moved northward with the expanding mining frontier and eventually pushed past the mining region into New Mexico, Texas, and California. Meanwhile, migratory Indians stole many horses and adapted their life and warfare to a new mobility acquired indirectly from Europe. Colonial ranchers used Spanish methods and terminology: their stock roamed free, and each year cowboys (*vaqueros*) rounded them up, separated them by owner's brand, and branded the colts and calves, which followed their mothers. After the work was done the cowboys demonstrated their riding and roping skills in a rodeo. Roundup entertainment also included barbeques, guitar music, singing, and dancing. The activities took place on *ranchos* (the larger ones were called *estancias*) and haciendas.

The hacienda was the characteristic economic and social institution of colonial Mexico. It was a large landed estate that provided some economic return, was used as collateral for cash loans, and give its owner, the *hacendado,* social prestige and political power. Frequently the owner resided in the provincial or viceregal capital for most of the year, leaving an overseer, or major-domo, to manage the property. Small estates grew into haciendas through purchase of additional farms or ranches, merger through marriage, foreclosure of mortgages, government grants, or seizure of adjacent lands. The creation of entailed estates (*mayorazcos*), and the law of primogeniture, whereby the oldest son inherited all the property, kept the landholdings intact. At the end of the colonial period there were more than a thousand large cattle ranches in New Spain and 3,749 haciendas. One of the largest of the latter belonged to the Marquisate of Aguayo. In 1760 it totaled almost 6,000 hectares (14,688,630 acres), and there were thousands of resident workers on the several estates making up that latifundium.

A typical hacienda had agriculture (maize, wheat, sugar, rice, or agave) and some livestock, but only a portion of the land was cultivated, and much land was unused even for grazing. It was a self-sustaining unit with an imposing residence for the owner, dwellings for an administrator and foremen, and rows of workers' huts. There were workshops and storage buildings, a store *(tienda de raya)* that sold dry goods, tobacco, sugar, and other items not produced on the estate, a bar or *cantina,* a chapel or church with a priest supported by the *hacendado,* and a cemetery. It was common for workers never to leave the hacienda where they were born, employed, married, and buried.

Most laborers on haciendas were resident workers called peons (day laborers) who tilled the land, cared for the livestock, and performed other services in return for a daily wage, housing in one-room shacks provided by the owner, and a small plot of garden land. A law of 1656 set the daily pay at three *reales* (there were eight *reales* in a peso); eighteenth century records suggest that wages were two to ten pesos per month, depending on the age and skill of the worker. Peons customarily were given advances on their wages or credit at the hacienda store. This practice led to debt peonage, which obliged workers to remain on the premises until the debt was repaid, a condition that was difficult because of the low wage scale and relatively high cost of goods and services such as cloth or funerals. Sometimes workers were paid in scrip or due bills negotiable only at the *tienda de raya.* Debt peonage kept workers in poverty and guaranteed the *hacendado* a steady labor supply at fixed low wages.

Although a majority of paid workers were employed in rural occupations, some lived in towns where they gained a living as craftsmen or laborers in factories. Manufacturing and processing activities·existed in New Spain in spite of official discouragement of industries that competed with those of the mother country. To meet the demand for clothing, *obrajes* (textile works) were organized as early as the 1520s, and they soon became notorious for their harsh working conditions. In the *obrajes,* men, using upright foot looms instead of the pre-Columbian backstrap loom used by women, produced inexpensive cotton *manta* cloth, woolens, and silks. Other colonial industries included shipyards, potteries, glassworks, tanneries, iron works, furniture factories, paper mills, and soap works.

Many of the artisans were organized into craft *gremios,* or guilds, which strictly controlled their membership and guided the men through stages from apprentice to journeyman to master. Eventually there were more than a hundred guilds in New Spain, including silversmiths, saddle makers, weavers, hatters, potters, candle makers, millers, and so forth. Guild members marched together in distinctive costumes at public celebrations or religious processions, and they congregated with their families for social affairs. A few guilds were organized as militia units, and the organizations served as mutual philanthropic and benevolent societies. Like their European counterparts, the guilds tended to be restrictive in their membership—some refused to admit Indians or blacks.

People from three continents, America, Europe, and Africa (plus a small number of Asians who arrived via the Philippine Islands) came together in New Spain, where they created a new society as well as some new ethnic strains. Although there was considerable miscegenation, a substantial part of each racial group maintained its own separate identity. Spanish colonial laws and customs recognized a hierarchical social system loosely based on race, but a person's cultural, social, and economic conditions were as important as ethnicity in determining his or her status. For example, legitimate birth was a crucial factor. The stratified system changed over the years, so that by the end of the colonial era the divisions were less rigid.

As Table 3 shows, the European-born Spaniards (peninsulars) never amounted to even 1 percent of the population; yet they ran the colony and obliged the lower classes to do the manual labor and support them through heavy taxation.

Those colonists who had been born in the home country — the Iberian Peninsula—were usually called *peninsulares,* or, derisively, *gachupines* (wearers of spurs). Members of this group had a virtual monopoly of the top positions: they controlled the government, the army, the universities, the secular Church, and the missions. Fifty-eight of the sixty-one viceroys and virtually all of the judges were Spanish-born. The same was true of the archbishops. As late as 1808 all but one of the sitting bishops were from the motherland, and those who had been born in Europe held key offices in the religious orders.

TABLE 3.
Ethnic Components of the Colonial Population

	1570	1646	1742	1793	1810
Peninsulars	6,644	13,780	9,814	7,904	15,000
Criollos	11,067	168,568	391,512	677,458	1,092,367
Mestizos	2,437	109,042	249,368	418,568	704,245
Indians	3,336,860	1,269,607	1,540,256	2,319,741	3,676,281
Mulattos and					
Zambos	2,435	116,529	266,196	369,790	624,461
Negroes	20,569	35,089	20,131	6,100	10,000
Totals	3,380,012	1,712,615	2,477,277	3,799,561	6,122,354

SOURCE: Gonzalo Aguirre Beltrán, *La población negra de México, 1519-1810* (Mexico: Fondo de Cultura Económica, 1972), 234.

About 300,000 Spaniards emigrated to New Spain during the colonial years; in addition, many men from the metropolis were assigned there temporarily. Married officials brought along their families or were soon ordered to send for them. Forty percent of the emigrants were from the southern provinces of Andalucía; others were from western or central Spain; and there were some Basques from the north. The majority of peninsulars were relatively poor people who sought economic opportunity overseas—many came at the request of relatives or townsmen already in New Spain. Some had no special skills; others were craftsmen, business agents, professionals, soldiers, or servants in the entourage of high officials, and a few were ne'er do wells. When they arrived in New Spain, all the peninsulars, regardless of their class or financial status, looked down upon those who had been born in the New World.

The second category of the colonial social hierarchy was composed of *criollos* (creoles), which at first meant American-born Spaniards or persons of all-European ancestry who had been born in the Indies. But soon the term came to mean "affluent Mexicans" and included racially mixed offspring of wealthy Spaniards, nor was it unknown to "purchase" the category. Many *criollos* became professionals: lawyers, physicians, teachers, scribes, religious friars, or secular priests. Others acquired status and wealth through ownership of haciendas, textile factories, or mines, and a considerable number of them engaged in commerce. A few—those who were descendants of conquistadors, related to distinguished families in Spain, or wealthy enough to have influence at court—obtained titles or decorations and formed part of the colonial aristocracy.

Peninsulars and *criollos* together constituted a socially superior elite group. They wore distinctive clothing of silk, velvet, linen, and lace—these materials were forbidden to Indians and blacks. Upper-class men were addressed with Don (Sir) prefixed to their Christian name, women with Doña (Lady). Elite women were called *damas* (ladies); the men were *caballeros*, a term that means both gentlemen and horsemen. Only the elite could ride horseback in parades— all ranks below had to ride mules, donkeys, or walk. Elite males could become priests or attend the universities— Indians and blacks were not eligible. And members of this upper class disdained manual labor—it was done by the lower classes. A wide social gulf separated the elite from all other ethnic categories.

The *mestizos*, persons of mixed Spanish and Indian background, had a special social status. They were considered to be *gente de razón* (people of reason); Indians and blacks were not. This class expanded rapidly because so many Spanish men took Indian wives and had large families. The widespread practice of concubinage produced a number of illegitimate *mestizos*, some of whom, rejected by both Spaniards and Indians, became vagabonds. When Indians abandoned their native ways—spoke Spanish, wore shoes, or worked at non-traditional occupations—they were regarded as *mestizos*. In the colonial era, *mestizos* comprised a lower middle class. A few had minor government positions; others were plantation, ranch, mine, mission, or factory foremen; and some were artisans, shopkeepers, farmers, or cowboys.

Indians, who were the great majority of the colonial population, were the peasantry of New Spain. Of course, there was a variety of native cultures and languages, as there still is. Many Indians lived on haciendas, and a great number lived apart in their own villages, where they governed themselves and tried to preserve their tribal language, dress, and customs. Some lived in *barrios* (districts) on the edge of colonial towns; while out on the frontier there were barbarian tribes like the Apaches, others that were semi-civilized, as well as natives who had lived in religious missions for a generation or more. In the early years Indian nobles, including the daughters of Moctezuma who married Spaniards, were part of the colonial aristocracy, but this element was soon assimilated. A few sons of Indian chiefs were educated at special Indian schools, and over the years several natives became Catholic priests in spite of various Mexican Church councils denying ordination to Indians and mixed castes.

Hereditary Indian chiefs were exempt from tribute payments and had other privileges; many of these *caciques* joined with Spaniards to exploit other Indians. Although the natives were considered to be minors in a state of tutelage, and as such were covered by protective laws that attempted to shield them from oppression, most of them were in a condition of semi-serfdom, subject to demands for their labor and tribute in goods. Exploitation of Indians led to a number of native uprisings, all of which were severely repulsed.

European diseases, especially smallpox, measles, and typhus, created a demographic disaster for the aboriginal population of Mexico. Indians had little or no immunity to the new maladies, and fourteen epidemics were recorded in the sixteenth century. Moreover, many Indians perished from hunger because roaming European livestock trampled their crops and ruined their irrigation systems. Scholars have estimated that the native population of central Mexico declined from twenty-five million to one million during the first century after the conquest. The dramatic decrease in Indian population was one reason for the importation of black slaves.

An African presence in Mexico began with the half-dozen blacks, one of them a free soldier, who arrived with Cortés.

In the subsequent three centuries about 200,000 African slaves, three-fourths of them males, were transported to New Spain. Miscegenation soon produced a sizable number of mulattos (offspring of the union of Spaniards and blacks) as well as *zambos* (progeny of a Negro and an Indian parent). A child's status, free or slave, was the same as its mother. Blacks worked as stevedores in Veracruz and Acapulco, labored in mines and factories, worked at plantations and sugar mills, were farm and ranch hands, found employment as artisans, and served as household servants in the large cities. Some free blacks became overseers of rural properties; others were put in charge of Indian workers. There were several slave riots in New Spain, and some runaway blacks, called *cimarrones* or maroons, managed to live in extremely isolated communities. (Descendants of these maroons still live in a few remote villages in the states of Veracruz and Guerrero.)

In spite of the harsh treatment of black slaves, mitigating features of Spanish law permitted slaves to marry a spouse of their choice, work for themselves in spare time to accumulate money, and buy their freedom or that of family members at the lowest market price. Many owners freed their slaves, sometimes because they had borne the master's children, performed extraordinary service, or were too old to work. At the end of the colonial era most of the blacks were free. However, prejudice against their color still kept them in the lower social and economic strata.

Negroes arrived in the New World without any baggage, but they brought with them a variety of skills and a panoply of African cultural traditions. Their knowledge and talents included plant cultivation and use of the hoe, animal husbandry, folk medicine, marketing techniques, and folk arts such as metal working, wood and ivory carving, basketry, and ceramics. Their musical forms and instruments, especially drums and marimba, had a great influence on Mexican music, and their oral traditions—legends, proverbs, fairy tales, riddles, heroic tales—were passed on to their own children as well as to white and Indian youngsters they nurtured. In the area of religion most African practices were suppressed or merged into acceptable modes of worship. A few blacks were baptized on Caribbean islands before they came to New Spain; those that were not soon took the first step to becoming Christians.

The Roman Catholic Church was the most important and influential institution introduced into the colony. Spanish Catholicism of the conquest era was a militant force that embraced all classes and races, and colonial residents demonstrated their faith through frequent public processions, liberal financial contributions for charitable works, endowment of convents, establishment of chaplaincies, and the general esteem that they had for churchmen. Personal diaries and private correspondence of the colonial era attest that the Catholic faith became deeply rooted in Mexican culture, and of course it still is.

The Church was united with the state in the task of transferring Spanish culture and civilization to New Spain. A series of papal grants in the late fifteenth and early sixteenth centuries established a special relationship between the Spanish crown and the Church. These concessions are known as the *patronato real,* the right of royal patronage. In return for accepting the obligation of Christianizing the natives of newly-found lands and for building the necessary churches and monasteries, the Spanish monarchs were permitted to nominate candidates for ecclesiastical offices—cardinals, bishops, abbots, canons, and so on—to collect tithes and allocate the revenues to pious purposes, to assign missionary orders to specific geographic areas, and to determine the boundaries of episcopal sees. In addition, the crown claimed the right to approve papal bulls and decrees before they could be promulgated in the Indies and to censor religious communications passing to and from the colonies. The royal prerogatives extended to virtually all Church matters except dogma and doctrine, and over the years those rights were exercised by the monarch, the Council of the Indies, and ranking colonial officers. One exception was the *fuero,* the special privilege of churchmen to be tried only in Church courts if they were accused of any crime.

Church work was carried on by personnel of both branches, the *secular* clergy, who served the public as diocesan or parish priests under the bishops and hierarchy, and the *regular* clergy, who were members of orders of monks and nuns. Missionary priests (regulars) established monasteries, hospitals, and schools in the settled areas, and they developed missions on various frontiers. When they completed their task of Christianizing and civilizing the mission Indians, they were supposed to turn over their church and charges to parish priests and move on to another mission field. Because of the shortage of secular clergy and the special frontier conditions in New Spain, many of the early bishops were members of religious orders.

Although conversion of the natives of Mexico was a tremendous undertaking, it proceeded rather quickly in the central part of the colony. A letter dated June 12, 1531, from the first bishop of Mexico, Juan de Zumárraga (a Franciscan), gives some details of the preliminary success.

We are very busy in the great task of converting the Indians. More than a million five hundred thousand of them have been baptized at the hands of our own Franciscan fathers. Temples of idols have been destroyed and more than twenty thousand idols ground to dust or burned. In many places churches have been built and the cross raised up and worshipped by the Indians. What seems most wonderful is that where formerly, in their infidelity, they were accustomed to sacrificing as many as twenty thousand human hearts, now they offer themselves not to evil spirits but to God, with innumerable sacrifices of praise, thanks to the teaching and excellent example of our priests, who are greatly respected by the children of the natives. Many of the converts fast and pray and discipline themselves with tears and sighings. Many of them know how to read and write and sing. They confess frequently and receive the holy sacrament with great devotion, and with joy preach the word of God to their parents, trained to do so by the priests. They rise at midnight for matins and are particularly devoted to Our Lady. They take the idols away from their parents and bring them to the priests, for which some of them have actually been killed by the parents and crowned by Christ in glory.

Each of our convents has a school alongside it and a dormitory, dining room, and chapel. The children are humble and obedient to the priests whom they love as fathers. They are chaste and quite clever, especially in painting, and have achieved a good heart before God.*

It is interesting to note that in those years, when Protestantism was eroding the power and membership of the Catholic Church in Europe, overseas missionaries were adding millions of converts, and secular priests were erecting new dioceses of the Church of Rome.

One factor that aided the conversion of Indians in New Spain was the cult of the Virgin of Guadalupe. According to tradition, the Virgin Mary appeared three times in December, 1531, at the hill of Tepeyacac near Mexico City, a site that was an ancient Indian sacred place identified with Tonantzin, "the mother of gods." Here the Virgin conversed with a Christianized Indian named Juan Diego and asked that a church be built on the hill. As a special sign she told the Indian to cut fresh roses that miraculously were blooming on the stony knoll and carry them in his cloak to the bishop. When he opened his cloak, there was painted on it a picture of the lady of his vision, a dark-haired, brown-skinned woman, Our Lady of Guadalupe. Under that title Mary became a special patroness of Mexico. A chapel (later a basilica) was erected at the site, renamed Guadalupe, and annually thousands of devout persons, especially Indians, have visited the shrine. Whether one considers the 1531 appearance a miracle or not, *Nuestra Señora de Guadalupe* became an important tradition that inspired many leaders and still forms an essential part of the Mexican psyche.

The Church touched virtually every phase of colonial life and was responsible for what we now call social services: education, hospitals, orphanages, and institutional care for the aged, poor, and mentally disturbed. Colonial churchmen planned and supervised construction of thousands of churches,

*Quoted in Charles S. Braden, *Religious Aspects of the Conquest of Mexico* (Durham: Duke University Press, 1930), 222–23.

The Virgin of Guadalupe with Juan Diego. Courtesy The Oakland Museum.

cathedrals, chapels, convents, monasteries, and oratories. (Most of the buildings are still extant, though not necessarily used for religious purposes.) Clerics and their institutions provided loans for capitalist ventures or for alleviation of suffering, they were sources of information for peasants or professionals, and they kept records of births, deaths, and marriages. They counseled government bureaucrats, they taught in primary and secondary schools, seminaries, and universities, and they directed choirs and orchestras. Furthermore, the priests, friars, and nuns acted as a moral force inspiring higher ideals in a frontier society. Of course there were some clerical scoundrels, but the great majority were devoted, sincere, and hardworking men and women.

During the colonial era the Church acquired considerable wealth, much of it donated by pious individuals. A few rich colonists financed the building of churches. José de la Borda, who acquired a fortune in mining, sponsored the beautiful Santa Prisca church in the town of Taxco. Others, especially those with no children, willed their property to religious establishments, and many of the faithful set up endowments or gave outright liberal cash gifts. The bulk of Church wealth was in land — early in the nineteenth century the conservative Mexican historian Lucas Alamán estimated that the Catholic Church owned half the real estate in Mexico. The system of Mortmain, under which the Church never sold any of its property, facilitated this vast accumulation.

Another source of Church wealth was the ecclesiastical tax known as the tithe or tenth part. Tithes were collected on harvested crops, livestock, mining profits, and on rental income from real estate. Distribution of tithe income varied somewhat from region to region, but the bishopric of Oaxaca serves as a typical example. There, half of the receipts were split equally between the bishop and the canons of the cathedral chapter; the remainder was divided into nine parts, with two-ninths assigned to the monarch, one-and-a-half ninths for the building and repair of the cathedral and parish churches, one-and-a-half ninths for the support of hospitals, and four-ninths to the curates or parish priests. Tithes were generally collected by government-appointed tax collectors, sometimes called "tax farmers," who paid in advance a lump sum for the privilege and then extracted what they could from the taxpayers.

Church and state were also allied in the establishment of the Holy Office of the Inquisition. This ecclesiastical court, which was set up to root out heresy and unify the empire, was formally established in New Spain in 1571. Before that time the bishops commonly functioned as inquisitorial officers. Indians were exempt from the jurisdiction of the Inquisition, but they remained liable to correction by bishops or, in frontier areas, by missionaries. Besides enforcing Catholic orthodoxy, inquisitors were concerned with public, and particularly clerical, morality. The great majority of investigations and trials involved such charges as bigamy, prostitution, sodomy, perjury, blasphemy, and the practice of astrology.

Procedures and practices of the Inquisition have been criticized, but they should be judged against the background of the times, when religious or political dissent was severely dealt with in Europe and England. In New Spain those accused by the Inquisition were tried in secret; some were tortured to elicit a confession, the first step to moral rehabilitation. Punishment of those found guilty varied with the type of crime. Many persons were censured publicly, others were fined, ordered to do public penance, or imprisoned. The death penalty was infrequent—during three colonial centuries only forty-three "unrepentant apostates" were turned over to civil authorities for capital punishment.

The Holy Office also served the state as a censorship agency to exclude from the Indies those books deemed heretical or which attacked the concept of divine right of sovereigns. Yet, many prohibited books did arrive in New Spain, as inventories of specific private libraries prove, and curiously, the study of mathematics at the University of Mexico included instruction in astrology as an aid to the compilation of almanacs.

As in Europe at the time, formal education in New Spain was limited to a select few. Although the great majority of the teachers were priests, missionaries, or nuns, there were also a few private tutors and secular instructors. The first schools were established in Mexico City, where they catered to children of the Spanish elite and to certain Indian and *mestizo* youths. By 1534 there were eight schools where women taught Indian girls the fundamentals of reading, writing, and arithmetic, as well as music, art, sewing, cooking, and homemaking. For over forty years Pedro de Gante, a Franciscan lay brother, directed the school of San José, where a thousand Indian boys studied Latin, Castilian, music, and religion, and adults were taught trades—carpentry, masonry, metalsmithing, and other crafts. New Spain's first viceroy dedicated the school of San Juan de Letrán, which for three centuries provided vocational education for orphaned or abandoned *mestizo* boys. A similar school for girls, Nuestra Señora de Caridad, opened in 1533.

One of the most famous Indian schools was the *Colegio* (secondary or preparatory school) of Santa Cruz Tlatelolco, established for training sons of Indian nobles to be teachers to their own people. It began in 1536, with sixty students who studied Latin, rhetoric, logic, philosophy, music, and Indian medicine. The faculty included such famous teachers as Juan de Gaona and Juan Focher, both trained at the University of Paris, and the distinguished ethnographer, Bernardino de Sahagún. About 1548, the Franciscans turned the *colegio* over to its Indian graduates, but within twenty years the experiment had failed. This was partly because of growing prejudice among the whites against higher education for Indians, and partly because Mexican Church councils, beginning in 1555, ruled against the creation of an Indian clergy—thus there was little reason for the natives to master Latin. And of course they were precluded from appointment to important government positions. Likewise, Indian women were forestalled from becoming nuns; yet many of them led a secluded, holy life—often as servants in convents.

A utopian experiment in Indian education was initiated by Vasco de Quiroga, a judge who later took Holy Orders. In 1531 he created the hospital-city of Santa Fe. This commune was based on social ideas from Plato and Thomas More. Two years later he moved to Michoacán, where he established similar communities among the Tarascan Indians who lived around Lake Pátzcuaro. The natives were taught rudiments of Christianity, new agricultural methods, and the use of European tools. Each village governed itself and specialized in a particular craft such as ceramics, weaving, or woodcarving; able-bodied adults worked six hours daily in the production of foodstuffs and crafts; and families shared equally in the division of produce. Quiroga's success led to his appointment as bishop of Michoacán in 1539, and he continued to found schools and hospitals and assist the Indians until his death in 1565. (To this day villagers of that region revere "Don Vasco" and continue their traditional crafts in the village pattern he arranged four centuries ago.)

Except for private tutoring, formal education for non-Indian children was generally available only to white males and a few upper-level *mestizos*. Following the European model, most women and the lower classes, rural or urban, remained unschooled; thus illiteracy in the colony was over 90 percent. The first schools for upper-class children were in monasteries of the mendicant friars. Later, secular priests established primary schools. Secondary education could be obtained only in larger towns where *colegios* were maintained by religious groups, especially by Dominicans and Jesuits. Besides teaching Latin grammar, they offered instruction in the liberal arts leading to a *bachillerato* (bachelor's degree), generally a prerequisite to entrance into a college or university. By the end of the colonial era New Spain had forty colleges and seminaries, half of which prepared students to take advanced degrees. The four institutions with university prerogatives were founded in Mexico City (1551), Mérida (1624), Guanajuato (1732), and Guadalajara (1792).

The major institution of higher education was the Royal and Pontifical University of Mexico. Two of the first professors were *audiencia* judges, and the rest were churchmen. Within fifty years the University had twenty-four academic chairs including Latin, rhetoric, philosophy, canon law, civil

Vasco de Quiroga, missionary and Bishop of Michoacán. Courtesy The Bancroft Library.

law, scriptures, theology, mathematics, medicine, and the
native Mexican languages Nahuatl and Otomí. (Indians were
excluded from the University, but their languages were considered suitable for scholarly study.) Schools of mining and
fine arts were added to the University in the eighteenth century. Most courses were taught in Latin; theology was a required subject; and students had to pay high fees in order
to graduate. During three colonial centuries, the University
granted about eighteen hundred licentiate, master's, and doctor's degrees. More than half of the diplomas were in theology. There were 595 law graduates, 150 in medicine, and 134
in arts. It is clear that the university curriculum was designed
to meet the needs of a very small cultural elite. Of course
many colonial priests, officials, and residents were peninsulars who had been educated in Europe, and a few *criollos* went
abroad to study.

Scholarship and the literature produced in New Spain
paralleled the colony's transition from a military outpost to
a sophisticated society. The earliest writings were chronicles
of discovery and conquest, a number of which preserved
much material about the native peoples. Cortés's lengthy
Letters from Mexico to Emperor Charles V are not only a
primary historical and ethnological source but also figure
among the first examples of New World literature. Writings
of other soldiers such as Andrés de Tapia and one who is
styled "The Anonymous Conquistador" preserve the record
of great deeds and are still read as heroic tales. Perhaps
the most famous and readable account is the *True History
of the Conquest of New Spain* written by the elderly veteran,
Bernal Díaz del Castillo, who recalled exploits of his compatriots in overthrowing the Aztecs.

Two *mestizo* descendants of Aztec nobles wrote important
historical accounts of their mothers' people. Hernando Alva
Ixtlilxóchitl's volumes are titled *Relaciones* and *Historia Chi-
chimeca;* Hernando Alvarado Tezozomoc, a grandson of Moctezuma II, wrote his *Crónica Mexicana* in Spanish and another
version in Nahuatl.

Missionaries penned the majority of books about the Indians of Mexico. With the help of his native students at the *colegio* of Santiago Tlatelolco, the Franciscan friar Bernardino de Sahagún compiled in Nahuatl and later translated into Spanish a monumental multi-volume work on Aztec culture known as the *Florentine Codex, or General History of the Things of New Spain.* Other noteworthy accounts by sixteenth-century missionaries are Toribio de Motolinía's *History of the Indians of New Spain;* Diego Durán's *The Aztecs;* Gerónimo de Mendieta's *Historia Ecclesiastica Indiana;* and Juan de Torquemada's three volumes, *Monarquía Indiana.* In his zeal to extirpate paganism among the Maya of Yucatán, the friar Diego de Landa destroyed some codices and idols, but he also wrote the first *Relación* (historical report) of that region and its native people. During the rest of the colonial era other missionaries continued to study and write about aboriginal cultures. One of the most important of the later works is the *Historia antigua de México* by the Jesuit scholar Francisco Javier de Clavigero, who was born in Veracruz in 1731.

Thomas Gage, an Englishman who spent twelve years (1625–37) in New Spain as a Dominican friar, later wrote a book in English with the modern title *Travels in the New World.* Although his writing was influenced by political and religious motives—by then he was back in England where he embraced Puritanism—the account has value as a record of daily life in Mexico and Guatemala.

Besides their historical writings, clergymen produced a number of religious tracts, sermons, and catechisms, as well as grammars and dictionaries of many native languages. Some of these manuscripts were printed in Spain, but about 1536, Juan Pablos established a printing press in Mexico City under the patronage of Bishop Juan de Zumárraga. Like other economic endeavors in New Spain, this printing office was a branch of a firm in Seville. Zumárraga's *Breve y mas compendiosa Doctrina Cristiana en lengua Mexicana* (1539) was one of the first books printed in the Western Hemisphere. More than three hundred works were printed in Mexico in the sixteenth century, the majority of them religious items.

Page of a book of anthems printed in Mexico, 1568. Courtesy Universidad Nacional Autónoma de México.

They appeared in ten native languages as well as Castilian. By the end of the colonial era the cumulative total of books printed in New Spain exceeded ten thousand.

Aside from conquest chronicles and religious books, writers in New Spain produced works in other genres. Doctor García Farfán, an Augustinian physician and inspector of pharmacies, published in 1579 a treatise on medicine that mentioned the pharmaceutical use of various native plants. Francisco Cervantes de Salazar's *Life in the Imperial and Loyal City of Mexico* described the viceregal capital and the virtues of its university, of which he was a founder and professor. And one of the earliest poets in the Americas, Bernardo de Balbuena, in 1603 published his epic poem *Grandeza Mexicana*, which contains 1,780 lines extolling the beauty of Mexico City.

The outstanding poet of New Spain, and one of the greatest in the Spanish language, was a seventeenth-century nun, Sor (Sister) Juana Inés de la Cruz (1648–95). A precocious child, she mastered Latin at an early age and at sixteen resided in the viceroy's court where nobles and intellectuals were astounded by the depth and variety of her learning. Still in her teens she entered a convent, where she devoted herself to contemplation, studying, and writing, while she amassed a library of four thousand volumes. She wrote plays and essays, but her lyric poetry earned her the title of "The Tenth Muse." Sor Juana, an early exponent of women's rights, lamented the unequal position of women in her day. In "Redondillas" (Seven-syllable Quatrains) Sor Juana expressed her feelings on the subject of courtship in no uncertain terms:

> *Stupid men, quick to condemn*
> *Women wrongly for their flaws,*
> *Never seeing you're the cause*
> *Of all that you blame in them!*
>
> *If you flatter them along,*
> *Earn their scorn, their love incite,*
> *Why expect them to do right*
> *When you urge them to do wrong?*

Sor Juana Inés de la Cruz, "The Tenth Muse." Courtesy Organization of American States.

COLONIAL INSTITUTIONS AND LIFE   157

You combat their opposition,
And then gravely when you're done,
Say the whole thing was in fun
And you did not seek submission.

You expect from action shady
That some magic will be done
To turn courted courtesan
Quickly into virtuous lady.

Can you think of wit more drear
Than for one with lack of brain
To smear a mirror, then complain
Since it is not crystal clear?

. . . .

Tempt us not to acquiesce,
Then with justice can you censure
Any girl who dares to venture
Near you, seeking your caress.

Women need be strong, I find,
To stay safe and keep unharmed
Since the arrogant male comes armed
*With Devil, flesh, and world combined.**

One of Sor Juana's friends and intellectual companions
was Carlos de Sigüenza y Góngora (1645–1700), a *criollo* savant
whose fame extended beyond the Spanish empire. Although
as a young man he was expelled from a Jesuit seminary for
an infraction of their strict rules, he was later ordained as
a secular priest. Afterward, he taught at the University of
Mexico for more than two decades. Sigüenza was a poet, historian, mathematician, astronomer, and he did research in
archaeology, agronomy, engineering, and applied science.
His many published works include biographies, a poem about
the Virgin of Guadalupe (known in translation as *Indian
Spring*), treatises on comets, and a history of the University.

*Willis Knapp Jones, ed., *Spanish American Literature in Translation; A
Selection of Prose, Poetry, and Drama Before 1888* (New York: Frederick Un-
gar, 1966), 208–209.

For a century after Sigüenza there were no outstanding literary figures, but in 1816, José Joaquín Fernández de Lizardi published his picaresque adventure story entitled *El Periquillo Sarniento* (translated as *The Itching Parrot*). This is considered to be the first true novel written in Latin America. New Spain's pioneer daily newspaper, *Diario de México*, appeared about that same time, although there had been weekly accounts, literary magazines, and short-lived gazettes since the appearance of *Primera Gazeta de México* in 1667.

Colonial music, dance and theater, like literature, followed patterns from the mother country. The Spanish guitar became the favorite instrument, and secular music varied from lullabies to ballads, *pasodobles, fandangos, jotas,* the minuet, and the martial music of bullfights. Churches, with their organs and choirs, spread Old World sacred music throughout the viceroyalty. The New World's first opera, *"La púrpura de la rosa"* (Blood of the Rose), was composed in Mexico in 1701. Based on a text by Pedro Calderón de la Barca, it was set to music by Thomas de Torrejón y Velasco. Morality plays, generally presented in Church buildings, were part of the drama scene, as were candle-lit secular theaters where plays by Spanish dramatists such as Lope de Vega were popular. A form of "street theater" occurred in the frequent masquerades, parades, and religious processions for which colonists dressed in costumes; some of them appeared on floats impersonating historical, mythological, or Biblical characters. Craftsmen spent untold hours designing and fabricating various elements for these pageants.

The Church was the major patron and client for colonial artists. Innumerable paintings and sculptures of religious subjects were made to adorn churches, chapels, convents, monasteries, schools, and hospitals. Artists also painted portraits of important Church and governmental officials, wealthy *hacendados,* or aristocrats and their families, but few were inspired to depict the unique landscapes or scenes of everyday life. Most of the colonial artists remain anonymous—many were Indian or *mestizo* craftsmen. Miguel Cabrera (1695–1768), an orphan from Oaxaca, was one of the most prolific painters. Dozens of his surviving works are displayed in various museums and churches; they include portraits of Sor Juana Inés de la Cruz, Viceroy Francisco Güemes y Horcasitas, Doña María Padilla y Cervantes, thirty canvases illustrating the lives of Saints Ignacio and Dominic, two murals in a Zacatecas convent, and a self-portrait.

Art critics consider Manuel Tolsá (1757–1816), a peninsular who taught at San Carlos Art Academy, the most talented colonial sculptor. His monumental bronze statue of King Charles IV astride a prancing horse is affectionately called by Mexicans the *"Caballito"* (little horse); it now stands in a traffic circle at the intersection of two of the capital's principal boulevards. Tolsá also was an architect. In addition to supervising construction of convents in Querétaro and San Miguel, he worked on the cathedrals of Puebla and Mexico.

Unquestionably the greatest expression of Spanish colonial art was its architecture. Every region of New Spain was embellished with magnificent churches, handsome plazas, *cabildos,* postoffices, and jails. Here and there were notable residential *palacios,* military posts, royal mints, granaries, sugar mills, stone bridges, and aqueducts. Many of these well-constructed monuments are still in use today. They lend charm and architectural integrity to modern Mexico.

Church buildings dominated colonial architecture—a recent engineering survey concluded that about thirteen thousand religious structures had been erected in the present territory of Mexico. The first ones were built like fortresses, but as the danger from Indian revolts subsided, and as financial support increased, the monasteries, parish churches, convents, and cathedrals became more ornamented, even flamboyant. Paralleling changing fashions, they were constructed in various styles: Gothic, Romanesque, baroque, rococo, and neoclassical. Some of the churches showed Islamic or Arabic details reminiscent of northern Africa or southern Spain, with lattice work, mudéjar paneling, arabesque traceries, and cupolas tiled in bright colors. The façades of the

Cloister of the Dominican monastery, Oaxaca.

Colonial government palace, Guadalajara. Courtesy The Bancroft Library.

churches of San Francisco Acatepec and Santa María Tonant-
zintla, both near Cholula, are covered with glazed ceramic
tiles, and so are kitchen and bathroom walls in a number of
Mexican convents and monasteries. Interior elements of
Mexican churches, such as altars, reredos, and pulpits are
often elaborate, with much use of carved wood, gold leaf,
and stucco. One critic remarked that the architecture was
lively "because the Spaniards felt a need to match a new
splendor against the former glories of the Indians so as to
displace their pagan gods; and also because . . . the natives
played an important role in these creative endeavors."

Outside the metropolitan capital, ten cathedrals were
erected in the colonial era; those at Guadalajara, Oaxaca,
and Puebla are considered to be architectural gems. The

The Cathedral of Mexico City. Courtesy The Bancroft Library.

cathedral in Mexico City, built principally of cut limestone, is the largest and most distinguished church edifice in all of Latin America. Although most of it was completed in the seventeenth century, it was under construction for 250 years. The last stages of work were done in the neoclassic manner so characteristic of the spirit of the eighteenth-century Enlightenment.

CHAPTER 6

Enlightenment and Independence

THE SPANISH EMPIRE reached its zenith in the sixteenth century, declined in the following hundred years, then revived in the eighteenth or Enlightenment century. Part of that revitalization arose from a change of ruling families from the Austrian Hapsburgs to the French Bourbons. This dynastic switch occurred because the last Spanish Hapsburg king, Charles II (1665–1700), had produced no heir and chose as his successor a French grandnephew named Philippe d'Anjou, henceforth known as Philip V of Spain. Thus, members of the House of Bourbon would rule both France and Spain, an arrangement opposed by the Hapsburgs of Austria, who had their own candidate for the Spanish throne and who, with allies including Great Britain, fought the War of Spanish Succession (1702–1713). The outcome was a victory for Philip V, who remained king of Spain.

Widespread reforms were initiated by the Bourbon monarchs and their French advisers, who introduced Parisian modes, attitudes, and policies into the royal court at Madrid. They also introduced the speculative ideas of the Enlightenment, which will be discussed later. These Bourbon reforms revised administrative practices, rejuvenated old institutions and created new ones, stimulated economic enterprises, and attempted to restore Spain's financial position and international prestige. Most of the changes affected the colonies as well as the mother country.

Spain experienced a dramatic economic expansion in the eighteenth century, accompanied by rapid industrialization in certain provinces. This was the result of royal policies aimed to generate wealth and taxes and regain control over colonial trade. The government sponsored new factories to produce woolen, silk, and cotton textiles; mirrors and fine glass; porcelains, pottery, paper, steel, hardware, and other items for home and overseas consumption. In 1700 only about one-eighth of the merchandise shipped from Cadiz to the colonies was of domestic origin—the great majority of items came from France, England, or Holland. These countries also traded directly and illegally with the colonies, thus avoiding Spanish taxes and freight charges. By 1788, Spanish products accounted for well over half of the imperial transatlantic commerce.

Meanwhile, the Bourbon reformers gradually ended restrictions on overseas shipping. First the monopoly of Seville and Cadiz was ended, then the cumbersome and expensive *flota* was replaced by a system of registered ships that could sail individually and directly between ports in the empire. In 1765 many additional ports in the Indies were opened to all Spanish merchants, and by 1788, with certain limitations, there was free trade within the Spanish empire—even intercolonial trade. These changes produced a fourfold increase in business, which tended to lower prices, eliminate foreign contraband goods, and provide more taxes for the government. Crown revenue was also increased through various measures that tapped the flourishing economy of New Spain.

Reforms in government at home and abroad involved restructuring and simplifying the bureaucracy, upgrading the quality of personnel, and achieving more responsiveness on the part of civil servants. Selling public offices to the highest bidder, a Hapsburg practice, ended; instead, officials were chosen on the basis of merit. The result was a distinct improvement in office holders. Also eliminated was "tax farming" whereby concessionaires had kept whatever taxes they extracted from the people. Under the Bourbons, tax collection became a direct responsibility of government officials. A similar improvement affected postal service when the crown abolished the system of private contracts and incorporated mail delivery into the royal administration.

Bourbon reforms occurred during the entire eighteenth century, but the second half was notable for momentous changes initiated under Spain's most enlightened monarch, Charles III (1759-1788). Although his program was designed primarily to increase administrative efficiency and augment the royal treasury, some of the changes had social implications. To carry out the reforms in New Spain the king appointed José de Gálvez as *visitador general.* During the years 1765-1770 Gálvez traveled around the colony gathering information and implementing new programs. He reorganized the treasury accounting system, eliminated some graft, inspected frontier military establishments, and organized the settlement expedition to Alta California. He also assisted the viceroy, Marquis de Croix, in carrying out the royal order for expulsion of the Jesuits.

One goal of the Bourbon monarchs was to insure that the power of the state was supreme, and when some of the king's advisors concluded that the Society of Jesus, or Jesuit Order, opposed this supremacy, the religious order was suppressed. The Jesuits, who had performed distinguished services as educators and missionaries, achieved much success, which resulted in wealth (land and buildings) and power for their order. This aroused the enmity of other clergy and laymen. Furthermore, regalists were concerned about the special Jesuit allegiance to the pope, and members of the ruling circle suspected Jesuits of political intrigue in Madrid. The culmination came in February, 1767, when Charles III decreed the expulsion of the "Black Robes" and confiscation of their property. The decree was kept secret until the following June 25. On that date military commanders throughout the empire opened sealed orders that obliged them to arrest the Jesuits in their district and send them to the Papal States.

The Viceroy of Mexico, Marquis de Croix, announced the startling news by the following public message, which was posted and read by town criers in principal cities of the viceroyalty:

I make known to all the inhabitants of this country that the King, our lord, on account of past incidents, and in order to fulfill the first obligation with which God has granted him the crown, that of

preserving intact its sovereign prerogatives and of keeping his
loyal and beloved people in subordination, tranquility, and justice,
and for other very serious reasons which he keeps secret, has
deigned to order, on the advice of his royal council and by the
decree issued on the 27th of last February, *that the religious of the
Society [of Jesus], priests as well as coadjutors or lay-brothers who have
made the first vows, and the novices who desire to follow them, shall be
banished from all his dominions in Spain, the Indies, the Philippine Islands, and the other adjacent territories, and that all the property of the
Society in his dominions shall be seized....*

I assigned this day for the proclamation of the supreme sentence
to the expelled in their colleges and houses of residence in this
New Spain, and also for announcing it to the people with the warn-
ing that all subjects of whatever rank, class, or condition, being
strictly obliged as they are to respect and obey the ever-just reso-
lutions of their sovereign, must honor, assist, and fulfill this one
with the greatest exactitude and fidelity. Because His Majesty
declares that the disobedient or the remiss in cooperating with its
fulfillment incur his royal indignation, I shall see myself compelled
to use the utmost rigor and military force against those who in
public or in private for this purpose may have conferences, meetings, assemblies, talks, or discussions by word or in writing; for
the subjects of the great monarch who occupies the throne of Spain
must henceforth know once for all that they are born to keep silent
and to obey, but not to discuss nor to judge the lofty affairs of
government.*

Expulsion of the Jesuits caused significant social change in
several parts of New Spain. During the previous two centuries
they had introduced Spanish civilization to the wilderness of
Sinaloa, Sonora, Arizona, and Baja California, where they
founded missions, established agriculture and livestock, explored and mapped the region, and served as frontier agents.
One of the outstanding Jesuit missionaries in this area was
Eusebio Francisco Kino (1645–1711), who worked among the
Pima, Pápago, and Yuma Indians. He founded two dozen
missions, among them San Xavier del Bac near Tucson, Ari-

*The Spanish text is in Vicente Riva Palacio, ed., *México a través de
los siglos,* 5 vols. (Mexico: Ballescá y cía., 1888–89), 2:842.

zona. At the time of their expulsion the Jesuits had 678 members in New Spain. They maintained more than a hundred missions and had the best schools, including twenty-three colleges and various seminaries. Their missions and schools were turned over to Franciscans and Dominicans, but these new overseers lacked sufficient manpower or adequate training for many of the posts. Education and intellectual life in the colony was severely stunted by the forced exodus of the "Black Robes."

Irate champions of the Jesuits rioted in half a dozen cities, including Guanajuato, San Luis Potosí, Pátzcuaro, and Valladolid. At the head of a large military force *Visitador* José de Gálvez suppressed the uprisings and meted out harsh punishments: ninety alleged leaders were executed, almost seven hundred rebels were sentenced to life imprisonment, and more than a hundred were exiled. Although peace was restored, hatred of the peninsulars simmered in this region until a greater rebellion against the Spaniards erupted in 1810.

The discontent of *criollos* and castes was somewhat ameliorated by improvements introduced by two of New Spain's greatest viceroys, Antonio María Bucareli (1771–79) and the second Count of Revillagigedo (1789–94). These men transmitted the spirit of the Enlightenment to the colony and were outstanding administrators who worked hard to improve the quality of life in the viceroyalty. Revillagigedo succeeded in achieving reformation of tax collection, encouragement of agriculture, mining, and industry, expansion of education, improvement of roads, paving and lighting of city streets, establishment of weekly mail service between the capital and northern military posts, sponsorship of exploration of the Pacific Coast to Alaska, and better administration of justice.

At the provincial level, New Spain's government structure was altered and invigorated after 1786 by the creation of twelve intendancies (*intendencias*), or sub-regions, each headed by an intendant whose authority embraced administration, justice, and treasury matters. The dozen crown-appointed intendants, only one of whom was a *criollo,* replaced some two hundred *corregidores* and *alcaldes mayores.* Intendants were

The Count of Revillagigedo II, fifty-second viceroy of New Spain, Courtesy The Bancroft Library.

supposed to protect Indians from their oppressors, eliminate graft and smuggling, encourage agriculture and commerce, organize local militias, and make detailed reports on vital statistics. Their powers constituted a check on all colonial officers from the viceroy down to parish priests; thus the new men encountered the opposition of entrenched officials everywhere. Although the system called for multiple talents that few men possessed, it generally provided greater efficiency, better government, and increased crown revenues. The intendant system did not cover the frontier provinces of California and New Mexico; they remained under military governors.

Spain's involvement in many foreign wars during the eighteenth century led to important reforms of the army and navy. Military units were reorganized, expanded, and modernized, new ships were built, and the Royal Corps of Engineers was created. More than a dozen of these engineers surveyed and made improvements at army forts and naval bases in New Spain. Their recommendations and those of other officers were responsible for the establishment in 1776 of the commandancy-general of the "Interior Provinces" in the northern part of the viceroyalty. This special military command with a series of "strike forces" was seen as a way to combat Apache, Comanche, and other roving Indians who constantly harassed Spanish settlements, missions, and mining camps.

Shocked by the British capture of Havana and Manila in 1762, Spanish leaders realized that New Spain was vulnerable, and they created a standing army in the colony. Before this date the only permanent troops had been the viceroy's guard and a company or two of infantry in the capital, plus some militia in the seaports and on the northern frontier. At times of foreign danger or Indian uprisings, local forces had been raised and armed for the emergency. The authorized strength of the new colonial army was three thousand regulars and eight thousand militia; by the end of the century the militia had been increased to twenty-three thousand, which was 70 percent of the total force. Heading the militia

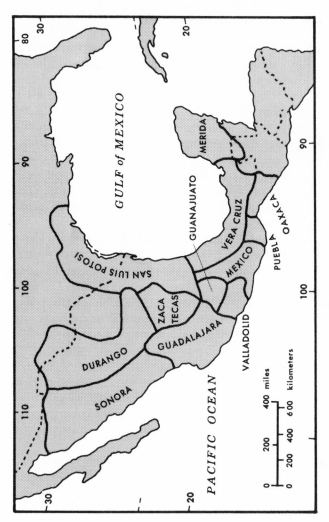

Intendancies in the Late Eighteenth Century

A colonial cavalryman armed with a lance and pistol. Courtesy Archivo General de Indias, Seville.

was a *criollo* officer class that achieved a powerful position through military *fueros,* or privileges of exemption from civilian control. Expansion of the militia provided promotion opportunities for *criollos* and *mestizos.* Until 1807, Indians and blacks were legally exempted from compulsory military service, but racial restrictions were not always enforced, and separate ethnic volunteer militia units with their own officers were acceptable and organized.

Army units participated in an accelerated extension of New Spain's settled frontier, a military strategy endorsed by the Bourbon regime. This policy was designed to forestall or curtail European encroachment on colonial Mexico. To

counter French settlements in Louisiana and Alabama, soldiers and missionaries from New Spain established presidios
and missions in Texas. San Antonio was founded in 1718.
Later, French trappers and traders from the Illinois country
were arrested when they appeared in New Mexico, but that
threat ended in 1763 when the French retreated from North
America, ceding New Orleans and the trans-Mississippi
portion of Louisiana to Spain. (Louisiana was returned to
France in 1800.) Spanish leaders also worried about the
British advance across Canada to the Pacific and, later, about
British naval officers such as Captains James Cook and
George Vancouver, who visited and charted the Northwest
Coast. Spanish-British rivalry in that area culminated in
the Nootka Sound Controversy of the 1790s after which the
Spanish withdrew to California.

Russian explorers and fur traders, who were based in
Alaska beginning in the 1740s, posed another threat to Spain
and led to the occupation of Alta California by forces sent
north from Mexico. Although settlement of Monterey and
San Diego had been contemplated for years, and money (the
Pious Fund) had been collected to help Christianize the California Indians, the plans were not put into effect until 1769.
In the succeeding years four *presidios* were built along the
Alta California coast, and Franciscan missionaries under the
heroic Junípero Serra and his successors directed the work
of establishing twenty-one missions along the *Camino Real*
(Royal Highway). Families recruited from Mexico and retired soldiers soon populated *pueblos* and *ranchos* in this
northernmost outpost of the Spanish empire.

To pay for the increased military presence in New Spain,
as well as for Spain's involvement in European wars, the
Bourbon monarchs maintained the oppressive tax levels of
their predecessors and added new assessments to be collected
in New Spain. Besides a general sales tax of 6 percent and
an average duty of 12 percent on all imported goods, there
were special taxes on the following commodities: wine, *pulque,*
tobacco, vanilla, leather goods, and even the ice brought
down from volcano peaks. The crown continued to collect
half of the first year's salary of all appointees to public office

as well as half of the first year's income attributable to newly elevated Church prelates. One of the larger revenue producers was the Indian tribute or head tax on adult males, which amounted to well over a million pesos annually by 1800. At the end of the colonial era, about half the royal income was used to pay costs of government in New Spain, one-sixth was applied to other colonies, and one-third was remitted to Spain.

In 1764 the government established a monopoly on tobacco and prohibited its cultivation except in the districts of Orizaba, Tezuitlán, and Córdoba, where it was grown under royal supervision. In the subsequent forty-five years the tobacco monopoly yielded more than 120 million pesos revenue, and it became the principal item of royal income from New Spain, as shown in table 4.

TABLE 4.
Royal Income From New Spain, 1803

SOURCE	REVENUE IN PESOS
Tobacco monopoly	4,500,000
Ten percent of precious metals	3,500,000
Sales tax (*alcabala*)	3,200,000
Tithes and temporalities	1,900,000
Mint profit (coinage)	1,500,000
Indian tribute	1,300,000
Tax on *pulque* liquor	800,000
Quicksilver monopoly	536,000
Import and export duties	500,000
Papal bulls and indulgences	270,000
Post Office	250,000
Gunpowder monopoly	150,000
Playing cards monopoly	120,000
Tax on salaries of appointees	100,000
Stamped legal paper	80,000
Tax on cockpits	45,000
Tax on ice	30,000
Total	18,781,000

SOURCE: Joel Poinsett, *Notes on Mexico Made in the Autumn of 1822* (Philadelphia: Carey and Lea, 1824), 107.

TABLE 5.
Colonial Silver and Gold Production

PERIOD	TONS OF SILVER	TONS OF GOLD
Sixteenth century	2,812	24
Seventeenth century	9,538	39
Eighteenth century	32,488	91

SOURCE: *Enciclopedia de México,* 1978 ed., s.v. "Minería."

The 10 percent tax on precious metals helped fill the royal coffers, since mining production increased dramatically during the eighteenth century, stimulated by pressure from Madrid and aided by new technology spawned by the Enlightenment. As shown in Table 5., production of bullion in the eighteenth century was a threefold increase over the previous century and ten times the amount produced in the sixteenth century.

Alexander von Humboldt, the Prussian scientist who visited New Spain in 1803–04, inspected a number of mining sites and collected data on production. He estimated that there were then about three thousand mines in the viceroyalty and that the value of registered gold and silver extracted since 1520 totaled £378,960,680. His figures do not include treasure that was mined but never minted because of evasion, smuggling, or hijacking, an amount he reckoned at one-seventh of total production.

One of the most important mining districts was Guanajuato, where von Humboldt noted that more than five thousand workers were employed in extracting and processing silver ore. In those days, before steam engines or electricity, the mines of that area used 14,600 mules to turn the mills and tread the amalgam. After descending into the famous Valenciana mine, von Humboldt wrote about the antiquated and sordid mining conditions.

A miner brought up in the mines of Freiberg, and accustomed to see many ingenious means of conveyance practised, can hardly conceive that, in the Spanish colonies, where the poverty of the minerals is united with a great abundance of them, all the metal which is taken from the vein should be carried on the backs of men. The Indian *tenateros*, who may be considered as the beasts of burden of the mines of Mexico, remain loaded with a weight of from 225 to 350 pounds for a space of six hours. In the galleries of Valenciana and Rayas, they are exposed ... to a temperature of from 22° to 25° [71°–77° F.]; and during this time they ascend and descend several thousands of steps in pits of an inclination of 45°. These *tenateros* carry the minerals in bags (costales) made of the thread of the pité [agave]. To prevent their shoulders from being hurt, (for the miners are generally naked to the middle) they place a woolen covering (frisada) under this bag. We meet in the mines with files of fifty or sixty of these porters, among whom there are men above sixty, and boys of ten or twelve years of age. In ascending the stairs they throw the body forwards, and rest on a staff which is generally not more than three decimeters [about a foot] in length....

The labor of a miner is entirely free throughout the whole kingdom of New Spain; and no Indian or Mestizoe can be forced to dedicate themselves to the working of mines.... The Mexican miner is the best paid of all miners; he gains at the least from 25 to 30 francs [£1 to £1.4.0] per week of six days....*

Von Humboldt's reconnaissance of Mexico was only one of half a dozen scientific expeditions aided or sponsored by enlightened Spanish officials at the end of the colonial era. From 1787 to 1796, biologists with the Royal Botanical Expedition to New Spain studied and collected flora and fauna from Vancouver Island to Nicaragua, inclusive. The group was headed by a Spanish physician, Martín Sessé y Lacasta, who also established the Royal Botanical Garden in Mexico City. He was joined by an outstanding Mexican physician-naturalist, José Mariano Moziño. When these two naturalists went to Spain they took along a large herbarium, copius field notes, and eighteen hundred expertly prepared botanical plates. During these same years Captain Alejandro Malaspina led a Spanish "round-the-world" scientific expedition.

---

*Alexander von Humboldt, *Political Essay on the Kingdom of New Spain*, trans. John Black, 4 vols. (London: Longman, Hurst, Rees, Orme, & Brown, 1814), 3:238–39, 246–47.

While his ships were anchored in Acapulco and other ports, the expedition's naturalists spent fruitful months ashore collecting natural history specimens.

Another type of scientific expedition was that of Francisco Javier de Balmis, who headed a medical mission to New Spain. For almost three centuries smallpox epidemics had ravaged the colony, being especially virulent among Indians who contracted the disease. Only five years after Edward Jenner published his discovery of the technique of vaccination with cowpox serum, the Spanish government dispatched teams of medical workers to the colonies to carry out a grand smallpox immunization program. Balmis, a Spanish physician who had worked previously in Mexican hospitals, returned there in 1804, and for the next two years he and his associates traveled from Zacatecas to Guatemala City, where they vaccinated tens of thousands of subjects. Perhaps more important, they trained Mexican doctors and *curanderos* (folk healers) in the new method.

Scientists who came to New Spain in the second half of the eighteenth century encountered colonial intellectuals whose ideas and work paralleled those of "men of the Enlightenment" in Europe, Great Britain, and the United States. Perhaps the outstanding Mexican savant of this period was José Antonio Alzate (1739–99), a *criollo* with multiple interests. He collected and studied specimens of natural history, visited archaeological sites and published descriptions of his findings, operated an astronomical observatory, experimented with electricity and lightning rods, and climbed volcanic peaks to make scientific observations. Alzate was a corresponding member of the Royal Academy of Science of Paris, the Royal Botanical Garden of Madrid, and the important Basque scientific organization, Sociedad Vascongada. He also established and edited a literary and scientific journal, *Diario literario* (later called *Gazeta de literatura*), which was published between 1768 and 1795.

In spite of censorship by Church and state, it is clear that aspects of the Enlightenment permeated intellectual circles of New Spain. Enlightened colonials, some of them priests, supported the idea of universal human progress and use of the empirical method in science. They studied the writings of Voltaire, Rousseau, Locke, Jefferson, and others, and agreed with some of the criticism of traditional doctrines and practices. On both sides of the Atlantic attention was focused on remnants of the Middle Ages: a rigid and very unequal class structure, restrictions on economic activities, religious intolerance, absolute monarchy, and the "divine right" of kings.

In addition to talk about natural rights, liberty, and social equality, there were vivid examples of transforming society through revolution. When the thirteen American colonies won their independence from mighty Great Britain, the new nation became a symbol and model for other discontented colonials. Literate Mexicans read and discussed radical phrases of the 1776 Declaration of Independence: "all men are created equal;" people have "certain unalienable rights;" governments derive "their just powers from the consent of the governed;" and "it is the right of the people to alter or to abolish" a government that becomes destructive to these ends. Next came the French Revolution, beginning in 1789, which overturned the old order and remade much of Gallic society. Mexican *criollos* condemned the extreme measures—regicide, conversion of Catholic churches into Temples of Reason, guillotine excesses, and even egalitarianism. Indeed, in many ways the *criollos* were conservative; certainly they did not want equality with the Indians or lower castes of Mexico. If they were shocked by what happened in France, they were horrified by the chaos and the massacre of whites when Haitian blacks fought their war for independence between 1790 and 1804.

Although some *criollos* talked about needed reforms, very few of them advocated independence until extraordinary events in Europe undermined Spanish authority. The rise of Napoleon Bonaparte to power in France, his Continental System to destroy the trade of Great Britain, and the British naval blockade against France and its ally Spain (after 1796) curtailed communications and trade between New Spain and

Europe. Then in 1807 a French army received permission from Madrid to march across Spain in order to take over Portugal; that accomplished, Napoleon pursued a plan to conquer Spain.

Government in Spain had degenerated under the weak and vacillating Charles IV, whose rule began in 1788. He was dominated by Manuel Godoy, the scheming, Francophile prime minister who also was widely reported to be the queen's lover. Godoy had engineered the French military corridor to Portugal, and he was considering further concessions in March, 1808, when there was a popular uprising against him supported by the ambitious crown prince Ferdinand. At that point King Charles resigned in favor of his son, who became Ferdinand VII. But Napoleon's agents intrigued; they persuaded Charles to withdraw his abdication, and that action widened the royal family rift. Offering to mediate the dispute, Napoleon lured Charles and Ferdinand to Bayonne, France, where he detained them, forced both men to renounce all claims to the Spanish throne, and gave them pensions and estates in France, where they were virtual prisoners. Then the French emperor appointed his own brother to head the Spanish empire.

On July 6, 1808, Joseph Bonaparte was proclaimed King of Spain. Although Spanish bureaucrats recognized the new monarch, the people overwhelmingly refused to acknowledge him; indeed, their guerrilla warfare in protest developed into the Peninsular War. Joseph Bonaparte was forced to abandon Madrid, and Spanish juntas sprang up to govern in the name of the exiled Ferdinand VII. Claiming to be the chief resistance government, the Central Junta operated first at Aranjuez near Madrid, then, ahead of French occupation troops it fled to Seville and finally to the fortified city of Cadiz. Late in 1808, Napoleon himself arrived in Spain with almost two hundred thousand soldiers, who put Joseph back on the throne in Madrid. Meanwhile, a British army invaded northwestern Spain to attack the French. Ultimately, the French were pushed back across the Pyrenees, but the chaos and warfare in the Iberian Peninsula had serious repercussions in the colonies.

News of the imprisonment of the Spanish monarch and the French invasion of Spain stunned colonial leaders in Mexico City and stimulated various factions to assert their view of what should be done. Rejecting recognition of Joseph Bonaparte as King of Spain, the *audiencia* judges favored submission to the Central Junta in southern Spain. The *criollo*-dominated *cabildo* declared for a junta in New Spain to rule in the name of the deposed Ferdinand VII; it also wanted popular sovereignty and equality with the provinces of Spain. The opportunistic viceroy, José de Iturrigaray, perhaps hoping that he might emerge as ruler if Mexico became independent, encouraged creation of a Mexican junta with provincial representation by *criollos,* and with himself as head. Naturally, the *audiencia* judges opposed this move, which would diminish their political role and which they viewed as treasonous.

At this point a group of peninsular Spaniards, organized as the "Volunteers of Ferdinand VII," made plans to oust the viceroy. On the night of September 15, 1808, they broke into the palace, took Iturrigaray prisoner and sent him to Veracruz to await passage to Spain, where he was later imprisoned. The peninsulars also arrested several prominent *criollo* leaders. General Pedro Garibay, senior military officer in Mexico, replaced the viceroy, but this octogenarian was senile and unable to reconcile various factions. In March, 1809, royalists forced Garibay to proclaim New Spain's adherence to the Spanish Central Junta. Four months later that body appointed the archbishop of Mexico to act as ad interim viceroy; he served about a year, until the arrival from Spain of a new executive, Francisco Javier Venegas. Thus, in this critical period of two years New Spain had four viceroys, all of whom had difficulty in stemming the tide of dissolution.

In scores of provincial towns small groups of *criollos* had been meeting to discuss the extraordinary political events. Some of these gatherings were Enlightenment-spawned clubs called *Amigos del País* (Friends of the Fatherland); others were literary societies where novels, plays, and political tracts were reviewed. At these meetings *criollos* vented their grievances, a principal one being their second-class status, imposed by *gachupines*. Mexican *criollos* did not consider themselves congenitally inferior to peninsulars, yet they did recognize that they were a distinct people with their own dialect (including many Indian words), their own non-Iberian cuisine (maize and chile peppers), and their own dependence on servile labor (Indians and blacks). And when *criollos* speculated about the future of Mexico, many hoped that they would supplant the Spanish-born rulers. A few groups actually made plans to sever the colony from Spain.

One independence plot was formed in 1809 in the town of Valladolid (later renamed Morelia), where the conspirators included government officials, clergymen, and an army lieutenant named José Mariano Michelena. Local Indian leaders pledged their support in return for a promise to end the native tribute system. In late December, just before the revolution was to be launched, the plan was betrayed and the ringleaders seized. Archbishop-viceroy Lizana was lenient with the conspirators—he simply kept them under light arrest. It is interesting to note that the principal strategist of the Valladolid plot was a Franciscan priest, Fray Vincente Santa María, who a year later escaped confinement and joined a subsequent insurrection that was also headed by a *criollo* priest.

Why were *criollo* clergymen in the vanguard of Mexico's independence movement? As highly literate members of the colonial society they were aware of Enlightenment ideas that challenged autocratic, unreasonable, and incompetent government. Clerics had a long list of grievances against the Madrid government, including a royal decree that banned creation of additional monasteries in New Spain, the king's expulsion of the Jesuits, and the Act of Consolidation, decreed in 1804, which sequestered the charitable funds of the Church and ordered the money sent to the royal coffers in Spain. This act required the Church to call in mortgages, which resulted in the alienation of many landowners from the mother country, and the act vastly curtailed the Church's social services.

Criollo priests and friars resented arrogant Spanish peninsulars who kept them from rising in the Church hierarchy— in 1808 all bishoprics except one, the majority of canon stalls, and the greater portion of rich curacies were held by peninsulars. There was a financial aspect too—Alexander von Humboldt reported that the annual income for a priest in an Indian village came to about 100 pesos, but yearly revenue from the diocese of an archbishop might amount to 130,000 pesos. Accumulated grievances of *criollos*—priests and laymen—smouldered until the crisis in Spain provided an opportunity to spark the flame of revolt.

The firebrand of Mexico's independence was Miguel Hidalgo y Costilla, an aging parish priest in the village of Dolores, Guanajuato. Born in 1753 to *criollo* parents of moderate wealth, Hidalgo spent his first twelve years on the hacienda where his father was administrator. Then for eight years he studied at two *colegios* in Valladolid, and in 1773 he went to the viceregal capital to be examined and receive his Bachelor of Theology degree at the University of Mexico. Returning to Valladolid, he lectured in philosophy and theology at the *colegio* of San Nicolás Obispo, and after ordination to the priesthood he became rector of the school. His extremely liberal ideas and conduct led to dismissal from that post, after which he was appointed successively to three pastorates. His last parish was Dolores, where he served between 1802 and 1810.

Twice the Inquisition investigated allegations concerning the orthodoxy and morality of Father Hidalgo. He was accused of reading prohibited books, advocating doctrines of the French Revolution, doubting the virgin birth of Mary, gambling, and keeping a mistress. Indeed, his household in Dolores included "two half-sisters, his younger brother, Mariano, and two daughters by Josefa Quintana." Other evidence showed that he had mastered the Otomí Indian language used by many of his parishioners, that he was beloved by them, and that he had worked hard to improve their economic welfare. He taught crafts and skills in night classes and established a pottery, tannery, saddlery, and shops for carpentry, blacksmithing, and weaving. Because he had introduced two illegal industries—winemaking and silk culture—government officials came to the village and destroyed the vines and mulberry trees.

In the city of Querétaro, about eighty kilometers (fifty miles) to the southeast of Dolores, there was a "literary club" that Hidalgo frequented. Members included the former *corregidor*, Miguel Domínguez; his wife Doña Josefa Ortiz de Domínguez ("La Corregidora"); two royal army officers, Ignacio Allende and Juan Aldama; and a few other *criollos*. Early in 1810, members of this group secretly plotted to separate Mexico from Spain. They planned to gather an army, seize the important towns, expel the peninsular Spaniards, and confiscate their property. Initially the revolutionary government was to operate in the name of Ferdinand VII, but at the opportune time it would declare independence. Father Hidalgo was selected to head the movement. Allende, a cavalry captain in the Queen's Regiment based at nearby San Miguel, would be the military commander for the revolt, which was set to coincide with a large regional fair in December, 1810.

News of the plot reached the ears of royal officials, who proceeded to investigate. On September 13 they arrested one conspirator in whose home they found a substantial cache of arms; two days later Domínguez and his wife were jailed, but not before "La Corregidora" sent a messenger to warn the others. At San Miguel, about twenty miles away, Aldama got the word in the late afternoon and immediately set out for Dolores to alert Father Hidalgo. Arriving about midnight, he found Allende already there, and the three compromised leaders decided that their only hope was to launch the revolution at once.

The revolt began at Dolores early in the morning of September 16 when bells summoned the townspeople to the parish church. Hidalgo harangued the congregation, telling them that the time had come to expel the Spaniards who had misgoverned them so long and who were plotting to recognize Joseph Bonaparte and the French regime in Spain. Two witnesses later said he also declared an end to the Indian tribute system. Hidalgo's exact words have not been preserved, but the sentiment of his *Grito de Dolores* was "Long live the Catholic religion! Long live America! Death to bad government!" Many of his followers later took up the chant, "Death to the *gachupines!*"

By mid-morning the rebel army set forth, armed with machetes, swords, knives, slings, clubs, axes, and a few muskets. Additional recruits were added when the local jail was opened and the former inmates given weapons. This practice was continued as each town was entered. From a church in a nearby village Hidalgo took a banner of the Virgin of Guadalupe that became the military standard of the crusade—this image of the dark-skinned Virgin was a powerful symbol to attract and hold Indian and *mestizo* supporters. At San Miguel the militiamen of Allende's regiment joined the seven hundred rebels, and by the time they reached Celaya their numbers had increased to twenty thousand. Hidalgo, now named "Captain-General of America," had difficulty controlling the unruly mob; the insurrection had become a race war as Indians and *mestizos* took peninsular Spaniards as prisoners and pillaged their homes and crops.

Guanajuato, capital city of the intendancy and an important mining center, was the next insurgent goal. Hidalgo wrote to the indendant requesting him to surrender, but that officer refused. Instead, he withdrew into the fortress-like granary (Alhóndiga de Granaditas) on the edge of the city, taking with him the local militia battalion of three hundred soldiers, almost all of the resident peninsulars, a few elite *criollos,* and the archives and treasury. The total value of gold, silver, and jewels was said to be over three million pesos.

On September 28 the rebels, augmented by mine workers from adjacent mining communities, reached Guanajuato, where they opened the jail and urged some three hundred freed prisoners to join them. Hundreds of common towns-

Hidalgo Initiates the War for Independence. *Mural by Juan O'Gorman. Courtesy Organization of American States.*

people, who felt they had been abandoned by their officials, joined the insurgents as they began an assault on the granary, whereupon many were shot down by royalist soldiers. Finally, a young miner nicknamed "El Pípila" (The Turkey), protecting his head and shoulders with a slab of stone, crept to the massive wooden doorway and set it afire. When the flames died, the attackers stormed into the central patio, where they killed those who resisted, imprisoned those who were still alive, and seized the treasure and supplies. During the next few days the town plebeians and insurgents sacked shops and houses of *gachupines*, disobeying Hidalgo's decree banning such action. At least three hundred peninsulars lost their lives in the battle for the granary and its aftermath. Casualties for the insurgents, who kept few records, were considerably higher.

Hidalgo and Allende were appalled by the pillage and excesses—they had anticipated a military rebellion with the taking of prisoners and confiscation of royalist funds, but they were witnessing a violent social upheaval. The lower classes were taking revenge on generations of oppressive conquistadors, *encomenderos, corregidores, hacendados,* mineowners, and land grabbers. Many peasants and miners also were frustrated by recent droughts and unemployment. In spite of their qualms, the *criollo* rebel leaders were heartened by early successes of the movement. The northern cities of San Luis Potosí, Zacatecas, and Saltillo acclaimed the revolution, and agents were working in the south and west to win over the masses.

In Mexico City the viceroy placed a price on the rebel leaders' heads, recruited troops, initiated a propaganda campaign, abolished the tribute in an effort to hold Indian loyalty, and asked Church leaders to condemn the uprising. Even before he heard of these royalist measures the bishop-elect of Michoacán, Manuel Abad y Queipo, a peninsular who had known Hidalgo for many years and was his religious superior, issued an edict excommunicating him along with the three chief military officers of the revolt. In a pastoral letter he condemned all revolution, called on the rebels to lay down their arms and return home, and forbade anyone to aid the insurgents, under pain of excommunication. Three weeks later as the revolutionary army approached Valladolid, the capital of Michoacán, the bishop and almost all the peninsular Spaniards fled. After Hidalgo arrived in that city, where he had spent twenty-seven academic years, he published a decree calling for the immediate abolition of slavery—with death for owners who did not comply—and he reiterated his earlier announcement that ended Indian tributes. He also appropriated 400,000 pesos from cathedral funds. News of these events and of the bloodshed in Guanajuato caused many *criollo* property owners to support the peninsulars and the royalist government.

From Valladolid the rebel force of sixty thousand, still led by Hidalgo, who now styled himself "Generalissimo" and refused to relinquish top command, moved on toward Mexico City. On October 30 at Monte de las Cruces, in the mountains overlooking the Valley of Mexico, the rebels fought a bloody battle with the royalists, forcing the retreat of the much smaller but well-disciplined army that was supposed to block the pass. Although the way was now open to the capital and a quick blow might have ended the war for independence, the insurgents did not move into the Valley; instead, they headed back the way they had come. Various reasons for this decision have been suggested by historians: high rebel casualties (two thousand killed, thousands wounded and deserted), disagreement among rebel leaders, shortage of ammunition and supplies, unwillingness to let a mob sack Mexico City, intimations that the metropolitan masses would not rise up in support, and reports of the imminent approach of a large royalist army. In the capital the *gachupines* attributed the rebel retreat to the intervention of their patroness, the Virgin of los Remedios.

Moving northwestward, the rebel army was surprised and routed by a royalist force near Querétaro, after which the remnants slowly headed toward Guadalajara. At this time Hidalgo changed his policy about *gachupín* prisoners and approved the execution of sixty in Valladolid, soon to be followed by more. Late in November, Hidalgo was well received in Guadalajara, where he established his headquarters and attempted to organize a government. Using the title *Alteza Serenísima* (Most Serene Highness), he published decrees abolishing government monopolies on gunpowder and tobacco; ordered lands returned to the native villages; appointed judges to court benches and commanders to military posts; coined revolutionary money; confiscated a press and chose an editor for the rebel newspaper, *El Despertador Americano* (The American Alarm); and sent a diplomatic representative to the United States (who was intercepted and jailed by the royalists). One of Hidalgo's lieutenants, Mariano Jiménez, was attempting to consolidate the rebel position in northern Mexico, and another subordinate, José María Morelos, was doing the same in the south.

Meanwhile, a royalist army of six thousand men—mostly peninsulars and *criollos*—under General Félix María Calleja marched in pursuit of the insurgents, while another Spanish army occupied Valladolid. In the *bajío* region where the revolt had originated, the royalists slaughtered many villagers suspected of aiding the rebels, and after Calleja recaptured Guanajuato and found that 138 *gachupín* prisoners had just been massacred, he ordered the execution of 69 residents, most of whom were selected by lot. On learning that Calleja's army was approaching Guadalajara, Hidalgo overrode the advice of his military staff and ordered his entire force to a position near the bridge of Calderón east of the city. When the opposing armies met in mid-January, 1811, the royalists were outnumbered twelve to one, but they had advantages in arms, training, and leadership. During the battle a Spanish artillery shell landed in a rebel ammunition wagon, exploded, and caused a grass fire in the midst of the rebel army. Panic ensued, and the insurgents' retreat turned into a rout.

With his closest advisers and twelve hundred followers Hidalgo fled north, hoping to secure aid in Coahuila, Texas, or the United States. Exactly six months after the *Grito de Dolores* the rebel remnant fell into a royalist trap in the northern desert; all were apprehended and the insurgent chiefs were taken in chains to Chihuahua City. After a military trial the non-clerical leaders were executed by a firing squad, but because he was a priest, Hidalgo was subjected to a lengthy hearing conducted by members of the Inquisition. Found guilty of heresy and treason, he was defrocked and turned over to the civil authorities, who ordered his execution on July 30, 1811. As a grim reminder, his head and those of Allende, Aldama and Jiménez were hung in cages at the four corners of the granary in Guanajuato, where they remained for a decade.

Although Hidalgo failed as a military leader, he succeeded in arousing a spirit of rebellion against control by Spain. His social program of abolishing black slavery and native tribute payments and championing Indian rights to their land was laudable, as was his personal courage. Mexicans justly revere Miguel Hidalgo as the father of their nation and symbol of their independence.

After Hidalgo's death the revolutionary movement continued under José María Morelos, a *mestizo* parish priest and a former student of Hidalgo. Before his ordination Morelos had been a muleteer on the route between Acapulco and Mexico City; later he served for a dozen years as curate in an isolated part of the *tierra caliente* (hot country) southwest of the capital. In October, 1810, Morelos conferred with Hidalgo, who gave him a military commission and ordered him to raise an army in the south. By that time most *criollos* would not support the revolution—they were opposed to its radical nature, especially the assault on private property. Thus Morelos relied on *mestizos* and Indians whom he trained in guerrilla warfare tactics.

Morelos never assembled a large army, but he managed to hold together a loose union of guerrilla bands and local chieftains. Besides hit-and-run raids, his strategy was to cut off the capital from both coasts. Late in 1811 his men controlled the city of Oaxaca; in 1812 they captured Orizaba on the Veracruz road; and in August, 1813, they took the seaport of Acapulco. The capital was almost isolated, and he turned to political affairs.

José María Morelos: priest, soldier, statesman. Courtesy Organization of American States.

In September, 1813, Morelos convoked a congress to serve as a government of the insurgent movement. Representing various dissident factions, the delegates first met in Chilpancingo, a village on the road to Acapulco, but military actions forced the congress to move frequently. On November 6, 1813, the congress issued Mexico's first formal declaration of independence, and a year later at Apatzingán it published a constitution. That lengthy document of 242 articles—which declared Mexico a republic, abolished slavery, and eliminated all class distinctions—was never put into effect, but it gave an aspect of legality to the rebel cause and served as a model for reformers much later.

Meanwhile, under the leadership of General Calleja, now elevated to viceroy, the royalists mounted an offensive against the insurgent bands. In December, 1813, they defeated Morelos' forces at Valladolid; then they took Oaxaca, Chilpancingo, and other rebel strongholds. Late in 1815, when government troops surprised Morelos, who was accompanying the congress on its way to Tehuacán, he created a diversion that allowed the congress to escape but resulted in his own capture. Taken to Mexico City, he was tried by the Inquisition, defrocked, and turned over to the state, which also convicted him and ordered him executed. Morelos was shot by a firing squad on December 22, 1815, at San Cristóbal Ecatepec, outside the capital.

By the beginning of 1816 the independence movement in New Spain reached its nadir, and for the next four years it was dormant. There was no overall leader, the congress disbanded, and a number of rebels made peace with the government. Only two guerrilla chiefs eluded the royalists, Guadalupe Victoria (who had changed his name from Félix Fernández) hid out in the back country of Veracruz, and Vicente Guerrero, who carried out sporadic raids from his base in the mountains near Acapulco. A liberating expedition by a foreign legion under Francisco Javier Mina was also repulsed by the royalists. Mina, a former Spanish military officer, purchased three vessels in the United States and enlisted about three hundred recruits there. Landing on the coast of Tamaulipas in April, 1817, the "Relief Army of the Republic of Mexico" proceeded south as far as Guanajuato. After several victories, they were finally defeated in October, 1817, and Mina and other leaders were executed. Royal authority was reasserted throughout most of the viceroyalty until 1820, when events in Spain caused a resurgence of the independence movement in Mexico.

While the Spanish monarch was in exile during the Napoleonic era, the Central Junta in Cadiz authorized the convocation of a *Cortes* with elected representatives from the homeland and overseas provinces. A number of deputies from New Spain attended the sessions and participated in writing Spain's first constitution, a liberal document promulgated in 1812. Two years later, upon his restoration, Ferdinand VII abrogated the constitution, abolished the *Cortes* and all its acts, imprisoned or exiled thousands of liberals, including many of the *Cortes* delegates, and organized forces to put down revolutionary movements in Spanish America. Opposition to his reactionary regime culminated in 1820 with a military revolt led by Colonel Rafael Riego, who marched on Madrid and forced the king to implement the Constitution of 1812. That document provided for a constitutional monarchy, sovereignty of the people, and freedom of the press, and its anti-clerical provisions led to attacks on the privileges and property of the Catholic Church. Mexican conservatives and clerical leaders, alarmed by radicalism in Spain, saw that one way to save their position was by establishing an independent Mexico. Ironically, these people who had opposed independence for so long now favored it.

During the early months of 1820, a small conservative group in New Spain, headed by Doctor Matías Monteagudo, rector of the University of Mexico and canon of the cathedral, met secretly and considered various schemes to achieve separation from liberal Spain. Some of them favored a bloodless coup d'etat similar to the one that had unseated the viceroy in 1808; others thought that they might have to cooperate with Mexican liberals. In any case they needed military support and the close cooperation of a high-ranking officer. The man who emerged for this role was a *criollo* colonel named Iturbide who shared their conservative outlook and misgivings about the liberal trend in Spain.

Born in Valladolid in 1783, Agustín de Iturbide was the son of a wealthy Basque landowner and a Mexican mother. At the age of seventeen he joined a royal infantry regiment with the rank of a second lieutenant. Ten years later, when Hidalgo began his revolt, Iturbide was offered a high rank in the rebel army, but he refused. His military actions against Hidalgo, Morelos, and Ignacio Rayón won him rapid promotion to colonel, but in 1816, having been accused, and then acquitted of mishandling of funds, he resigned from the army and took up residence in Mexico City. In the fall of 1820, Iturbide's conservative friends persuaded the viceroy to reinstate him in the army and commission him to undertake a campaign against the only active rebel leader, Vicente Guerrero. Iturbide was promoted to brigadier general, given command of twenty-five hundred men, and, in mid-November, his army left the capital headed for the rugged mountains in the south.

After weeks of maneuvering and a few skirmishes, Iturbide persuaded Guerrero to meet with him at the village of Iguala on the Acapulco road. In preliminary negotiations the royalist commander pointed out certain common goals, and then he made an astonishing proposal—that they join forces and fight for the independence of Mexico. On February 24, 1821, the two commanders proclaimed the *Plan de Iguala,* a program that outlined the principles to be embraced.

Designed to win the support of all classes and races, the Plan of Iguala contained twenty-four articles, but it is best remembered for its "three guarantees"—independence, religion, and equality. First, Mexico would be declared independent as a constitutional monarchy; the crown would be offered to Ferdinand VII or, if he declined, to another European prince. Second, Roman Catholicism would be the state religion and the only one tolerated, and clergymen would retain all their rights and privileges. The third guarantee was for racial equality; it specified that "All the inhabitants of New Spain, without any distinction between Europeans, Africans, and Indians, are citizens of this monarchy with the right to hold any office, according to their merit and virtues." Another provision called for a junta or council to rule until a monarch could be selected and elections held for a constituent assembly. Meanwhile, an "Army of the Three Guarantees," called the *Trigarantes,* would uphold the principles agreed upon.

Iturbide then took steps to consummate the independence of Mexico under the Plan of Iguala. He sent messengers to the principal army officers and Church dignitaries to secure their collaboration; he acquired a printing press and newspaper to publicize the program; and he increased his war chest by half a million pesos when he intercepted a merchant silver train enroute to Acapulco.

Viceroy Apodaca rejected the Plan of Iguala and called Iturbide a traitor, but the majority of military units and cities soon declared their support. It was an appealing program to Mexicans, who were weary of a decade of war and whose nationalism had been aroused during that period. The Plan did not call for "death to the *gachupines*" or even their banishment; instead it guaranteed that all Church and state officials who supported the Plan would keep their positions, and those who opposed it would simply be replaced. The Plan also promised there would be no interference with property rights. Faced with overwhelming opposition and aware that his replacement had already been named, the viceroy resigned. At that moment the Spanish red and gold royal colors were flying in the capital and in only two other major cities, Veracruz and Acapulco. Elsewhere the country was under the triumphant red, white, and green flag of the *Trigarantes*—one color for each guarantee.

When the last appointed viceroy, General Juan O'Donojú, a Spanish liberal of Irish descent, arrived in Veracruz at the end of July, 1821, he found that the colony was virtually independent and he never assumed office. Hoping to salvage whatever he could from the inevitable collapse of the royal establishment, he arranged a conference with Iturbide at the village of Córdoba on the Veracruz–Mexico City highway. The outcome was the Treaty of Córdoba, signed by the two leaders on August 24. This document recognized the independence of the Mexican empire; it accepted most of the terms of the Plan of Iguala; it said that if no European prince could be persuaded to become emperor of Mexico, anyone else could be designated; and it gave O'Donojú a place in the provisional governing junta of Mexico. In his capacity as the ranking Spanish military officer, O'Donojú arranged for royalist troops to leave the capital and go to the island fortress of San Juan de Ulúa, preparatory to their return to Spain.

Riding at the head of the *Trigarantes*, Iturbide came into Mexico City as a conquering hero on September 27, 1821. The *cabildo* gave him golden keys to the city, O'Donojú received him at the palace, and the archbishop offered a *Te Deum* in his honor at the cathedral. On the following day a governing junta was established, and Iturbide as its spokesman issued a decree proclaiming to the world that the colony of New Spain had ceased to exist. Mexico was now an independent nation.

CHAPTER 7

First Empire and Early Republic

AMID the joy and enthusiasm over Mexico's independence in the autumn of 1821 there were serious concerns about the future. Would the new nation be able to get diplomatic recognition from the major powers? Would it be able to survive economically? What kind of government would be created? At its birth, independent Mexico had no executive, no constitution, and no legislature. But it had a *caudillo,* the military hero, General Agustín Iturbide, who would play an important role in fashioning a new government.

In accordance with the Treaty of Córdoba signed by Iturbide and Spain's last viceroy-designate, General Juan O'Donojú, the provisional governing junta began its work immediately. Its twenty-eight conservative delegates were all appointed by Iturbide, who was also a member and chief spokesman. The junta functioned as an interim congress, and it named the five members of a regency, presided over by Iturbide, that was to act as interim executive. None of the noted guerrilla leaders such as Guerrero or Victoria served on these boards; O'Donojú was a member of both, but he died unexpectedly within a few days of his appointment.

The junta arranged for the election of an official Congress to write a constitution for Mexico. Deputies for this assemblage were elected indirectly — the town councils chose electors who selected delegates for provinces, but each province had to have one secular clergyman, one military representative, and one judge or lawyer in its contingent. A certain number of seats were set aside for the nobility, mining, commerce, and industry sectors. Thus, the Congress was in the hands of conservatives, professionals, the wealthy, and the aristocracy — no seats were available to the lower classes.

While Congress deliberated, news of Mexico's independence reached Spain, where it stunned imperial policy makers. In mid-February of 1822 the *Cortes* declared that O'Donojú's acquiescence had been treasonous and the peace treaty he had signed was null and void. The Spanish government not only refused to recognize the independence of Mexico (for eighteen years), it even threatened to use military force to bring the area back into the empire. And when Ferdinand VII and his brothers scorned the idea of accepting a Mexican crown, that put it within the reach of Iturbide, who sought it.

Iturbide was the man of the hour in Mexico. He was a military hero, a popular idol, and he was considered to be a political genius for having designed the plan that united opposing forces at Iguala. The regency gave him a twelve-league *rancho* in Texas and the title of generalissimo, with an annual salary of 120,000 pesos. Church dignitaries called him *"elegido de Dios"* (God-chosen). But he did not have control of the Congress, which was split into factions that spent much time in recriminations and sterile debates. A few liberals favored a republic, a number of conservatives wanted a monarchy headed by a European prince, while Iturbide's partisans maneuvered to have their man crowned. As the weeks wore on, the majority of delegates became increasingly hostile toward the generalissimo, and he realized that it was time for action.

The coup occurred on the evening of May 18, 1822, when there was a "spontaneous demonstration" by soldiers who filled the streets in the center of the capital shouting "Long Live Agustín I, Emperor of Mexico!" Their rockets and artillery salvos brought thousands of civilians to the area, and part of the mob congregated outside of Iturbide's stately house, where they demanded that he declare himself emperor immediately. Feigning reluctance, the generalissimo said that he would need the consent of Congress.

The following morning he appeared before that body, where a claque filled the aisles while his cohorts declared that the manifestation of May 18 had been "a true plebiscite."

Augustín de Iturbide, Mexico's first emperor. Courtesy The Bancroft Library.

Overlooking the lack of a legal quorum, the assembly, by a vote of 66 to 15, named Agustín Iturbide constitutional emperor of Mexico. Two months later in an impressive ceremony in the cathedral the military hero and his wife, Ana María, were solemnly crowned emperor and empress of Mexico.

One of the first preoccupations of the Mexican empire was to create a royal court patterned after those of Europe. A French baroness who had been at Napoleon's court designed uniforms for chancellors, stewards, grooms, pages, lords of the bedchamber, ladies-in-waiting, and a variety of personnel who were to wait on the sovereigns, their nine children, and other princes of the imperial household. Busts of Agustín I appeared in public buildings, and his profile was stamped on coins. The emperor instituted knighthood when he created the Order of Guadalupe. Those who were inducted received jeweled collars, they promised to make special devotions to the Virgin, and they swore to defend the Plan of Iguala, the grand master of the Order, and the monarch.

To many people the future of the Mexican empire looked brilliant. Had not Baron von Humboldt reported on the enormous mineral riches of the country and its unrealized agricultural potential? And perhaps there were undiscovered valuable resources in the vast territory that stretched from northern California to Panama. Agustín invited the Central American provinces, which had secured their independence from Spain without bloodshed, to join his empire. Except for Panama, they were annexed to Mexico, helped along by an army sent to reinforce the invitation. Diplomatic recognition by the United States was another achievement—although President Monroe and his advisors in Washington certainly would have preferred a republic to a monarchy.

As it turned out, the Mexican empire was a house of cards that collapsed within ten months. Beyond the façade were colossal problems that would have been difficult for any nation to solve. After eleven years of civil war, the country's economy was shattered. The important mining industry was in disarray if not ruin: many owners and managers had been killed, others had fled to the capital or returned to Spain, innumerable workers who had left to fight in the wars never returned, mining machinery was damaged, mines flooded, and production had declined drastically. Agriculture and ranching were similarly impacted by the independence struggle. *Hacendados* had been murdered, their manor houses damaged, stored crops requisitioned, fields burned, livestock killed or dispersed, and the labor supply disrupted. In an attempt to forestall further attacks on their property, the elite resorted to a garrison state.

Commerce was at a standstill, now that trade with Spain had ended and new suppliers and supply lines had not been established. The port of Veracruz was blocked by the Spanish military occupation of the island fortress of San Juan de Ulúa, an occupation that was prolonged when Spain refused to recognize Mexico's independence. Most of the peninsular Spanish merchants returned home with their capital, but some were arrested in Mexico because they refused to submit to forced loans imposed by the imperial government. That violation of the Treaty of Córdoba apparently did not worry Agustín or his advisors.

Undoubtedly the most serious problem for the empire was the lack of revenue to cover expenses and the inability to secure a large loan. In 1822 Mexico's treasury receipts amounted to eight million pesos and the expenses exceeded thirteen million. The following year's income was expected to be slightly more, but the budget increased one and a half times as shown in Table 6.

One immediately notes that military expenses were almost half the imperial budget. To stay in power, the government had to pay the army, so it resorted to forced loans, confiscations, and depreciation of the currency by an unchecked issuance of paper money. The government even seized a convoy carrying more than a million pesos of private money destined for Spain.

Joel Poinsett, who later became the first United States minister to Mexico, was not impressed by the emperor or his

TABLE 6.

Mexican Budget for 1823

Imperial Household	1,500,000
Ministry of State	333,820
Ministry of Justice	709,240
Ministry of Treasury	3,473,202
Ministry of War & Navy	9,759,530
Unforeseen Contingencies	442,198
Interest on National Debt	1,000,000
Deficit of 1822 & Forced Loan	2,800,000
Administration & Publications	310,750
Total	20,328,740 pesos

SOURCE: *Guía de la hacienda de la República de México, año de 1826, parte legislativa,* 2 vols. (Mexico, 1826), 1:163–64.

chances for success. In his published *Notes on Mexico* he recalled his first visit to the royal palace on November 3, 1822:

I was presented to His Majesty this morning.... The emperor was in his cabinet and received us with great politeness. Two of his favorites were with him. We were all seated, and he conversed with us for half an hour in an easy unembarrassed manner, taking occasion to compliment the United States, and our institutions, and to lament that they were not suited to the circumstances of his country. He modestly insinuated that he had yielded very reluctantly to the wishes of the people, but had been compelled to suffer them to place the crown upon his head to prevent misrule and anarchy....

I will not repeat the tales I hear daily of the character and conduct of this man. Prior to the late successful revolution, he commanded a small force in the service of the Royalists, and is accused of having been the most cruel and blood-thirsty persecutor of the Patriots, and never to have spared a prisoner. His official letters to the viceroy substantiate this fact.... His usurpation of the chief authority has been the most glaring and unjustifiable; and his exercise of power arbitrary and tyrannical. With a pleasing address and prepossessing exterior, and by a lavish profusion, he has attached the officers and soldiers to his person, and so long as he possesses the means of paying and rewarding them, so long he will maintain himself on the throne; when these fail he will be precipitated from it....

To judge Iturbide from his public papers, I do not think him a man of talents. He is prompt, bold and decisive, and not scrupulous about the means he employs to obtain his ends.*

Agustín's unscrupulous and arbitrary acts hastened his fall from "the cactus throne." Criticism of the emperor by jouralists led to the suppression of several liberal newspapers, and an alleged conspiracy by congressmen resulted in the arrest of nineteen deputies. When other congressmen protested, Agustín dissolved the Congress at the end of October, 1822. Thus he became a dictator—the first of many Mexican military *caudillos* who would suppress constitutions, dismiss congresses, and rule by fiat.

Had the army remained loyal, the emperor could have continued his reign, but several dissatisfied commanders conspired to overthrow him. Many of the officers belonged to Freemasonry lodges where they associated with civilian liberals who championed representative government. Some of the military leaders became outspoken republicans and opposed the autocratic monarch; others were disgusted with rising inflation and delays in receiving their pay or promotions. The revolt took definite form in December, 1822, when Antonio López de Santa Anna, the military commander of Veracruz, proclaimed a republic. This young *criollo* officer had fought with the Spanish infantry against the insurgents during the wars for independence until 1821, when he joined Iturbide's army in support of the Three Guarantees. Less than two years later he was instrumental in overturning the Mexican empire.

Santa Anna's revolt against Iturbide was supported by the heroic insurgent leaders Guerrero, Victoria, and Bravo, who endorsed the Plan of Casa Mata. This plan, which called for a new congress and national representation, was first signed by Santa Anna and General Echávarri, the imperial officer ordered to suppress the uprising. (Echávarri's agreement with his "enemy" resembled Iturbide's pact with Guerrero

*Joel Poinsett, *Notes on Mexico Made in the Autumn of 1822* (Philadelphia: Carey and Lea, 1824), 67–69.

two years earlier.) In the capital, Iturbide resurrected the old Congress, but it was hostile. Finding himself abandoned and his situation hopeless, he abdicated on March 19, 1823.

The Congress granted Iturbide an annual pension of twenty-five thousand pesos, and in May the ex-emperor embarked with his family for exile in Europe. A year later he returned, claiming that he wanted to defend his country against a supposed Spanish plan to reconquer Mexico. Apparently unaware of a congressional decree that called for his death if he ever set foot in Mexico, Iturbide landed near Tampico, where he was apprehended and shot by a firing squad on July 19, 1824. It was an ignominious end for this audacious son of Mexico.

Upon the fall of the First Empire, a provisional government negotiated a loan of sixteen million pesos from Great Britain and encouraged a constituent congress to draft a new framework of government for the nation. In October, 1824, the Constitution of the United Mexican States was promulgated. Patterned after that of the United States, it made Mexico into a federal republic with a president, vice-president, two branches of legislature (Senate and Chamber of Deputies), and a judiciary. The country was divided into nineteen states, each with its own government, and five territories administered by the central government. Religious liberty was not guaranteed—indeed, the framers were true to Spanish tradition and the Plan of Iguala by permitting only the Roman Catholic religion to be practiced.

Historians call the subsequent era "The Early Republic." It was a period marked by political instability, financial chaos, and humiliation in dealing with foreign powers. Part of the trouble stemmed from lack of experience in self-government, the imposition of democratic institutions on a people inured to despotic leadership, and a national illiteracy rate of over 90 percent. Another factor was the preponderant role taken by military officers whose ambition exceeded their ability as statesmen and whose *fueros* exempted them from civilian control. And the expulsion of all Spaniards (except some clergy), decreed in 1829, resulted in an exodus of many educated and talented persons.

After independence, the members of the educated elite in Mexico soon were divided into liberal and conservative camps. For the next half-century, control of the government changed back and forth between representatives of these factions. Upon taking power, the new group not only changed key government personnel, it also rewrote laws and even the constitution to reflect its philosophy. Often the "outs" fled or were forced into temporary exile until their party regained office. The cleavage between "right and left" widened over the years. It split Mexican families, divided the clergy, and resulted in revolutions and civil war.

Most liberals supported federalism (which in Latin America means states' rights, not centralized control), freedom of the press, an egalitarian society, curtailment of privileges and titles, toleration of all religious sects, and public education rather than Church-controlled schools. Those liberals who favored moderate social reforms called themselves *moderados;* others who wanted a radical restructuring of society were known as *puros.* Liberals came from a variety of backgrounds, but many were middle-class intellectuals, journalists, teachers, lawyers, or small entrepreneurs. Three leading liberals were Valentín Gómez Farías, a physician and politician originally from Jalisco; Lorenzo de Zavala, a publisher and congressman from Yucatán; and José Luis Mora, an economist, doctor of theology, and lawyer from Guanajuato.

Opposing the liberals were the conservatives. They favored a centralized state, even a dictatorship; a certain amount of censorship; a class system with rule by an elite; preservation of privileges, *fueros,* and titles of nobility; monopoly of religion by Roman Catholicism; and Church control of education. Conservative membership came from the Church hierarchy, army officers, the landed elite, mineowners, and the great merchants. Peasants and Indians also generally supported conservative positions. Three prominent conservatives were Lucas Alamán, a mining engineer, statesman, and histo-

Lucas Alamán, conservative leader and historian. Courtesy The Bancroft Library.

rian from Guanajuato; Nicolás Bravo, a general from Guerrero who had fought with Morelos in the independence war; and Carlos María Bustamante, a lawyer and publisher from Oaxaca.

The basic idealogical cleavage was also manifested in branches of Freemasonry to which many leaders, including Catholic priests, belonged. Conservatives were generally Scottish Rite Masons (*escoceses*); liberals tended to belong to the York Rite (*yorkinos*). As a secret society organized into lodges, Masonry provided meeting places and support for politicians and plotters during the earliest years of the Mexican republic.

In Mexico's first presidential election, in the fall of 1824, the state legislatures, acting as an electoral college, chose two men from opposing factions to become president and vice-president. Guadalupe Victoria, a *yorkino* and federalist, assumed the highest office; his vice-president was Nicolás Bravo, grand master of the *escoceses* and a centralist. Victoria was a national hero because of his valor and suffering during the independence wars, but he lacked the talent to run a nation. He was indecisive, showed poor judgment in picking cabinet and other officials, and was unable to address major domestic problems confronting the nation. Of utmost concern were the bankrupt treasury and a national debt that totaled over seventy-five million pesos.

Although Victoria lasted out his elected term—the only president to do so for the next forty years—in 1827 he had to put down a serious armed revolt led by his vice-president. Ultimately defeated by forces under General Guerrero, grand master of the *yorkinos,* Vice-president Bravo was captured, tried, and exiled. These internal struggles reduced the influence of Freemasonry on Mexican politics, but the strife continued in the form of bitter feuding between conservatives and liberals.

Factional rivalry marked Mexico's second presidential election in 1828, when the liberal, Vicente Guerrero, opposed the *moderado* ex-minister of war, Manuel Gómez Pedraza, who had conservative support. Although Guerrero apparently was the more popular candidate, he lost in a close election by the state legislatures, whereupon the liberals challenged the decision with arms. General Santa Anna "pronounced" in favor of Guerrero; so did General José Lobato in the capital, where his troops and a mob of five thousand *léparos* (vagabonds) provoked by *puro* Lorenzo de Zavala demonstrated in the main plaza. Their enthusiasm became a riot during which they sacked and destroyed the Parián Market, where many foreign traders sold their wares. Finally, the elected chief executive went into exile, and in April, 1829, Guerrero was installed as president, with a conservative vice-president, General Anastasio Bustamante. As a reward for his role in the uprising Santa Anna was promoted to major general, the highest rank in the army.

Guerrero's tenure as president was brief—he lasted only eight and a half months. During that period his administration abolished slavery by a law that was unopposed except in Texas, where Anglo-American colonists had been bringing in black slaves. The president also enforced the decree of March, 1829, expelling virtually all of the remaining Spaniards.

The expulsion of Spaniards and reports of civil strife in Mexico prompted the Spanish government to launch an ill-conceived attempt to reconquer the former colony. In July, 1829, three thousand Spanish soldiers from Cuba landed at Tampico and soon occupied the principal fort, which had been abandoned by the Mexican defenders. But it was a quixotic adventure. The landing site was too far from the center of population and government, the expeditionary troops could not move inland because they were beseiged by a Mexican army, yellow fever and tropical heat decimated their ranks, and their supply and retreat line had been cut when the Spanish transports returned to Cuba following a dispute between army and navy commanders. Finally, on September 11, the Spanish general peacefully surrendered to the Mexican zone commander. That defender of the coast was General Santa Anna, who thereafter was known as the "Victor of Tampico."

At the end of 1829, Guerrero left the capital to put down a revolt against him led by his conservative vice-president, Bustamante, who had the support of the army. One cause of the revolt was the liberal president's refusal to relinquish the extraordinary powers granted him at the time of the foreign invasion; thus, Bustamanate posed as a champion of constitutionalism and called Guerrero a dictator. Early in 1830 the vice-president took over the president's office, and Congress disqualified Guerrero, declaring him *imposibilitado* (unfit) to govern the republic.

Bustamante's administration improved government finances and checked banditry in the countryside, but the conservative president also created a dictatorship. He suppressed opposition newspapers and intimidated the legislature and judiciary by the threat of military force. With the aid of the army he replaced liberal governors and jailed, exiled, or executed liberal leaders. One victim of the firing squad was Guerrero, who was captured through treachery and bribery. (Seventeen years later the former president's name was given to a new state created by Congress.) Guerrero's execution shocked many Mexicans and triggered another military revolt.

Santa Anna was one of the first military commanders who rebelled against Bustamante early in 1832. Uprisings also occurred in Texas Tamaulipas, Zacatecas, and the port of Acapulco. After suffering an initial defeat, Santa Anna's forces eventually occupied the city of Puebla as they pushed on toward the capital. Finally, at the beginning of 1833, Bustamante went into exile, and General Gómez Pedraza was recalled to serve out the last three months of the term to which he had been elected five years earlier. A subsequent election resulted in the presidency of Santa Anna, Mexico's latest *caudillo.*

Antonio López de Santa Anna was a principal historical figure in Mexico for more than three decades. He helped topple Mexico's first empire and on eleven different occasions between 1833 and 1855 he served as chief executive of the nation. The Mexican general was a talented military

General Santa Anna, the Napoleon of Mexico. Courtesy Library of Congress.

commander revered as a hero for his battle victories, and his personal magnetism could attract a devoted following of soldiers or civilians. Santa Anna was intelligent and dynamic; he was also a clever politician who was able to shift his policies when public opinion changed. Several times he was sent into "perpetual" exile, but when there were troubles in Mexico, he returned to be hailed as savior of the nation.

During Santa Anna's first presidency he retired to Manga de Clavo, his hacienda in the state of Veracruz, and permitted his more liberal (*puro*) vice-president, Valentín Gómez Farías, to act for him. Gómez Farías and his radical theoretician, Doctor José María Luis Mora, wanted to implement sweeping reforms such as: separation of Church and state; establishment of public education; an end to privileges held by the nobility, military, and clergy; suppression of monastic institutions; and transfer of surplus Church property to private individuals, preferably those with little or no land. Of course, they also favored freedom of the press and a guarantee of individual liberties.

Gómez Farías persuaded the national Congress and state legislatures to enact laws in the reform spirit. They abolished the death penalty for political crimes, reduced the size of the standing army, and eliminated the military *fuero* of trial in the special military courts for civil and criminal violations. Ecclesiastical changes were the most revolutionary: the right of *patronato* was granted to the central government, which meant that it had the power to name bishops and other Church officials; members of monastic orders—priests, nuns, and lay brothers—were permitted to retract their religious vows; payment of Church tithes was changed from compulsory to voluntary; the Franciscan missions of California were secularized and their funds and property sequestered; and the University of Mexico, where most of the professors were priests, was closed. A new office of public instruction was charged with organizing a system of government schools from primary to college level.

Rallying around the cry of *"Religión y Fueros,"* the conservatives rose in revolt and called for annulment of the liberal-sponsored laws. During the second half of 1833, Santa Anna alternated between exercising the executive power and delegating it to his vice-president while he tried to put down the uprisings. The following year he succumbed to entreaties by the conservatives to become their leader and protect their prerogatives. Assuming absolute power in April, 1834, he ousted Gómez Farías, revoked the reforms, dissolved Congress, replaced liberal governors, and exiled the principal radicals. A new conservative Congress abolished the federal system and replaced it with a centralized one whereby the states became military departments headed by *caudillos* appointed by the president. This arrangement was eventually incorporated into the Constitution of 1836, sometimes called the *Siete Leyes* (Seven Laws). Meanwhile, opposition to this centralization was one of the causes of a revolt in the province of Texas—a revolt that proved disastrous to Mexican pride and to Santa Anna.

The difficulties in Texas arose from the presence of Anglo-American settlers who chafed under Mexican culture and laws. In the 1820s, Mexico had encouraged colonization of this northern province—proper settlement was seen as a barrier to future United States aggression. But more North Americans moved into Texas than did Mexicans from states farther south. Attracted by the abundance of arable land suitable for cotton cultivation, Stephen F. Austin and a few other entrepreneurs from the southern United States applied for colonization grants in Texas. Austin received a vast tract of land, the greater part of which he agreed to convey to immigrant families that he would bring to the state. Each family was permitted to purchase at least 640 acres at about ten cents an acre. The right to bring Negro slaves to Texas was a special inducement; so was the exemption from payment of general taxes for ten years and customs duties for seven years. All colonists were required to become Mexican citizens and to profess Roman Catholicism. Austin's grant authorized the introduction of three hundred families the first year; within a decade he had given out twelve hundred titles.

By 1830 about nine thousand former United States citizens had migrated to Texas. Their part of the population was triple that of the Spanish-speaking component. For various reasons the two societies did not integrate. Anglo-Americans settled on rural estates remote from the old population centers, they continued to use English almost exclusively, most were Protestants, and they used black slave labor to grow cotton for export to England and the United States. In contrast, the Spanish-speaking residents of Texas lived in towns, much of their social life centered around the Catholic Church, ranching and small-scale farming was their major economic basis, and they did not own slaves or export surpluses abroad.

Serious conflicts developed between impetuous Anglos and Mexican authorities in Texas. In 1826 Haden Edwards, claiming to have an *empresario* (entrepreneur) grant in eastern Texas, fortified his settlement and declared it to be the independent Republic of Fredonia. This ill-conceived revolt, which was opposed by Austin and the majority of American settlers, collapsed before Mexican troops arrived to quell it, but the uprising exacerbated the rift between the two cultures. Black slavery was another problem. When the Mexican Congress abolished all slavery in 1829, the Anglo-Texans protested vehemently and were allowed to keep their slaves but prohibited from further importation of bonded workers.

Belatedly, officials in Mexico City tried to remedy the problems in Texas. New regulations in 1830 closed the border to additional colonists from the United States (but not from Europe). Trade across the frontier was severely restricted, and new customs duties were levied on imports and exports. This affected the Anglos who regularly brought in American goods and shipped their cotton to Louisiana. Although additional Mexican revenue officials and army reinforcements were sent to implement these regulations, they could not patrol the long border—Americans continued to move westward across the Sabine River, thus becoming illegal aliens ("wetbacks") in Texas. By 1834, when the anti-Yankee immigration clause was set aside, the Anglo-Americans numbered

20,700 and the Spanish-speaking sector 4,000. Nevertheless, the Anglo majority was politically neutralized because in 1824 Texas had been combined with Coahuila, which had nine times the population of its northern neighbor. Another control factor was the distance to the state capital of Coahuila-Texas, which was located at Saltillo until 1833, when it moved to Monclova—both cities more than five hundred kilometers (three hundred miles) southwest of San Antonio.

Troubles in Texas escalated in the 1830s; as more Yankees arrived, so did more Mexican soldiers. Stephen Austin went to Mexico City on a futile mission to petition for separation from Coahuila, Mexican statehood for Texas, and a more convenient state capital. His demands were rejected, and he was imprisoned for a year because authorities intercepted an inflammatory letter in which he advised Texans to form a separate state "even though the general government refuses its consent."

Meanwhile, Texans armed themselves, gathered in protest meetings, and debated what to do. Some advocated independence; others, who declared their allegiance to the defunct 1824 federal constitution, hoped for reforms and reconciliation; and a few talked of union with the United States or Great Britain. A number of Spanish-surnamed residents of Texas joined Anglos in opposing the Mexican dictatorship; foremost among these was Lorenzo de Zavala, an ousted liberal politician originally from Yucatán, who had held the posts of congressman, treasury minister, and diplomatic representative to France. Zavala was also a land speculator in Texas associated with David G. Burnet in the Galveston Bay & Texas Land Company. Reports that a Mexican centralist army would be sent to "occupy" Texas unified the war and peace parties and galvanized public opinion there.

When centralist forces under General Martín Prefecto de Cos, brother-in-law of President Santa Anna, moved into Texas in September, 1835, they met armed resistance. Hostilities erupted in October when colonists at Gonzales refused to surrender a small cannon to a detachment of soldiers— instead they opened fire on the troops. A week later, rebels captured the military post at Goliad. Then, late in the month, Stephen Austin led three hundred volunteers, half of them Spanish-surnamed, to San Antonio, where they laid seige to the invading army of more than seven hundred soldiers. Six weeks later General Cos surrendered; he and his soldiers were permitted (or obliged) to leave the province. Clearly, a war for separation had begun, and in March, 1836, delegates to a convention at Washington-on-the-Brazos declared independence and chose David Burnet as president and Lorenzo de Zavala as vice-president of the Republic of Texas.

Mexico's chief executive, General Santa Anna, who in April, 1835, had led a force that crushed an anti-centralist revolt in Zacatecas, determined to put down the Texas rebellion. Gathering an army of 6,000 men, he marched north in the winter of 1835–36. In late February as he approached San Antonio with half of his army, the Texans ordered the city evacuated and positioned 150 men under William Travis in an abandoned Franciscan mission known as the Alamo. Thirty-two volunteers arrived later to join Yankee frontiersmen Davy Crockett, Jim Bowie, and the other defenders. For ten days Santa Anna besieged the fortress and demanded unconditional surrender; when Travis refused, the Mexican commander signaled an all-out attack with no quarter or clemency. Santa Anna won the battle, his soldiers killed all the defenders, and Texas military units stationed elsewhere got a battle cry, "Remember the Alamo!"

The war lasted another six weeks. Late in March near the village of Goliad a unit of Texans under Colonel James Fannin was surrounded and outnumbered by a Mexican army under General José Urrea. Fannin surrendered in the belief that he and his men would be treated as prisoners of war, but Santa Anna enforced a recently-passed "piracy" law and ordered all 365 prisoners to be shot. They were. The situation looked bleak for the remaining eight hundred Texas soldiers under General Sam Houston. They were retreating toward the eastern border when suddenly, on April 21, 1836, near the San Jacinto River, they attacked Santa Anna's army and won a stunning victory. Almost the entire Mexican force of fourteen hundred men were captured or killed, and Santa Anna himself was taken prisoner.

Some Texans wanted to execute their distinguished prisoner, but Houston realized that he could be very useful to the Lone Star Republic. On May 14, as president of Mexico and general-in-chief of the Mexican army, Santa Anna signed two treaties with David Burnet, president of Texas. The first Treaty of Velasco was public; it specified that hostilities would cease, all Mexican troops would withdraw to the other side of the Rio Grande without delay, there would be an exchange of prisoners, and Santa Anna would not take up arms against Texas or cause others to do so. In the secret agreement, made public later, the Mexican general was guaranteed transportation back to Veracruz in exchange for his promise to work for Mexican recognition of the Republic of Texas.

Santa Anna did not return to Mexico for nine months. First he was taken to Washington, D.C., with a Texas delegation that sought diplomatic recognition of the new republic and eventual annexation by the United States. After a series of meetings President Andrew Jackson sent the Mexican general to Veracruz aboard a United States warship. At home, Santa Anna found himself in disgrace for the Texas debacle, so he retired to his hacienda. In April, 1837, the Congress named General Bustamante president; his government repudiated the treaty that Santa Anna had signed and refused to recognize the independence of Texas. Moreover, various officials talked of reconquering the province, but internal revolts and foreign threats precluded any such action.

A dispute between France and Mexico came to a head in 1838 with a military engagement known as the "Pastry War." The derisive name came from the claim of a French baker whose shop had been demolished by Mexican soldiers during disorders in Mexico a decade earlier. This claim and those of other French citizens amounted to over 600,000 pesos, according to an ultimatum presented by the French minister in March, 1838, and backed up by a French fleet that appeared off Veracruz. When the demand was not met, Mexico's chief port was blockaded. In October the Mexican government agreed to pay the claims, but France now demanded an additional 200,000 pesos—the cost of the blockade. Mexico would not pay that amount, so in late November the French ships bombarded the fortress of San Juan de Ulúa and forced its surrender. The following day the Veracruz garrison capitulated.

Responding to its citizens' charges of military incompetency and intimations of treason, the Mexican government declared war on France, repudiated the capitulations signed by the commanders of San Juan de Ulúa and Veracruz, and entrusted General Santa Anna with command of the forces sent to combat the French. When he heard about the French bombardment, Santa Anna offered his services and hastened to the port, where he arrived on December 4. The next day three thousand French soldiers landed in Veracruz, but they were forced back to their ships by the Mexican troops. Finally, after negotiations both parties agreed to a peace treaty which set the indemnity at 600,000 pesos. One result of the Pastry War was Santa Anna's serious battle wound in his left leg, which had to be amputated below the knee. More than once thereafter his peg-leg gave him a claim to honor and respect as a wounded veteran and national hero.

Fanny Calderón de la Barca, Scottish-born wife of Spain's first minister to Mexico, met Santa Anna, several times. In her fascinating book, *Life in Mexico,* she recorded her impressions of him when she and her husband visited Manga de Clavo in December 1839. She said he spoke often of his amputated leg, "Otherwise, he made himself very agreeable, spoke a great deal of the United States, and of the persons he had known there, and in his manners was quiet and gentlemanlike, and altogether a more polished hero than I had expected to see. To judge from the past, he will not long remain in his present state of inaction. . . ."

Between 1839 and 1846, Mexico experienced half a dozen internal revolts. Most of these were *cuartelazos,* military uprisings, with one general trying to unseat another from the presidency. A few were inspired by civilian leaders such as

Gómez Farías, who wanted a return to federalism. That same goal caused the province of Yucatán to declare itself independent in 1839; four years later it finally succumbed to central control.

After a military revolt in 1841, Santa Anna became the dictator of Mexico for three years. This period was characterized by a large increase in the size of the army and civil bureaucracy, huge budget deficits, foreign borrowing, forced domestic loans, import duties increased by 20 percent, widespread graft and corruption at all levels of government, lucrative mining concessions sold to English investors, and lavish extravaganzas. Santa Anna basked in self-glorification. His amputated leg was reburied in an elaborate ceremony in the capital attended by cabinet members, congressmen, and foreign diplomats; statues and busts of the dictator appeared in public buildings and along thoroughfares; and a new national theater was named *El Gran Teatro de Santa Anna*.

In his *Recollections of Mexico* the United States minister, Waddy Thompson, recalled some aspects of social life for the middle and upper classes during this era:

The new Theatre in the street Bergara, which was finished in 1843, is said to be the finest in the world, except that of Saint Carlos in Naples. I can conceive of nothing of the kind more elegant in its architecture, or perfect in its arrangements. I have seen in it a concourse estimated at seven or eight thousand, and it was not full. There are eight tiers of seats, with a pit sufficient to accommodate a larger audience than the whole of any ordinary theatre. In the rear of each box there is room for the accommodation of those who occupy the box. These boxes, in certain tiers, rent for two and three thousand dollars per annum, some of them I believe for even more. The whole theatre is lighted by splendid chandeliers. . . .

Of all the spots in Mexico, the Alameda is the most beautiful. It is a public square on the western border of the city, containing about forty acres, enclosed by a stone wall. It is covered with a thick growth of poplar trees [*álamos*] and hence the name; the whole square is intersected with walks paved with flag-stones; all these walks unite in the centre where there is a beautiful *jet d'eau,* and from this point they diverge in every direction, and again unite in

Interior view of the Gran Teatro. Courtesy The Bancroft Library.

four or five smaller circles. There is a carriage-way inside of the
wall entirely surrounding the square.

A short distance from the Alameda is the Paseo—the fashionable
ride. It is a broad road just on the outside of the city, of perhaps
a mile in length, and terminating at the aqueduct. Here every one
in Mexico who has a coach of his own, and every one who has not,
who has the money to pay the hire of a hackney coach, assemble,
besides hundreds and often thousands of horsemen. . . . I have frequently seen a thousand carriages and more than five thousand
horsemen in the Paseo.*

Mexico's gala social life and public fiestas masked serious
political and economic troubles. Military revolts continued.
In December, 1844, Santa Anna was ousted and exiled to
Cuba, being replaced by another general, José Joaquín Herrera. The latter was overturned a year later by General
Mariano Paredes, who had to cope with problems that were
developing on the northern frontier.

Mexico never had recognized the independence of Texas
and strongly objected to plans for its annexation by the
United States. During the nine years it was an independent
nation the Lone Star Republic repeatedly petitioned to join
the Union, but the issue of slavery prevented it. Then in
1844, James Polk was elected president of the United States
on the platform of acquiring "Texas and Oregon too." Congress, by a joint resolution on March 1, 1845, invited Texas
to become a state if the people there ratified the agreement.
One week later Mexico suspended diplomatic ties with the
United States, the American minister soon returned home,
and on July 21, Mexico's president asked his Congress for a
declaration of war to take effect at the time of United States
annexation or invasion of Texas. The stage was set for the
United States–Mexican War.

Besides annexation there was another problem—the disputed boundary between Texas and Mexico. For more than
two centuries the southern limit of Texas had been the Nueces

*Waddy Thompson, *Recollections of Mexico* (New York and London:
Wiley and Putnam, 1846), 125–26.

Woman wearing a mantilla. Courtesy The Bancroft Library.

River — all the old maps showed it that way — but when Texas became independent, it claimed the Rio Grande *(Río Bravo)* 240 kilometers (150 miles) farther south, as its frontier. Furthermore, it claimed the land east of the Rio Grande all the way to its source in Colorado; that exaggerated claim put half of New Mexico, including Santa Fe and Albuquerque, in Texas. After annexation the United States supported the Texas boundary claim and sent an occupation army under General Zachary Taylor to the Nueces River.

In the fall of 1845, when Polk was informed that the Mexican government would receive a commissioner to discuss the Texas question, he dispatched John Slidell to Mexico City as "Envoy Extraordinary and Minister Plenipotentiary." Slidell was charged with negotiating an acceptable Texas boundary. He also was authorized to settle Mexico's defaulted payment of more than two million dollars in claims of Americans against Mexico; and he carried secret instructions to offer twenty-five million dollars as a purchase price for California. The emissary arrived in the Mexican capital on December 8; a week later a revolt against the central government erupted, and a council of government decided against receiving Slidell, because this would involve diplomatic recognition. Hoping for a reversal of this decision, Slidell remained in Mexico until the following March.

Upon learning of Mexico's rebuff of Slidell, President Polk ordered General Taylor to move his army from the mouth of the Nueces to the Rio Grande. By the end of March, 1846, the Americans had begun construction of a six-sided fortress across the river from Matamoros. From that city the commander of Mexico's Division of the North, General Pedro de Ampudia, ordered the Americans to return to the Nueces or face hostile action. Taylor replied that his orders did not permit a withdrawal.

Hostilities erupted in the disputed territory along the Rio Grande in the spring of 1846. Even before the inevitable military clash, President Paredes declared that the American army had invaded Mexico, and he said, "From this day [April 23] defensive war begins." Two days later, across from

Matamoros an American scouting party was ambushed by a Mexican cavalry unit. Eleven Yankees were killed, six wounded, and sixty-three were taken prisoner. Taylor rushed this news to Washington, where President Polk had been reviewing with his cabinet the American grievances against Mexico.

A declaration of war soon followed. Polk sent Congress a bellicose message noting, "Mexico has passed the boundary of the United States, has invaded our territory and shed American blood upon the American soil." Only a few congressmen questioned whether that incident actually took place on American soil—the overwhelming majority voted on May 13 to declare war on Mexico. In Mexico City the official congressional declaration of war occurred on July 2. It was announced publicly a week later by President Paredes, who also said that the clergy would furnish one million pesos to pay for the war.

America's military offensive was multi-pronged; while naval units controlled Mexico's Gulf and Pacific ports, four separate armies would invade the republic. The Army of the West was to take New Mexico, then go on to California; the Central Division would march southwest from San Antonio down Mexico's central corridor; the Army of Occupation was ordered to cross the Rio Grande and attack Monterrey; and an amphibious force, the Veracruz Expedition, was destined to land on the east coast and follow Cortés's route to Mexico City.

The Army of the West under Colonel (soon promoted to General) Stephen Watts Kearny encountered the least Mexican opposition. Late in June, 1845, at the head of fifteen hundred men he departed from Ft. Leavenworth, Kansas, headed for New Mexico. His movement was slowed by the desert terrain and the enormous size of his train: more than fifteen hundred wagons and nineteen thousand head of livestock. When the Americans approached Santa Fe, Governor Manuel Armijo was waiting for them in Apache Canyon with about four thousand men, only ninety of them regular Mexican soldiers; but suddenly he disbanded his army and fled

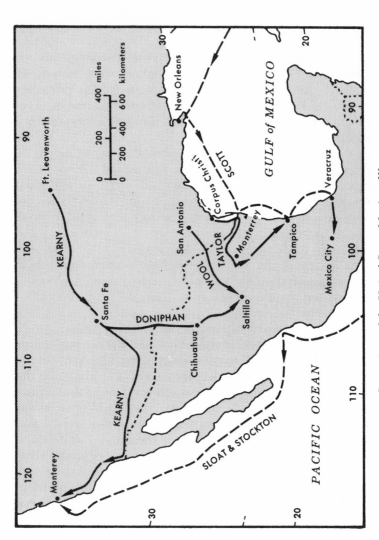

Campaigns of the United States-Mexican War

south to Chihuahua. Some say that his troops refused to fight; others suggest that Armijo was bribed by the Yankees. In any case, Kearny's men hoisted the Stars and Stripes over the governor's palace on August 18 and fired a thirteen-gun salute. Those were the only shots fired in the takeover.

After organizing a government in New Mexico, Kearny assigned part of his troops as an occupation force, ordered others under Colonel Doniphan to invade Chihuahua later in the year, and set off for California with one hundred dragoons and a pack train. In mid-December the hungry and exhausted men straggled into San Diego after having been attacked by a detachment of California lancers. Monterey, California's capital, had been seized six months earlier by American naval forces under Commodores John Sloat and Robert Stockton, but Los Angeles was under Mexican control when Kearny arrived on the coast. A joint force under Kearny and Stockton captured Los Angeles, and on January 13, 1847, the Mexican *Californio* army under General Andrés Pico surrendered to Major John C. Frémont, who had marched south with his battalion of mounted riflemen. The surrender ended organized resistance to American occupation of California and turned attention to the main theaters of war.

General Zachary Taylor's penetration of northern Mexico with the Army of Occupation resulted in a series of victories that made him a hero at home. He crossed the Rio Grande in May, 1846, and set up camp near Matamoros. Then in July and August the Americans went by steamship upriver to Camargo, staging point for the march south to Monterrey. By that time Taylor's army totaled six thousand officers and men. Defending Monterrey were seven thousand Mexican soldiers under General Pedro de Ampudia, who fortified the city and awaited battle. Taylor began the attack on September 20, and four days later victory seemed inevitable, when the Mexican commander suddenly proposed an armistice. Ampudia agreed to evacuate the city and retire with his troops and arms to Saltillo; in return, Taylor promised not to advance that far for eight weeks or until the armistice was disavowed by either government.

American army in Monterrey during the Mexican War. Courtesy The Bancroft Library.

Meanwhile, early in July, 1846, an American agent had gone to Cuba to confer secretly with the exiled General Santa Anna. The former Mexican dictator agreed that if the United States passed him through the blockade and allowed him to return home, he would try to regain power and would then negotiate for peace. America's peace terms were stated to him: no indemnity, settlement of the old financial claims, and purchase of the disputed Rio Grande territory as well as New Mexico. Santa Anna arrived at Veracruz in mid-August and promptly forgot his promises to the United States. Within a month he was given command of the Mexican army and headed for San Luis Potosí, where he organized and trained a force of twenty thousand men to oppose Taylor's thrust into northern Mexico. At the end of the year Santa Anna was "elected" president by a constituent congress; during his absence from the capital Gómez Farías was to exercise the executive power.

While Santa Anna was consolidating his position, another American army, the Central Division, marched into north-central Mexico. Under General John Wool, this column left San Antonio in mid-August, crossed the Rio Grande near present Eagle Pass, Texas, then marched south to Monclova, arriving there in November. A month later it occupied the town of Parras. From there, General Wool's two thousand men moved to Saltillo to join Taylor's Army of Occupation.

A showdown between the armies of Taylor and Santa Anna occurred south of Saltillo near the hacienda of Buena Vista. (Mexicans call the battlefield Angostura, from another place-name.) Santa Anna took the offensive after his men intercepted a message directing Taylor to send almost half his troops to the Gulf Coast, where they would embark for Veracruz. The Battle of Buena Vista, fought February 22 and 23, 1847, was bloody—American casualties totaled 14 percent and Mexican losses were even greater. Both generals claimed victory, and both had enemy flags and other trophies to bolster their claims. After the battle, Taylor remained in control of northern Mexico, while Santa Anna's troops retreated southward. The Mexican *caudillo* returned to Mexico City where he ousted Gómez Farías, then turned toward the east to meet another invading army.

General Winfield Scott planned and executed the major United States campaign against Mexico; his Veracruz Expedition was destined to carry the war to Mexico's heartland. Landing unopposed south of Veracruz on March 9, 1847, the army of ten thousand Americans moved behind the walled port city, cut off its fresh water and supply route, then bombarded it for four days. At least one hundred Mexican civilians and eighty soldiers were killed in the shelling; Mexican estimates run as high as five times that figure. Finally, at the end of March, the besieged garrison of thirty-three hundred soldiers, plus a thousand men stationed at the offshore fortress of San Juan de Ulúa, surrendered. Veracruz became the base of operations for the Yankee march inland.

While Scott assembled his men and supplies, President Santa Anna organized the Army of the East to block the approach from Veracruz. Before leaving Mexico City he borrowed two million pesos from the Church to finance the operation, and he appointed Pedro María Anaya as acting-president during his absence in the field. In mid-April, when the opposing armies clashed at the mountain pass of Cerro Gordo near Jalapa, Santa Anna was defeated and barely escaped with his life after Americans surrounded his supposedly impregnable position. He hoped to make another stand at Puebla, but officials there would not cooperate, so he retreated to Mexico City to direct the defense of the capital.

United States forces occupied Puebla in mid-May and remained there for almost two months while recuperating from wounds and illness (malaria, yellow fever, and dysentery), waiting for reinforcements, and trying to negotiate a peace. Scott quarreled with a State Department official, Nicholas P. Trist, who came with a draft treaty, but finally the two men agreed to advance ten thousand dollars to Santa Anna with the promise of a million dollars upon the signing of a peace treaty. After receiving the down payment Santa Anna was unable to prevail upon the Mexican Congress to repeal a law it had passed making it high treason for any official to treat with the Americans; nor would the Congress authorize any discussions with the invaders. It was clear that Scott would have to advance on the capital.

Continuing in the footsteps of Cortés, the Yankee conquistadors moved over the pass between the volcanoes and down into the Valley of Mexico. The defenders had erected massive redoubts at a fortified hill, El Peñon, and near Mexicalzingo, blocking the main eastern approaches to the capital, but Scott's wily engineers pioneered a route south of Lakes Chalco and Xochimilco, which permitted the invaders to attack the capital from the south. On August 20, 1847, two major engagements were fought at Contreras (Padierna ranch) and Churubusco. The Mexican commander at the first location, General Gabriel Valencia, disobeyed Santa Anna's orders to withdraw to San Angel, and his exposed position contributed to his defeat. General Manuel Rincón's fifteen hundred men of the National Guard put up a spirited defense at a fortified convent in Churubusco, but they were overwhelmed by a combination of American artillery bombardment and waves of infantry attacks.

General Scott reported to Washington the casualty statistics for both sides in the battles of August 20. He noted that the American army "made about 3,000 prisoners, including eight generals (two of them ex-presidents), and 205 other officers; killed or wounded 4,000 of all ranks — besides entire corps dispersed and dissolved. . . . Our loss amounts of 1,053 — killed, 139, including 16 officers; wounded, 876, with 60 officers."

Among the prisoners taken at Churubusco were seventy-two men who had deserted American ranks at different times and places and joined the Mexican army as part of the San Patricio (St. Patrick's) Battalion. Most of the defectors were foreign-born, and 40 percent were Irish. Following a court-martial, those who had deserted before the declaration of war were branded with a "D," whipped, and imprisoned; seven had their sentences remitted; and the remaining fifty were hanged for desertion during wartime.

After the battle of Churubusco the American commander decided to halt outside the gates of Mexico City. Scott thought that the devastating defeats inflicted on Santa Anna's army and the desire to avoid destruction of the capital would force the Mexicans to negotiate, but a two-week armistice produced no concessions on either side. In the interim Santa Anna had reinforced his defenses within the city and stopped the sale of provisions to the Americans; these violations of the agreement led Scott to terminate his armistice.

The Americans fought two more battles before they could enter the "Halls of Montezuma." On September 8 they attacked and occupied El Molino del Rey, which they thought was a foundry for cannon. It was a pyrrhic victory, because there was no factory, and the two-hour fight cost the Yankees almost eight hundred casualties. Five days later came the successful assault on Chapultepec Castle at the crest of a hill dominating several approaches to Mexico City. It was defended by about nine hundred Mexican soldiers and forty-seven cadets of the Military College that was located there. Six of the teen-aged cadets died in the engagement—these *Niños Héroes* were later commemorated by a large monument erected at the base of the hill.

Santa Anna and his remaining troops retreated from the capital, allowing American occupation of the city on September 14. Two days later the Mexican leader renounced the presidency and marched toward Puebla, where he tried unsuccessfully to cut the American line of communication. When a large part of his army deserted, and he was ordered to appear at a Mexican court-martial investigating his conduct of the war, Santa Anna found exile on the island of Jamaica. Meanwhile, Mexican guerrilla bands, one led by a Spanish priest, continued to harass American supply depots and hospital trains on the Veracruz highway.

Although the Yankees occupied Mexico City, it took some months to get a peace agreement signed and sealed. On February 2, 1848, American commissioner Trist and the interim president of Mexico, Manuel de la Peña y Peña, met at the village of Guadalupe Hidalgo, where they signed a tentative treaty that was ratified by both countries on May 30. Under the treaty terms Mexico gave up all claims to Texas and agreed to a new frontier with the United States: from the mouth of the Rio Grande to the southern boundary of New Mexico, then west to a point just south of San Diego, California. Mexico lost two-fifths of her territory but less than half of 1 percent of her population, and residents of the ceded area could choose their citizenship. Not counting Texas, this Mexican cession of land to the United States amounted to one and a third million square kilometers (529,017 square miles)—an area larger than Spain, France, and Italy combined. For this territory the United States agreed to pay $15 million and to assume all outstanding claims of its citizens against the Mexican government.

Mexico's tragic loss of soldiers, battles, and territory was a psychological blow that shattered the nation's honor and dignity. In addition it engendered a deep feeling of "Yan-keephobia" that still persists, openly as well as below the surface. Clearly, leaders in the United States had aggressive designs on Mexican territory, but most Mexican historians recognize that the threat could have been parried better had there been less financial irresponsibility and political chaos in their own country. A modern Mexican source gives the following comparison between the two antagonists:

> While the United States came together to win the war, and there was unity of command in each campaign, Mexico disintegrated into anarchy: President Paredes was imprisoned; the form of government and the Constitution were changed; there were seven presidents; six generals successively directed the campaign against Taylor; insurrections continued; and only seven of the nineteen states which then formed the Mexican federation contributed men, arms, and money to the national defense.*

The end of the war left Mexico dismembered, demoralized, and subject to another period of turmoil out of which Santa Anna would again emerge to rule the country. There were

*Enciclopedia de México, 1978 ed., s.v. "Guerra de E.U. a México."

Indian raids in the north; roving bandits along the highways; military revolts in the states of Puebla, Aguascalientes, Jalisco, and Guanajuato; and a barbarous racial war in Yucatán, where Maya Indians turned on their white oppressors in the Caste War (1847–53). To rescue the country from anarchy, the most respected conservative leader, Lucas Alamán, persuaded Congress to call Santa Anna back for one year while a search would be made for a monarch. The former leader took over the presidency in mid-April, 1853, but unfortunately Alamán soon died, and with no restraining influence on his actions Santa Anna imposed a despotic regime. He also adopted monarchical trappings and assumed the title of His Most Serene Highness.

To obtain money for his "court" and for the army, Santa Anna sold to the United States, for $10 million, the Mesilla Valley in southern Arizona and New Mexico. American promoters wanted the tract of 76,768 square kilometers (29,640 square miles) for a railroad right-of-way to connect Texas and California. This alienation of territory, known in the United States as the Gadsden Purchase (1853), aroused deep resentment in Mexico and served as a catalyst for the tyrant's enemies, who initiated a movement to overthrow him.

A group of young liberals, many of whom had been persecuted by Santa Anna, joined with the old insurgent leader Juan Álvarez in drawing up the Plan of Ayutla issued in March, 1854. This manifesto called for overthrowing the dictator, a provisional presidency under Álvarez, and convocation of a constituent assembly to give the nation a constitution that would reflect the advanced liberal ideas of the century. The revolution of Ayutla was successful. Santa Anna fled to his final exile, and Álvarez took over the government in the summer of 1855. The Santa Anna era had finally ended, and the new leaders hoped to restructure the government and regenerate the nation.

CHAPTER 8

Juárez and Maximilian

ONE of the handsome boulevards in Mexico City is called Paseo de la Reforma; it is named for a liberal movement, *La Reforma* (the Reform), which altered the course of Mexican history after 1855. This reform program was headed by a new group of liberal leaders who championed social justice. Many of them had been jailed or exiled by Santa Anna. Among other goals they wanted to reduce the political power of the army and the Church, and they opposed special legal rights *(fueros)* that benefited clergy and military personnel. In many ways this movement was a rebirth of the radicalism of the previous generation and a continuation of the liberal-conservative struggle.

Three important leaders of *La Reforma* had legal training and served as liberal governors. They were Melchor Ocampo, governor of Michoacán and a scholar of Rousseauvian inspiration; Santos Degollado, a legal clerk who became a general in the revolution of Ayutla and later was governor of Jalisco and Michoacán; and Benito Juárez, the Zapotec Indian governor of Oaxaca who was a man of amazing integrity and ability.

Juarez's life story has been an inspiration to countless Mexicans. Orphaned at an early age he found a benefactor who sponsored his admission to a seminary; later he received a law degree and entered politics. He served in the state and national legislatures and was elected governor of Oaxaca for a four-year term beginning in 1848. Juárez's policies led to his exile by Santa Anna, whereupon he joined Ocampo and other liberals in New Orleans. In 1855 he returned to join the revolution of Ayutla as secretary to the old leader, Juan Álvarez, and when the revolt was successful, Juárez

Benito Juárez, the Indian president. Courtesy Organization of American States.

became minister of justice in President Álvarez's cabinet. Two years later he was elected chief justice of the Mexican Supreme Court, and the following year he became president of the nation. During all his years in office, Juárez lived a simple life and set a fine example as a dedicated public servant.

When the liberals took power in 1855, they began a legal assault on vestiges of colonial feudalism and special privileges. One of their first significant reform laws was the *Ley Juárez*, named for its sponsor, who was then minister of justice. Issued in November, 1855, the new law abolished religious and military *fueros* — the right of soldiers and clerics (and their dependents) to be tried in their own courts for alleged violations of civil or criminal law. Ecclesiastic and military courts were not abolished; instead their jurisdiction was restricted to cases involving canon or military law. The *Ley Juárez* provoked violent opposition by conservatives, and it split the liberals into moderate and radical (*puro*) factions. By the end of the year, when Álvarez and most of his cabinet had resigned, the presidency devolved on the moderate Ignacio Comonfort, a general who had been minister of war and navy.

A second controversial reform law was the *Ley Lerdo*, drafted by Comonfort's minister of treasury, Miguel Lerdo de Tejada. Promulgated in June, 1856, it forbade all institutions, including the Church and villages, from owning landed estates. They could keep any land and buildings necessary for their operation, but they were forced to sell all surplus property. The excess property was not expropriated or confiscated; instead it was to be auctioned, with the sale price going to the institution. Proponents said this law was designed to achieve three goals: it would raise money for the government through a tax on all sales or transfers; it would emasculate the wealth and power of the Church (contemporary estimates reckoned that half of the nation's real estate belonged to ecclesiastical corporations, most of it acquired through gifts over three centuries); and it would create a new class of yeoman landowners (who would be loyal to the liberals). Unfortunately, the law had other results —

the amount of revenue generated was meager, and because few peons or Indians could pay the purchase price, the auctioned lands passed into the hands of bourgeois friends of the liberals, speculators, or wealthy *hacendados.* These new owners exploited the workers in ways the Church had not, nor did they offer the social services provided by ecclesiastical ownership. The forced sale of communal village lands known as *ejidos* took ancestral plots away from Indian families, thus compelling them to seek employment as landless peons on haciendas.

A third reform law, the *Ley Iglesias,* initiated by cabinet member José María Iglesias, struck more directly at the clergy. It limited the fees or stipends charged for performance of baptisms, marriages, and burials—the poor would receive the sacraments free, and those with means would pay only a modest amount. Other laws transferred the registration of all births, marriages, and deaths from the Church to the state. The reformers considered themselves good Catholics—they did not attack Church dogma but only Church control of what they considered to be civil matters.

A high point of the Reform was the Constitution of 1857, which had been drafted under liberal, anti-privilege, and anticlerical inspiration. Few conservatives participated in writing the document, and the old liberal, Valentín Gómez Farías, was the first president of the constituent assembly. Instead of a vice-president, the new Constitution provided that the head of the Supreme Court would take over in the event of the death or incapacity of the executive. Another innovation was a unicameral legislature (a Senate was added in 1878); and suffrage was extended to all males of twenty-one or, if married, eighteen years or older. Slavery and compulsory service were abolished, as were all titles of nobility. There was a bill of rights guaranteeing freedom of speech, press, assembly, and education; freedom of worship was tacitly recognized because it was not mentioned, nor was Roman Catholicism made the state church.

Churchmen opposed the new Constitution and attempted to nullify it. They objected to various parts of the document, such as freedom of education, which they claimed contradicted canon law, and they maintained that abolishing compulsory service could be interpreted as permitting nuns and priests to renounce their vows. Pope Pius IX supported the Mexican Church hierarchy by declaring, "We raise our Pontifical voice in apostolic liberty. . . . to condemn, reprove, and declare null and void everything the said decrees and everything else that the civil authority has done in scorn of ecclesiastical authority and of this Holy See." When Mexican bishops threatened to excommunicate anyone who supported the Constitution, it presented a real dilemma for civil servants and military personnel who were obliged to swear allegiance to the new basic law of the land or forfeit their positions. Thus the Constitution and its implementation split Mexico into two irreconcilable camps; the dichotomy led to civil war and, eventually, to foreign intervention.

Conservatives—especially ranking army officers, Church officials, aristocrats, and big landowners—challenged the Constitution by supporting a revolt that became known as the War of the Reform (1858–60). In December, 1857, under the leadership of General Félix Zuloaga they proclaimed their Plan of Tacubaya, which denounced the Constitution and called for another convention. Marching on the capital, they dissolved Congress, arrested Juárez, and tried to win President Comonfort to their side. The president vacillated, and when he resigned his office and abandoned the country, a junta declared Zuloaga chief executive. Meanwhile, Juárez, who as head of the Supreme Court was constitutionally next in line for the presidency, had escaped to Guanajuato where he assumed the presidency and declared that constitutional government had been reestablished. Leaders of eleven states supported his position, and he moved the liberal government to Veracruz, where it could use the customhouse receipts to secure arms and outside support. Consequently Mexico had two presidents and two governments—one in Mexico City under the banner of *Religión y Fueros,* and the other in Veracruz proclaiming *Constitución y Legalidad.*

The War of the Reform, sometimes called the Three Years'

War, was a bitter civil conflict that transcended racial and class lines. Old alignments and antagonisms were complicated by religious or economic factors, while some participants were drawn into the struggle through following a trusted leader. Indians were found on both sides. Those who had been dispossessed by application of the *Ley Lerdo* were opposed to the liberal cause. So were loyal followers of the Indian *cacique,* Tomás Mejía, who was a crack general in the conservative army; yet many other natives supported the Indian "civilian *cacique,*" Benito Juárez. Rich property owners also were represented in the two opposing forces and central governments; their attitudes about privilege often determined their allegiance. Some conservatives supported the liberals in order to acquire Church lands. Like most wars fought for ideas, it was a vicious conflict marked by excesses and atrocities; conservatives shot prisoners without a trial, liberals seized Church property and killed priests who refused the sacraments to their men, and many noncombatants had their property confiscated or destroyed.

In the midst of the war Ocampo drafted and Juárez signed additional reform laws that were more radical than the earlier ones. Because Church wealth was being used to sustain the conservative revolt, Juárez declared that all remaining Church property and assets were to be nationalized without compensation. In addition, every male religious order and brotherhood was dissolved; convents of nuns were allowed to continue, but they were put under the control of bishops and no new novices were permitted to take the veil. Marriage was made a civil contract; to be legal it would have to be performed by a civil official. Cemeteries were removed from control of the clergy, many religious holidays were eliminated, and freedom of worship was established. Although affairs of Church and state were separated by a law of July, 1859, it is clear that the Juárez government's decrees and actions of that year went well beyond "separation."

The war came to a head in 1860. Liberal soldiers under General Santos Degollado tried to take Mexico City in April, but they were defeated by the army of General Leonardo

Márquez. That same spring General Miguel Miramón, who had replaced Zuloaga as head of the conservative government, marched seven thousand soldiers on Veracruz and blockaded the port by sea, but without avail. By mid-1860 the fortunes of war began to favor the liberals; in the fall they took Guadalajara and Oaxaca, and in late December General Jesús González Ortega won the last formal battle on the plains of Calpulálpan northeast of the capital. Miramón fled to exile, and Juárez returned to Mexico City in January, 1861.

Although Juárez won the presidential election in March, 1861, the country was far from unified. Indeed, even the liberals split over Juárez's policy of granting amnesty to the former enemies. Ocampo was one of the radicals who resigned; he returned to his hacienda, where he was kidnapped and murdered by a conservative guerrilla band that also killed Degollado in the summer of 1861. The liberal triumph in the civil war provided only a temporary peace, because foreign complications developed.

Mexico's postwar desolation was tragic—the Reform War had left its toll of death and destruction; unemployment was severe; and the nation was bankrupt. Although $45 million worth of Church property had been nationalized, less than 2 million pesos had reached the treasury through sales, and that was soon spent. Furthermore, the government owed more than $80 million to foreign powers and individuals. Customs receipts comprised the main source of government income, but 90 percent of them were allocated just to pay the interest on the foreign debt. Some of the loans had been negotiated at exhorbitant rates—for example, while Miramón was in power he dealt with a Swiss banker, Jean B. Jecker, who provided $750,000 in immediate cash in exchange for the Mexican government's promise to pay $15,000,000 plus interest. Juárez's government did not repudiate these agreements, but Congress voted in July, 1861, to suspend for two years payment of principal and interest on the foreign debt.

As a result of Mexico's moratorium on payment of its debts, representatives of France, Spain, and Great Britain met in London, where they signed a treaty in October, 1861. That agreement called for joint armed intervention to seize military forts and customhouses along Mexico's Gulf Coast. The announced purpose was to collect debts owed to their governments or to their subjects; however, there were other grievances and motives.

For some time a number of Mexican monarchists, conservatives, and Church officials had been in Europe, where they tried to interest the pope and various sovereigns in aiding their cause and returning them to power. General Miramón was in Spain; the bishop of Puebla, Pelagio de Labastida y Dávalos, had been banished and was in Italy; and General Juan Almonte consorted with José Hidalgo, José Gutiérrez de Estrada, and other arch-conservative emigres in Paris. These last three men often met with the very devout French Empress Eugénie, who was Spanish-born and who listened to their pleas for European military intervention against the anticlerical radicals under Juárez. Doubtless she relayed to the emperor some of her hopes for Mexico.

Besides supporting their subjects who were creditors of Mexico, at least two of the European monarchs had ulterior designs. Spain was then engaged in an attempt to rebuild a world empire — Spanish troops invaded Vietnam (1858-62), Morocco (1859), and the Dominican Republic (1861). The opportunity to get a foothold in Mexico was rationalized by complaints about unkept treaties and Juárez's expulsion of the Spanish minister. Napoleon III of France, anxious to win popularity and fame through a spectacular foreign policy, had plans to expand French commercial and cultural influence in Latin America. By backing the claims of Jecker, the Swiss financier who had recently become a French subject, the emperor saw a chance to make Mexico into a puppet state. The British government based its actions on Mexico's default of payments to bondholders as well as the wartime seizure of two shipments of silver belonging to British mineowners — one waylaid by Márquez was valued at $600,000, the other, taken by Santos Degollado, was worth a million pesos. And because the United States was preoccupied with its Civil

War, President Abraham Lincoln could not enforce the Monroe Doctrine against European intrusion into the Americas. The intervention in Mexico began in December, 1861, with the arrival at Veracruz of a Spanish military squadron that was joined the following month by French and British troops. The European allies proclaimed that they had come to assist a people suffering from internal disorder; they were going to help in the "regeneration of Mexico." After only three months, friction between the tripartite military commanders and civilian commissioners led to complete withdrawal of the British and Spanish contingents. They recognized that France had a more aggressive policy than debt collection; indeed, the French soon increased their military force to sixty-five hundred men and marched toward the Mexican capital. When they attacked the fortified city of Puebla on May 5, 1862, Mexican soldiers under General Ignacio Zaragoza and the young Brigadier General Porfirio Díaz humiliatingly defeated the French invaders. Ever since then, Mexicans have celebrated the *cinco de mayo* (fifth of May) in honor of that victory.

About a year later, after the arrival of thirty thousand additional soldiers, the French expeditionary force under General Elie Forey advanced toward Mexico's capital. Again the major obstacle was the city of Puebla, which had been reinforced by General Jesús González Ortega, who was in command after the untimely death of Zaragoza. A two-month siege with heavy bombardment finally forced the defenders to surrender, and the way was open to Mexico City. President Juárez, who had made preparations for the capital's defense, realized the hopelessness of the situation and fled north with his cabinet and remnants of the republican army.

Meeting no opposition, the French army entered Mexico City, where the Gallic commander organized a provisional government. The junta that emerged selected for its executive a triumvirate composed of two conservative generals, Juan Almonte and José Salas, and the archbishop-designate, Pelagio Labastida. Then the junta appointed 215 Mexican citizens, all residents of the capital, who would join with them to constitute an "Assembly of Notables" which would determine the future government of the country. After a short discussion the Assembly declared that Mexico would thereafter be a hereditary monarchy with a Catholic prince as emperor. Their principal candidate was the Austrian archduke, Ferdinand Maximilian von Hapsburg, who already had been selected by Napoleon III. While a delegation went to offer the crown to Maximilian, the French forces extended their control over Mexico. Opposition by Mexican guerrilla bands was persistent but too scattered to stop the French penetration. Even so, the French never were able to dominate more than a large wedge of the country fanning out from Veracruz, but it included most of the nation's principal cities. The dwindling forces of Juárez retreated to the northern desert provinces, while those of Porfirio Díaz operated in the south.

Meanwhile, diplomatic maneuvering in Europe prepared the way for Mexico's Second Empire. In October, 1863, Maximilian accepted the offer of a crown on the condition that it be approved by the Mexican people. Marshal Achille Bazaine, the new French commander in Mexico, engineered a plebiscite, and to no one's surprise, the referendum indicated overwhelming approval of the Austrian archduke. In April, 1864, at Maximilian's castle overlooking the Adriatic Sea, his agent and one from Napoleon III signed the Treaty of Miramar, which detailed the relationship between the empires of France and Mexico. It specified that Mexico would pay the costs of the French military expedition: 270,000,000 francs to July 1864, and after that date one thousand francs a year for each man. Regular French troops were to be evacuated as soon as Maximilian could organize a Mexican imperial army, but the French Foreign Legion of eight thousand men was to remain in Mexico for at least six years. In addition, France demanded that Mexico pay all the claims of French subjects and indemnify them for any wrongs they might have suffered. By ratifying this treaty Maximilian tripled Mexico's foreign debt.

Before sailing for Mexico in April, 1864, Maximilian and

Maximilian, the Austrian-born emperor of Mexico. Courtesy The Bancroft Library.

his wife Carlota—Marie Charlotte Amélie, daughter of the king and queen of Belgium and cousin of Queen Victoria of Great Britain—paid a farewell visit to relatives and friends in Vienna. A crisis developed when Austrian Emperor Francis Joseph required his younger brother, Maximilian, to sign a document renouncing all claims to the Austrian throne, and Carlota had to give up certain privileges and income due her as an Austrian duchess. Then the royal couple visited Rome, where they received the personal blessings of Pope Pius IX; Maximilian declared his loyalty to the Church and its principles, but he also confessed his moderate liberalism. Finally, they boarded the Austrian frigate *Novara* and arrived at Veracruz on May 28, 1864. Two weeks later Mexico's new emperor and empress made a triumphal entry into their capital, Mexico City.

Maximilian was thirty-two and Carlota twenty-four when they began their tragic Mexican adventure. He was an impressive figure: tall, handsome, fair-skinned, and full-bearded —in a way he was another "fair god" in the tradition of Quetzalcoatl or Cortés. Carlota was brooding, haughty, and high-strung; although she was of average height for a European woman, she rose above any crowd of *Mexicanas*. The imperial couple established their residence at Chapultepec Castle, which had been built in the eighteenth century as a viceregal palace and was later used as a military academy. During Maximilian's reign it was the focus of court life, although some state functions and balls were held at the National Palace that fronted on the *zócalo* or main plaza. An American guest described one of the frequently-held grand balls:

The invitation, in French, was in the name of the Empress. It bore the Imperial arms, and was left at the hotel by a liveried messenger from the palace.... The Belgian sentinal saluted us as we passed the principal gateway and fell in with the stream of fashionable humanity....

Presentations over, the master of ceremonies and his attendants were actively engaged preparing for the formal opening of the ball, and presently the crash of a German band was the welcome signal.

Empress Carlota, a tragic figure. Courtesy The Bancroft Library.

Far as the eye could reach down the bright vista, uniforms and rich dresses flashed and floated, multiplied everywhere in the numerous mirrors, presenting a picture not less strange than captivating. But the centre of attraction was the Empress. On the eastern side of the hall a throne had been erected, where, seated in state, and supported by her ladies, she awaited the forming of the sets. It was, of course, the privilege of royalty to select its own partner, and [José Fernando] Ramírez, formerly an influential Liberal, but now Minister of State under the Empire, was honored with the choice.... Upon her being again seated, the early formalities of the ball yielded to the round dances, and the waltz, schottische and redowa were in full blast, upborne on the wind of the great orchestra.... There were present perhaps a thousand persons, among them almost everybody of note or distinction in the city. Officers of several national armies were represented.... and ambassadors accredited from every great Power in Europe.*

Maximilian and Carlota were charmed by Mexico and seemed genuinely interested in developing the country. They spoke Spanish whenever possible, traveled through many provinces, often wore regional costumes, served Mexican food, and the childless couple adopted Agustín Iturbide, a grandson of Mexico's first emperor, hoping thereby to continue the dynasty. The imperial couple tried to inspire a literary, artistic, and scientific revival. They sponsored architectural renovation, cultural societies, and scientific reconnaissance of their domain. Maximilian wanted to expand industry and build railroads—only a small part of Mexico's first rail line from Veracruz to Mexico City, begun in 1837, had actually been constructed—so he put men to work building trestles and laying tracks. He also encouraged immigration from Europe, Asia, and Africa and actively recruited hundreds of former Confederates who fled the southern United States with their Negro slaves when the Confederacy collapsed. His policy of restoring slavery, euphemistically called "black peonage labor," was reactionary, but in other spheres the Mexican emperor was a moderate liberal.

*William V. Wells, "A Court Ball at the Palace of Mexico," *The Overland Monthly* (Aug. 1868), 1:107–108, 110.

Maxmilian's attitude toward the Church disappointed the conservatives, although it paralleled the French army's liberal position. Marshall Bazaine had followed Napoleon's orders of July, 1863: "Do not become reactionary; do not retract the sale of clerical property." When the military commander forced the rock-bound archbishop out of the governing regency, the prelate excommunicated the entire French occupation army. Maximilian stepped into this impasse and soon became disillusioned by what he saw and heard of the reactionary Mexican clergy. He tried to arrange a concordat with the Vatican, but the ultra-conservative pope and his nuncio would not compromise their position. After weeks of fruitless negotiation, the Mexican emperor finally unilaterally issued a series of decrees that defined the Church-state relationship in his empire.

The major points of Maximilian's ecclesiastical decrees, published in February, 1865, were the following: Roman Catholicism was recognized as the state religion, but all other sects would be tolerated; sales of Church property that already had taken place were confirmed; those sales that were irregular in any way were to be reviewed by the office of nationalized property and would be validated if they met legal tests; Church entities were to show religiously valid cause for retaining lands that the republic had declared liable for nationalization; and the Church could acquire no additional property. In effect, these decrees confirmed the Reform Laws of a decade earlier. If Maximilian's policy was designed to win over liberals to the empire, it did not have that effect; at the same time it alienated conservatives and churchmen, especially Pope Pius IX.

In the field of foreign relations Maximilian's empire secured recognition by the Holy See and twenty-one European states, mostly monarchies, plus Russia and Turkey, but it failed to establish diplomatic ties with either the American government in Washington or the Confederate States of America. President Lincoln's government supported the nomadic Mexican republic through the entire period—even after the imperialists had forced Benito Juárez and his ragtag army to the northern border at El Paso del Norte (later renamed Ciudad Juárez). In an effort at domestic concilia-tion Maximilian released all political prisoners serving terms less than ten years, and he offered important positions to liberals, including Juárez. The Indian president scorned any cooperation with the European invaders, but some of his former supporters accepted appointments in the Mexican imperial government.

The peak of the French intervention was reached in 1865 when all of the provincial capitals flew the imperial flag. By April, Marshal Bazaine commanded sixty thousand troops; half were French, two-fifths were Mexican, and the remainder were Austrian and Belgian. To put an end to the constant harassment of his forces by irregular guerrilla bands and remnants of the republican army, Bazaine wanted to treat them as outlaws. For some time Maximilian resisted this course, hoping to win over his domestic enemies, but finally, on October 3, 1865, he signed the famous "Black Flag Decree," which was published in Spanish and Nahuatl and posted throughout the kingdom. It mandated that any person caught bearing arms against the empire be executed within twenty-four hours. The same fate was set for "all persons belonging to armed bands or corps, not legally authorized, whether they proclaim or not any political principles." Almost immedi-ately a number of republicans, including two generals, were caught and executed without a trial. This extreme measure failed in its purpose—instead of weakening the opponents, it intensified their hostility, and it cost the emperor support of many moderate Mexicans. It was also one of the factors that ultimately led to Maximilian's own fate.

During the second half of 1865 the Juarista forces were gaining strength, while various props supporting the Mexi-can empire were weakened. After the termination of the American Civil War and the end of the embargo on arms exports, tons of surplus military equipment were transferred to the Mexican republican forces on the border, and about three thousand discharged veterans of the Union army went to Mexico and joined Juárez's forces. Meanwhile, the Mexican imperial army, reinforced by two thousand former Confederate soldiers, was not being paid. The treasury was empty, all customhouse receipts were in control of the French, and Napoleon III declared that he would not provide additional credit. Furthermore, the French emperor was under pressure to recall his expeditionary army — French intellectuals and members of the Chamber of Deputies protested the costly and bloody campaign, the United States government insisted on a pullout, and the rapid rise of Prussia as a power and threat made it urgent that the French army be concentrated and strengthened at home. In January, 1866, Napoleon announced that all his forces would be withdrawn from Mexico in three detachments or phases, beginning that year.

Shocked by Napoleon's determination to abandon them, Maximilian and Carlota wrote urgent letters to him and to Empress Eugénie imploring them to reverse the decision. When that produced no results, Carlota decided to go to Europe to beg for assistance. She left Mexico in July, 1866. In Paris her impassioned pleas were not successful, so she decided to visit the Holy Father. On the way to Rome the first symptoms of her psychosis were noted — she complained that Napoleon's agents were trying to poison her. At the Vatican it became apparent that she was mentally unbalanced, and the terrible news was cabled to Maximilian and to her brother, the king of the Belgians. Carlota was taken to Belgium, where she lived on for sixty years hopelessly insane, never realizing that her consort had reached an equally tragic end.

Maximilian vacillated about whether he should abdicate, a policy urged by the French, or remain in Mexico as advised by his mother, who reminded him of "his duties as a Hapsburg." Grief-stricken by Carlota's condition and ill himself from recurrent fevers, in October, 1866, he decided to take up residence in tropical Orizaba, two-thirds of the way to Veracruz. At that port two Austrian warships were loaded with thousands of crates containing the Mexican imperial archives, household furnishings, and personal effects of the royal couple. And Prince Agustín Iturbide was sent back to his mother in Europe. While resting in Orizaba, Maximilian spent most of the days netting and mounting butterflies for his collection. Finally, at the end of the year, various conservatives, including Generals Miramón and Márquez and the German Jesuit Father Augustín Fischer, who had become the emperor's advisor, persuaded Maximilian to remain in Mexico and return to the capital.

In mid-January, 1867, an Assembly of Notables was convoked in the imperial palace of Mexico to determine the future of the nation. Although Maximilian did not attend, all his ministers were there; so were Marshal Bazaine, the archbishop, General Márquez, Father Fischer, and other leaders. Speaking first, Bazaine reported that as soon as French troops had withdrawn from various cities, republicans had occupied them. He saw no chance for the emperor's survival after the imminent departure of the remaining French troops; thus he urged Maximilian to abdicate and leave Mexico. The archbishop refused to commit himself on this issue, but two-thirds of those present voted in favor of continuing the empire. Of course their positions and personal security depended on the monarchy. About this time Maximilian and Bazaine broke off relations; they refused to speak or communicate with each other thereafter. About 350 Austrians and a larger number of French soldiers chose to become Mexican subjects and stay in the country, but all the other foreign troops were evacuated by mid-March of 1867.

In February, Maximilian rode north to Querétaro and took command of the main element of his imperial army. The garrison of about nine thousand men was soon surrounded by Juarista armies that converged on the city and besieged its defenders. By then the empire controlled only four isolated cities, Veracruz, Puebla, Mexico City, and Querétaro. At the end of March, twelve hundred cavalrymen under General Márquez managed to slip through the lines and ride to Mexico City, where they were supposed to procure money and reinforcements to break the siege. However, Márquez traitorously remained in the capital, assumed supreme power, and instituted a "reign of terror" marked by forced loans, arbitrary arrests, and lavish decorations bestowed on his favorites. When Querétaro fell on May 15, Maximilian and all his troops in that city became prisoners of the republican forces under General Mariano Escobedo. Because the emperor had been captured in uniform and armed, it was decided that he must stand a military trial.

During the month between his surrender and his trial, Maximilian was confined in a former convent in Querétaro. There he conferred with European diplomats about his legal defense, dictated a codicil to his will, and was involved in a complicated escape plan. A central figure in this fantastic scheme was Princess Agnes zu Salm-Salm, a Vermont-born woman who had married a Prussian prince; together they had arrived at Maximilian's court in 1866 and had accompanied him to Querétaro. The princess's role was to bribe key republican officers to permit the escape, but her failure to seduce a certain Colonel Palacios resulted in frustration of the plot and her own arrest.

The court-martial of Maximilian and his captured generals, Miramón and Mejía, took place in a Querétaro theater in mid-June, 1867. Seven republican army officers presided over the trial and acted as judges. Pleading illness, Maximilian was excused from attending the proceedings; his defense attorneys questioned the court's jurisdiction to try the emperor, and they asked for clemency, assuring that if he were permitted to leave the country, he would never again set foot in Mexico. Among the thirteen charges leveled against Maximilian, the most important was his infamous decree of October, 1865, which had resulted in the death of many Mexicans. After two days of testimony the court pronounced a verdict of guilty and by a close vote sentenced the three prisoners to death. In spite of dozens of pleas to spare his life—telegraphed to President Juárez from abroad and from Washington—Maximilian was executed by a firing squad in the early morning of June 19, 1867. It is an interesting coincidence that Mexico's great Indian president, Benito Juárez, was at least indirectly responsible for the death of Maximilian, a lineal descendant of Charles V, in whose service Hernán Cortés had put to death the Mexican Indian emperor, Cuauhtemoc.

Mexico's second empire collapsed with the death of Maximilian, and the following month Juárez entered Mexico City in his simple black coach. (Today that vehicle sits alongside the emperor's ornate gilded carriage in the National Museum of History at Chapultepec Castle.) One of the first tasks of the president was to regularize his position. His term had expired in 1865, and because of the impossibility of holding elections then, he had declared that he would continue in office for the duration of the war. In the elections of October, 1867, Juárez was elected for a third term. His dedication to the Constitution and his resistance to foreign domination had made him a hero and a symbol of national unity.

Mexican scholars acknowledge that the liberal-republican victory of 1867 marks the beginning of a new era in their nation's history, and they call the first decade of this period the "Restored Republic." Juárez and his followers began to rebuild the nation, which had been shattered by ten years of war. The reconstruction took place in various spheres, political, economic, and cultural. In order to lessen military influence, the civilian president reduced the size of the army from sixty thousand to twenty thousand men. That action embittered many high ranking officers, and of course it swelled the unemployment figures, but it did subordinate the armed forces and it decreased national expenditures. By creating and supporting the *rurales,* a national rural police force modeled on the Spanish Guardia Civil, the Juárez administration curtailed banditry and made highway travel safer. Conspicuous in their handsome uniforms, mounted *rurales* watched the stage lines and guarded shipments of merchandise; their presence aided commerce and industry.

Reviving the national economy was a high priority of the Restored Republic. José Iglesias, who served as secretary of the treasury to 1869, and his successor, the brilliant Matías Romero, planned and directed the economic recovery program. They reduced the national debt to a fifth of its postwar figure, revised tax and tariff structures, spurred revitalization and modernization of the mining industry, and promoted expanded planting of the chief agricultural exports: tobacco, cacao, vanilla, coffee, sugar, and cotton. Convinced that the modernization of their country depended upon foreign capital and technology, the governing liberal elite encouraged foreign capitalists to invest in Mexico, and they granted concessions for petroleum exploration, fishing rights, telegraph and steamship lines, and railroad construction.

The Juárez administration continued to subsidize construction of the *Ferrocarril Mexicano* (Mexican Railroad), which was to link the capital with Veracruz, the principal port connecting Mexico with the outside world. Renewal of the concession held by a British company brought on criticism of Juárez because it violated a law that cancelled concessions with companies or individuals who had dealt with Maximilian's empire. But the president said that the project was more important than partisan politics. When the rail line was finally opened on January 1, 1873, Archbishop Labastida attended the public ceremony and gave his blessing. His presence signified an improvement in Church-state relations.

Orders of nuns and priests traditionally had maintained Mexico's schools, but their suppression by the government had created an educational vacuum. Juárez and his advisors attempted to establish a new system of public education because they believed that material progress and the effective functioning of democracy depended on widespread literacy. They selected Gabino Barreda as head of a commission to organize secular instruction at all levels. Barreda, a physician and professor of anatomy, had studied in Paris under Auguste Comte, founder of the system of Positivism, and he brought to Mexico the new emphasis on physics, mathematics, and natural science. The commission sponsored several laws that, for the first time in Mexico, made elementary education free and compulsory; one law required all towns with over five hundred people to have primary schools. Among the new government-sponsored secondary schools was one in Mexico City for young ladies and another, called the National

Preparatory School, which opened in February, 1868, under the direction of Barreda. Although primary schooling was declared to be compulsory, the law was seldom enforced, and universal education remained a goal rather than a reality.

Juaréz's hope for a democratic society operating under the Constitution of 1857 was thwarted by insurrections, Indian unrest, and the existence of regional *caudillos,* such as Manuel Lozada of Nayarit, who had private armies and would not submit to a federal system that might decrease their power or tenure. To cope with these problems the president was forced to use "less than democratic" methods. For example, he suspended constitutional guarantees. His arbitrary actions caused some of his contemporaries (and a few historians) to accuse him of dictatorship, and the controversy resulted in a split within the liberal faction.

Juárez was frustrated not only by traditional enemies but also by the political ambitions of erstwhile colleagues and supporters. His former student from Oaxaca, General Porfirio Díaz, became a rival in 1867 and opposed the president in the election of that year. Four years later, when Juárez announced his determination to seek a fourth presidential term, Díaz, by then retired from the army, again became a candidate and accused the president of seeking dictatorship and violating his own principles. Juárez, who had succumbed to a passion for politics and desire for power, claimed that his continuance in office was necessary in order to preserve the liberal reforms in the face of internal disorders. Sebastián Lerdo de Tejada, until then the president's closest associate for more than a decade, also campaigned for the highest office. One observer cleverly remarked that "Juárez believed he was indispensible, while Lerdo regarded himself as infallible and Díaz as inevitable." When no one candidate received a clear majority, the election devolved on Congress, which determined Juárez to be the winner, and second-place Lerdo then became president of the Supreme Court. But Díaz, who garnered only three congressional votes, disputed the outcome.

In November, 1871, Porfirio Díaz and his followers declared

a revolt under their Plan of La Noria, named for the general's hacienda near the city of Oaxaca. Accusing the Juárez government of dictatorship and of rigging the vote, they called for "free and honest elections." Although Díaz was supported by Indian strongman Manuel Lozada and other regional *caciques*, the revolution was not successful. With the sudden death of President Juárez on July 18, 1872, the movement lost its *raison d'être* and it sputtered out.

Benito Juárez was a unique and majestic figure in many ways. His transition from illiterate, Indian shepherd boy to the first magistrate of the nation was most remarkable in a society with vestiges of a class system. Another unusual aspect was that he was a civilian in a period plagued by civil wars and foreign intervention when most of the principal leaders wore military uniforms. As a lawyer and statesman he distinguished himself by defending the Constitution, and like his contemporary, Abraham Lincoln, he preserved the republic in time of great danger. Lincoln's secretary of state, William H. Seward, who was acquainted with many of the most distinguished men of his age, visited Mexico in the fall of 1869 and, in a speech in Puebla, declared that Juárez was the greatest man he had ever met in his life.

The Zapotec president's inspired leadership and popularity generated a resurgence of Indianism that caused many Mexicans to appreciate their Indian ancestry. That this nativist and nationalistic movement was reflected in the arts is verified by many examples, including the following: Alfredo Chavero, a leading literary figure of the period, wrote a three-act dramatic tribute to the Aztecs entitled *Quetzalcoatl;* about the same time musical composer Aniceto Ortega wrote the short opera "Guatimotzín" (Cuauhtemoc), which premiered in September, 1871; and José María Velasco, the preeminent Mexican landscape painter of the nineteenth century, depicted Indians and *mestizos* in dozens of his large canvases.

With the death of Juárez in 1872, Sebastián Lerdo de Tejada became interim president; then in October he won 93 percent of the votes when he ran against Porfirio Díaz. President

Lerdo retained most appointees of his predecessor and continued Juárez's policies: enforcing the Constitution, attacking remnants of privilege in society, expanding education, pacification of regional chiefs (Manuel Lozada was captured and shot), and unification of the nation through improved communications. Contracts were let for construction of several new rail lines, notably the Mexican Central Railroad, which ran north from the capital to the United States border, and the Isthmus of Tehuantepec line, which would cross Mexico from the Gulf to the Pacific. In an attempt to link all the state capitals with the metropolis, more than twenty-five hundred kilometers (sixteen hundred miles) of telegraph wire were strung during these years.

Lerdo backed two significant political reforms that were approved by Congress. First, he proposed that the unicameral legislature be changed to a two-house system, and in 1875 a Senate was added to the Chamber of Deputies. The president hoped that this modification would aid executive influence on Congress and further his goal of centralization. Also in 1875, the Reform Laws, which affected Church-state relations, were incorporated into the Constitution; thus they became basic law of the land.

Lerdo's intransigence toward Church control of what he considered state functions led him in 1874 to expel the last remaining order of nuns, the Sisters of Charity. Members of that order had operated various shelters and schools. One of their largest and most successful establishments was a hospice in Guadalajara that had been founded about 1796 by Bishop Juan Cruz Ruiz Cabañas. An American who visited the Hospicio Cabañas in 1870 was impressed by the structure itself, which covered "six or eight acres of ground," and he left a record of what went on inside:

This establishment . . . now holds within its walls sixteen hundred human beings, from the foundling just brought in from the street to the young woman or man ready to go forth into the world as a teacher, artizan, house-servant husband or wife. It is superintended by the Sisters of Charity of whom there are some twenty in the establishment, and managed with an amount of economy and skill wonderful to witness. In its sixteen different departments it is at once a foundling hospital, reform school, juvenile school, orphan asylum, asylum for the aged and indigent, boy's and girl's high school, school of arts, workshop, college and hospital.

In one department we saw thirty foundlings, two of which had just been brought in. . . . They are neatly dressed, nursed by Indian women, and well cared for. In another ward were one hundred and five boys, arrested by the police as vagabonds on the streets and sent here to be reformed. They were drilling as soldiers when we came in. The City pays six and one quarter cents each, per day, for the support of these boys, and they all have to learn useful trades before leaving the institution. I noticed many among the children who had lost one or both eyes, and was told that in the Indian villages it is not uncommon for the parents to thus mutilate their children in infancy, to fit them for begging, or to enable them to avoid military duty. . . .

In another ward, two hundred children, between two and five years of age, one hundred boys and one hundred girls, belonging to parents too poor even to dress them, were being taught orally. . . . All the cloth for the clothing of the pupils is made within its walls, and all the clothing, and boots and shoes required, are made up by the boys and girls. . . .

We spent four hours wandering through this great establishment, and after partaking of a collation, listened to a brass band of thirty pieces, played by boys instructed in the place, and operatic music by the young ladies, and then left because night had come and we could wait no longer.*

Many of President Lerdo's policies and actions—such as expulsion of the nuns—were unpopular, and he was criticized severely by the press; nevertheless, he determined to seek re-election in 1876. Early that year Porfirio Díaz and his supporters launched a revolt and issued the Plan of Tuxtepec, which called for no re-election of the president and state governors. Various generals supported Díaz, while others remained loyal to Lerdo; their skirmishes took place from Nuevo León to Oaxaca. In the fall, when Congress

*Albert S. Evans, *Our Sister Republic: A Gala Trip Through Tropical Mexico in 1869-70* (Hartford: Columbian Book Co.; 1870), 123–26.

recognized the electoral triumph of Lerdo, the president of the Supreme Court, José María Iglesias, announced that the re-election was "null because of fraudulence," and he declared his own rebellion, hoping to overthrow Lerdo and gain the presidency himself. General Díaz was the victor of this three-way struggle. After his troops defeated government forces at the Battle of Tecoac, Lerdo and Iglesias sought exile in the United States. Once again Mexico was in the hands of a *caudillo* who had come to power through revolution.

CHAPTER 9

The Age of Porfirio Díaz

THE COUP D'ETAT that brought Porfirio Díaz to the presidency in 1876 ended a long period of governmental instability and ushered in a generation of political peace. During the nation's first fifty-five years of independence, Mexican governments had lasted less than a year on the average, and only two administrations completed their full term. Díaz not only concluded his first presidential period, but after a lapse of four years he served six additional terms, giving him a total of more than thirty years in the highest office. Such a remarkable record suggests that it was achieved by an exceptional individual—an astute and tenacious man.

Porfirio Díaz Mory was forty-six years old when he took control of Mexico in 1876. Born in the city of Oaxaca, to a family of modest means, he was of mixed Spanish and Mixtec ancestry. Like his older acquaintance Benito Juárez he began studies for the priesthood but left the seminary to pursue a law career. Díaz did not finish law school, and during the War of Reform he found his true vocation, the army; while aiding the liberals in their struggle he rose from the rank of captain to colonel. Promoted to general during the French intervention, he was one of the heroes of the *cinco de mayo* battle. He was twice captured by the invaders, but escaped and led troops that liberated Oaxaca (October 1866), Puebla (April 1867), and Mexico City (June 1867) from the imperialist armies. Soon after the end of that war he retired from the army and moved to La Noria, an hacienda given him by supporters in the state of Oaxaca.

By 1870, Díaz had become involved in national politics, first as a member of Congress representing his district of Oaxaca. In 1872, as a liberal, he opposed the re-election of

257

President Juárez and led an unsuccessful rebellion; later that year, after the sudden death of the popular Indian president, Díaz was defeated in his electoral bid for the presidency. Four years later, against Lerdo de Tejada he raised the cry: "effective suffrage and no re-election," and by the military revolt of Tuxtepec forced President Lerdo to abandon his office and the country. After seizing power, Díaz called for a special election in May, 1877, that resulted in his being chosen as president for a four-year term. At that time the general was popular; for more than twenty years he had backed liberal principles, he was a military hero, and his *mestizo* background earned him considerable support, as did his image as a *macho* (virile, masculine) leader.

Beginning with his first presidential period, Díaz consolidated his personal power and worked to extend his tenure. He carefully masked his maneuvers and appeared to operate in conformity with the Constitution and other laws. Although he had been an advocate of "no re-election," Díaz wanted more than one term, so he subtly promoted modification of the electoral laws. In 1878 a constitutional amendment was enacted that prohibited immediate re-election but permitted it after a lapse, and in 1880 the wily politician stepped aside while General Manuel González, his friend and client, assumed the presidency for one term. González's administration was marred by financial arrangements that almost bankrupted the country and by scandals involving his friends and cabinet members, so in 1884 the "indispensable" Díaz was returned to the presidency. Three years later he sponsored a law that permitted one immediate re-election, and in 1890 a constitutional amendment abolished all limits on presidential terms. Finally, in 1904, the chief executive's term was extended to six years. Thus, Díaz's ambition to remain in power was paralleled by removal of legal barriers.

As president of the nation, Díaz worked to establish internal stability and stimulate economic growth. He and his advisors proclaimed that order and progress were inseparable, and they maintained that unifying and modernizing their country would have the additional benefit of fortifying it against

General Porfirio Díaz, the durable dictator. Courtesy Instituto Nacional de Antropología e Historia.

encroachment by the powerful neighbor to the north. Díaz is reported to have said, "Poor Mexico, so far from God and so close to the United States!" To put an end to civil discord, Díaz became the national *cacique* who reconciled by force the disparate elements; if they would not accommodate, they were extinguished or expelled from the country. Thus he became a dictator whose apologists justified the authoritarianism by pointing to the nation's past history of anarchy and regional *caciques;* they said that "Mexico was not ready for democracy."

During the years of his presidency, called the Porfiriato by Mexicans, Díaz cleverly created a "constitutional dictatorship"—a despotic regime that functioned behind a façade of legality. Using his power of appointment, control of the political party apparatus, his affiliations within the career army officer corps, the police and *rurales,* and the *cacique* structure of provincial Mexico, he was able to impose his will on the Congress, the state governors, and the judiciary. Civil service rolls were expanded by 900 percent from 1876 to 1910, while government employees and other citizens became dependent on the executive for their jobs and even for their freedom.

Díaz's policy of *pan o palo,* (bread or the stick) rewarded those who conformed to the regime and punished those who opposed it. A number of critics lost their positions, some were imprisoned or exiled, and not a few suffered fatal "accidents." The *ley fuga* (fugitive law) also claimed its victims, persons who were reported as "shot while trying to escape." Other nonconformists were conscripted involuntarily into the army or forced into labor gangs that worked on huge plantations. Treatment of the press during the era illustrates the "cooperate or else" policy. Editors who praised the chief and defended his policies were subsidized. One example was Rafael Reyes Spindola, director of the important daily newspaper *El Imparcial,* who received about fifty thousand pesos annually. Newspapers that opposed the regime were suppressed; among them were *El Universal, El Monitor Republicano, La Humanidad, El Debate,* and *Diario del Hogar.*

As in most dictatorships, control of the military forces was a crucial element. Díaz favored a small, disciplined and professional army that would depend exclusively on the central government and whose forces would be scattered throughout the country. By 1910, army numbers had been reduced to thirty thousand. While insuring the loyalty of the officers through generous pay, pensions, and other benefits, he controlled appointments to key positions and frequently shifted regional commanders to prevent their building a local power base. Some potential rivals were assigned duties as attachés or diplomats at overseas capitals where they no longer were a threat.

As a counterweight to the army, Díaz expanded and strengthened the corps of federal rural police, the *rurales*. The mission of this unit was to maintain order in the countryside, where most of the population lived, and it became an enforcement tool of executive policy. An American who spent a few years on a coffee *finca* (farm) near Jalapa had the following to say about order and security during the Porfiriato:

Besides the small but businesslike policemen with large, visible revolvers who seem to be on every corner and who materialize in swarms at the slightest infringement of the code, the highways are patrolled by that picturesque body of men known as rurales, of whom there are between four and five thousand. . . . Under President Díaz they have attained a high degree of efficiency, and while their practically limitless powers in isolated and inaccessible parts of the country are no doubt sometimes abused, their reputation for fearlessness, supplemented by a revolver, a carbine, and a saber, has a most chastening influence."[*]

The same author also commented that "The frequency of the policemen is equaled (or exceeded, one sometimes feels) only by the frequency of the churches."

The Catholic Church was another element upon which Díaz

---

[*]Charles Macomb Flandreau, *Viva Mexico!* (New York: D. Appleton and Company, 1908), 270–71.

A member of the Rurales *(Rural Guards). Courtesy The Bancroft Library.*

depended for support. In return for a conciliatory state policy, the hierarchy, priests, and religious newspapers were expected to favor the regime. Liberal legislation of *La Reforma* remained the law of the land, but those laws that were antagonistic to the Church were not enforced, and the anticlerical spirit of government officials diminished. Some writers have credited Díaz's pious second wife, Carmen Romero Rubio, with influencing her husband to seek a Church-state reconciliation. Whatever the cause, during the Díaz era the Church enjoyed a comeback.

Statistics for the period between 1876 and 1910 indicate that the national population increased by 62 percent (9,500,000 to 15,200,000) while the growth of Church personnel and real estate holdings was much greater. During those years the priesthood went from 1,700 to 4,405; the hierarchy grew from 4 to 36. Five new archbishoprics and eight new dioceses were created; Church properties doubled in number and value; the number of buildings used for worship tripled; and the number of Catholic schools increased by six times. Some convents and monasteries were reactivated to serve as schools, orphanages, or charitable institutions, and two new religious orders were established, the Guadalupan Sisters, and Servants of the Sacred Heart of Jesus. This quantitative resurgence was paralleled by an expansion of clerical prestige and influence. Symbolically, whenever Díaz dedicated a government project, a robed priest stood beside him to add his blessing.

New churches, government buildings, and monuments erected in the Díaz era reflected current European fashions— artistically there was a "Europeanization" movement visible throughout the republic. Mansard roofs, Italianate details, Victorian Gothic, and the new use of iron and steel replaced Spanish and Mexican motifs and techniques. Lacy, cast-iron uprights and lintels graced new kiosks in the plazas of dozens of cities, and iron and steel beams spanned large openings in railroad stations and factories. Foreign architects designed three important buildings in Mexico City: the Post Office, built in Italian Renaissance style; the neoclassical Legislative

Díaz era kiosk in the plaza at Puebla.

Palace (its unfinished dome later converted to the Monument to the Revolution); and the National Theater, now called the Palace of Fine Arts. Marble for the latter structure was imported from Italy even though Mexico has great quantities of marble; the twenty-two-ton glass curtain for the stage was designed and made in the United States by Tiffany; and structural steel members were imported, as were mechanical devices such as passenger elevators. The Díaz regime's downgrading of things Mexican and widespread adoption of foreign values permeated the fine arts and even the clothes and manners of the elite.

Painting, sculpture, and music during the Porfiriato imitated patterns from across the Atlantic. Except for *costumbrista* (genre) canvases, most Mexican paintings resembled those done in France or Italy; one painter, Germán Gedovius, even did a self-portrait in the clothing and manner of Rembrandt. The numerous busts and statues commissioned to commemorate national or cultural heroes followed the European fashion. Two notable examples were statues of Benito Juárez—one in the Alameda park in Mexico City, and the other a large marble figure in Oaxaca that was sculpted by an Italian who never knew Juárez or visited Mexico. Foreign music and dances also were copied. An Otomí Indian, Juventino Rosas, in 1891 composed the famous set of waltzes *"Sobre las Olas"* (Over the Waves), and other Mexicans wrote lyrics and music for operas that were sung in Italian and portrayed Classical themes.

Most of the literature produced during the Porfiriato turned its back on native traditions—indeed, writers like Francisco Bulnes (1847-1924) scorned Indians and ridiculed Mexico's national heroes. The most important literary development was a new movement called *Modernismo;* eventually embraced throughout Latin America and Spain, it was exotic, artificial, and based on French models. Identified with Modernism were three of Mexico's best poets: Manuel Gutiérrez Nájera (1859-95), who used more than twenty pseudonyms and founded the literary journal *Revista Azul;* Enrique Gonzáles Martínez (1871-1952), who attained renown through employing the poetic symbols of the swan and owl; and Amado Nervo (1870–1919), an early editor of *Revista Moderna*, who entered the diplomatic service in 1906 and subsequently published most of his poetry abroad.

Justo Sierra (1848–1912) was a leading journalist-historian-educator of the era. He was sub-secretary of Public Instruction in 1901 and four years later became head of that department, where one of his great accomplishments was refounding the National University, which had been dormant for forty years. Although Sierra urged his disciples to study French literature, he himself wrote a great synthesis of Mexican history that emphasized the role of the *mestizos*. Printed in Mexico in 1910, it was later translated into English and published as *The Political Evolution of the Mexican People*. Sierra was the only member of Díaz's cabinet who openly questioned the positivist orientation of the dictator's chief advisors.

Positivism, the system of philosophy developed by Auguste Comte, permeated intellectual and ruling circles in the Díaz era. Its theme of "Order and Progress" neatly dovetailed with the goals of Díaz and his cohorts, and it provided justification for the dictatorship. Members of an influential group of positivist adherents, some of whom were cabinet members, became known as *científicos* (scientists), because they emphasized using science, statistics, and sociology to attain positive knowledge, achieve material progress, and solve problems, even social problems. An important leader of this group was José I. Limantour, a financial genius who served as secretary of treasury after 1893. He subscribed to the theory that "liberty constituted a privilege of the select; the weak would have to yield to the superior men." Along with other Mexican positivists he was influenced by the Social Darwinism popularized by Herbert Spencer.

Científicos justified the regime's hostile policy toward Indians by citing "Survival of the Fittest" doctrines. Not only were the Indians downgraded racially, but their lands were taken by *mestizo* and *criollo hacendados*. When the *Ley Lerdo* was enforced against remaining communal tribal lands, the former *ejido* farmers were reduced to peonage. In the northwest state of Sonora dozens of bands and settlements of Yaqui and Mayo Indians resisted white encroachment on their tribal lands, but army campaigns between 1885 and 1909 forced many of them to submit; others were killed in battle, and thousands were transported forcibly to Yucatán, where they were sold as laborers on henequen plantations that supplied twine to the world. Similar military actions reduced groups of unintegrated Maya Indians in the Yucatán peninsula. Mexico's government leaders saw this as progress.

Those who consider the Porfiriato a highly successful period are impressed by the economic and financial statistics. When Díaz first took office, the nation was virtually bankrupt (some historians accuse his predecessor, Lerdo, of looting the treasury); by 1895 there was a surplus of $2 million, which increased to $62 million by 1910. In the same period the value of exports and imports increased fivefold to $500 million pesos. Moreover, the government paid off its past foreign debts, established a banking system, simplified and modernized tax collection, and created a sound international credit reputation.

The combination of internal security, government concessions and subsidies, cheap and docile labor, and the natural resources of the country attracted many North American and European capitalists to Mexico. By 1910, foreign investments amounted to about $2 billion dollars, half from the United States. This outside capital and its concomitant technology spawned significant development and material progress in Mexico, and of course it also generated vast profits for the foreign investors. Under Díaz, foreigners were assured of definite and generous returns; they also enjoyed tax exemptions and were given protection in the courts. Some critics remarked that "Mexico had become a mother to aliens and stepmother to her own citizens." In an effort to keep American capitalists from gaining supremacy, concessions also were granted to promoters from various European powers. Industrial development was encouraged by the *científicos* who wanted to impose modern capitalism on semi-feudal Mexico. While accomplishing their program, many of them became extremely wealthy through graft or by working closely with the foreign capitalists.

A major achievement of the Díaz era was the construction of an extensive railroad network—from 617 kilometers of rails in 1876 the system expanded to almost 25,000 by 1910. All but six of the state capitals and five of the principal seaports were connected by rail with the national capital. The following major lines were built during the Porfiriato:

1. The Mexican Central (Mexico City to Ciudad Juárez, with branches to Guadalajara, Colima, and Tampico)
2. The Mexican National (Mexico City to Nuevo Laredo, with a branch to Uruapan, Michoacán)
3. The Isthmus (Coatzacoalcos on the Gulf of Mexico to Salina Cruz on the Pacific)
4. The Pan American (Ixtepec, Oaxaca, to Tapachula, Chiapas)
5. The Interoceanic (Veracruz to Mexico City via Jalapa, and projected to Acapulco)
6. The Mexican Southern (Puebla to Oaxaca)
7. The Mexican International (Piedras Negras, Coahuila, south to Durango)
8. The Southern Pacific of Mexico (Nogales, Sonora, down the West Coast to Tepic, Nayarit)

Built with government subsidies, most of the railroads were foreign owned (chiefly by United States banks and holding companies) until 1908, when the Díaz government acquired ownership of more than half of the lines and merged them into the National Railways of Mexico. By comparing Mexico's development with other Latin American countries one sees the importance of the railroad system—it revitalized vast regions of the country, made it possible to market surplus farm goods, and connected the sources of raw material with refineries, ports, and smelters.

Mexico's mining industry was expanded and modernized by an infusion of foreign capital and technology. Besides generous tax exemptions, the extractive concerns benefitted from a change in the mining law authorized by Díaz in 1884. According to this new code, all subsoil deposits belonged to

Railroad train alongside the Querétaro aqueduct. Courtesy Library of Congress.

the owner of the surface; before that date the government (the crown in colonial times) had held title to underground resources and received royalties from their exploitation. Silver production quadrupled during the Porfiriato, and Mexico became the world's second largest copper producer, supplying metal for the booming electric industry. By 1910 more than 3,000 silver, copper, lead, zinc, and iron mines were in full production; new smelters used the cyanide process to separate metals from ore; and more than 100,000 Mexicans were employed in mining. Of the 1,030 mining companies that operated in Mexico in 1910, 840 were North American, 148 Mexican, and the rest British or French.

Three North American companies dominated the mines and smelters of northern Mexico. In 1890, when Daniel Guggenheim secured a concession to build a silver-lead smelter in Monterrey, the city granted "exemption from all municipal and state taxes to the company or companies he may organize, on the capital he may invest in this city." His family's American Smelting and Refining Company soon had mines and smelters in the states of Chihuahua, Durango, Aguas Calientes, and San Luis Potosí. The Montezuma Copper Company, which operated in northern Sonora, was a subsidiary of the vast Phelps Dodge Company, and nearby in Cananea was William C. Greene's Consolidated Copper Company, which in 1906 employed fifty-five hundred men. A few years later Greene's company merged with a larger American mining concern, the Anaconda Copper Company.

Petroleum was another sub-surface mineral that interested foreigners. Exploration began in the 1860s, and for the next forty years more than a hundred prospectors — Mexican and foreign — unsuccessfully drilled wells and attempted to refine oil from the bituminous outcroppings along the Gulf Coast. Finally, in 1901, Edward Doheny, an American who had made a fortune in California oil, acting on the advice of Mexican geologist Ezequiel Ordóñez, struck oil at El Ebano about forty miles west of Tampico. Doheny spent $3 million in the next three years drilling other wells and building a refinery. He also sold asphalt to several Mexican cities for street paving, and he got a contract to supply oil for locomotives of the Mexican Central Railroad. By 1916 his Mexican wells were producing more than a million dollars worth of oil each week. Doheny eventually sold his interests to the Standard Oil Company.

Doheny's petroleum bonanza was soon matched by Weetman Pearson (later knighted as Lord Cowdray), who was head of a British firm that renovated and operated the Isthmus of Tehuantepec Railroad, dredged Veracruz harbor and built new docks there, and constructed the drainage tunnel that freed Mexico City from flooding. Convinced that he could find oil, and aided by the Petroleum Law of 1901, which authorized tax-free entry of machinery, Pearson drilled more than a hundred dry wells before striking oil in 1906 near Tuxpan. A series of gushers made his Águila (Eagle) Petroleum Company the second largest oil producer. By 1910, Mexico's crude oil output averaged ten thousand barrels a day.

Industrial development during the Porfiriato accelerated rapidly as thousands of new factories were established. Furthermore, more than two-thirds of the total new investment came from Mexican capital. The new plants included mills for processing sugar, flour, paper, textiles, and chemicals as well as breweries, glass works, potteries, shoe manufacturies, and cement plants. Although there were iron foundries in Mexico before the Díaz era, the first integrated steel mill in any part of Latin America, Fundidora de Fierro y Acero, was established in Monterrey in 1900, and it began producing three years later. By 1910 the company's annual production was fifty-five thousand tons. This steel mill reflected Mexico's modernization, as did the construction of electrical generating plants and installation of electric lights, streetcars in several cities, and telephones that linked Mexicans with each other and to the world. But this urban and industrial progress scarcely touched the majority of the people — the rural population.

The policies of the Díaz regime impacted negatively on the *campesinos,* or rural folk, who comprised three-fourths of the nation's population. Many small farmers and Indians lost their lands through renewed application of the *Ley Lerdo* or the aggressive policies of *hacendados* or land developers, who, taking advantage of any irregularity of titles, dispossessed the occupants and forced them into peonage. When those who lost land protested, the *rurales* rushed in to "restore order." Unequal distribution of land had been a primary social evil for years, but land ownership became even more concentrated during the Porfiriato. Latifundia increased in number and size — the Terrazas family holdings in Chihuahua totaled over 405,000 hectares (1,000,000 acres), and great haciendas developed with the assistance of new land laws enacted between 1883 and 1894.

A land law of 1888 authorized formation of companies to survey *terrenos baldíos,* unclaimed and vacant lands in the national domain. As compensation the companies received one-third of the area surveyed; the remainder was usually sold by the government at ridiculously low prices to the land companies or to favored individuals. In nine years nearly 40,000,000 hectares (98,840,000 acres) were surveyed and most of the land transferred to a few companies or to private persons. Aliens purchased huge tracts and generally hired foremen to manage the properties in a way to produce maximum profits; this system contributed to anti-foreignism in Mexico.

Statistics on landholding in the Díaz era are astonishing. Between 1883 and 1894, one-fifth of the entire area of the republic was conceded by the administration to a few companies and individuals. By 1910 about eight hundred *hacendados* owned more than 90 percent of the rural land; fewer than 10 percent of the Indian communities had any land; and less than 3 percent of the agricultural population owned any land whatever. The 1910 census revealed that of Mexico's total population of 15,160,000, there were 834 *hacendados* and between 9 and 10 million landless peasants (3,143,271 *peones* and *vaqueros* plus their families). Clearly, the hacienda became the principal form of land tenure; at the same time it was also a social system.

Peons who resided on haciendas (*peones acasillados*) had various arrangements with the owners. Some mainly worked the owner's lands, receiving wages and a dwelling or permission to build a dwelling, and in their spare time could tend small garden plots allotted to them, from which they derived their basic subsistence. A second kind were primarily tenants or sharecroppers, but they also were required to work the owner's portion during part of the year. Cowboys and shepherds were a third type of hacienda peon. Peasants who lived in neighboring villages frequently worked part-time on haciendas, particularly at planting and harvest seasons.

In 1901 an Englishwoman, Ethel Tweedie, visited the hacienda of San Gabriel in the southern part of the state of Morelos. The historic estate was then owned by the Amor family, whose four sons had been educated in England and who maintained a fine stable of thoroughbred race horses. Besides describing the luxurious mansion where "there is always one and sometimes there are two servants allotted to each member of the family," the visitor wrote about the peasants:

The village, containing nearly three thousand souls, belongs to the hacienda. The people pay no rent, and the owners of the hacienda hold the right to turn them out. The peasants are lent the ground on which they build their own houses—such as they are— merely bamboo walls roofed with a palm leaf sort of thatch. They are all obliged to work for the hacienda, in truly feudal style, whenever called upon to do so. Each man as a rule has an allotted number of days on which he is bound to render service. Generally about one thousand people—or one-third of the entire population of the village are constantly employed; but the women in Mexico never work away from their homes, though in busy seasons children, and even old men, are pressed into service to cut the sugar-cane. . . .

As a rule all the employees on the hacienda are paid in cash each Saturday night, and a little on account every Wednesday. . . . A man and his family live on six or eight cents [centavos] a day (a cent is about a farthing), and men earn fifty cents per week on an average. . . . Everyone is paid by the day, and the books are most intricate. An hacienda of this kind is quite a colony, and requires a clever head to manage.

In the evening about sundown all the hands come up from the fields and pass before the book-keeper, who sits behind a large table on the balcony at the bottom of the house stairs, and as he calls out the names each man answers in turn. It naturally takes some time to register one thousand or more names.*

*[Ethel B.] Mrs. Alec Tweedie, *Mexico As I Saw It* (London: Hurst and Blackett, 1901), 338–41.

Recording peons' labor at Hacienda Peotillos, San Luis Potosí. Courtesy Library of Congress.

Conditions of labor on the haciendas varied from one region to another—they were far worse in Yucatán than on the central plateau—yet everywhere there were low wages, a minimum standard of living, and the system of debt peonage. Custom and tradition, rather than law, fixed the obligations for *hacendado* and peon. From time to time the government examined rural working conditions and published reports. The following typical report is from the Department of Pichucalco in the state of Chiapas:*

*Mexico. Secretaría de Fomento, *Informes y documentos relativos a comercio interior y exterior, agricultura e industrias*, no. 6 (Mexico, 1885), 84.

Here the workers are divided into two classes: free laborers and those bound by debt. The first receive 25 *centavos* daily in addition to subsistence, or 38 to 50 *centavos* without it. The laborers bound by debt are those who receive a sum in advance to cover a debt to their former employer, which debt frequently amounts to 500 or more pesos.

The monthly compensation of these laborers is:

Free laborers		Laborers bound by debt	
cash	7.50	cash	4.00
500 ears of corn	3.31	500 ears of corn	3.31
20 pounds of beans	.62	20 pounds of beans	.62
salt	.07	salt	.07
		2 percent interest on half the debt	4.00

To this amount should be added the value of the following:

house rent	1.00	house rent	1.00
medicines given	1.00	medicines given	1.00
garden plots	.33	garden plots	.33
2 bottles alcohol	.25	2 bottles alcohol	.25
Total pesos	$14.08	Total pesos	$14.58

The hacienda system had many inherent evils. Because the mere ownership of land gave prestige, power, and borrowing ability to the *hacendado,* he felt no obligation to utilize all the property. Thus great tracts of arable land lay fallow year after year. Few *hacendados* or their overseers kept abreast of developments in agriculture or ranching; their archaic methods maintained production at a stable level even when population and demand increased. Marketing techniques were little understood by owners or managers. If they had a superabundant harvest one year, the surplus often remained unsold and unutilized. Many *hacendados* were absentee landlords who lived abroad or in provincial capitals, therefore they were unaware of, or insensitive to, the miserable living and working conditions on their property. Wages for peons were the same as they had been for a century, while prices of staple foods and necessities had doubled or tripled. Peons were compelled to buy at the company store where they received credit and typically were in debt. Since they could not leave while owing their employer money, this debt peonage amounted to a kind of serfdom, tying the people to the land. Schools were virtually non-existent on the haciendas, thus the peons and their children were condemned to perpetual illiteracy.

Opportunities for education during the Porfiriato barely kept pace with the population growth. In 1878 there were about five thousand primary schools in the entire nation, with an enrollment of about fifty thousand pupils; by 1910 there were twelve thousand schools with a million students. However, the census of 1910 showed that only one in three children aged six to twelve was enrolled in school, and their attendance record was erratic. This was certainly an inadequate base upon which to build a literate society—in 1910 the illiteracy rate was almost 80 percent. It was much higher in the rural areas than in the cities.

Human degradation and social injustice were common in urban areas as well as in the countryside. Factory workers received more pay than peasants—six to eight pesos a week— but they were obliged to labor twelve to fifteen hours a day, and at times of full production many were not given a day of rest. There were no protective rules for women and children; there was no extra compensation or insurance for hazardous work, job-related accidents, or industrial illnesses. Payroll deductions were made for religious services; workers were obliged to trade at the company store; and many had to live in housing provided at the work site with no space for a garden, chickens, or a cow. Some foreign company compounds had their own police and court system, where Mexican law was secondary to foreign law or company rules.

In spite of harassment and legal obstacles erected by the dictatorship, labor organizers finally succeeded in forming unions and organizing protests against working conditions. Not all labor leaders were affiliated with radical political movements, but some called themselves socialists and others were anarchists who advocated collective ownership of factories and farms. A strong current of anarchism and syndicalism came from Spanish immigrants, whose numbers increased dramatically during the Porfiriato. Between 1880 and 1900 there were seventy-five strikes in the textile industry, sixty in the railroad sector, and thirty-five among tobacco workers. Industrial and agricultural labor strife continued in the first decade of the twentieth century, when it was also influenced by members of the Industrial Workers of the World (IWW), whose aim was "to unite skilled and unskilled workers for the purpose of overthrowing capitalism and rebuilding society on a socialist basis." Mexican government sources attributed the labor unrest to political enemies of Díaz, Marxists, and agitators in the United States.

Foremost among the radical opponents of Díaz were the Flores Magón brothers, Ricardo, Enrique, and Jesús. In 1892, Ricardo Flores Magón was jailed following a student demonstration against the regime; in 1900 he was one of the founders of *Regeneración,* an opposition newspaper that was suppressed by the government; and two years later he edited *El Hijo de Ahuizote,* a periodical that caricatured and ridiculed leading members of the government. The Flores Magón brothers and Camilo Arriaga established Liberal Clubs — eventually there were more than fifty — and were prime movers in the Liberal Party (which was more radical than liberal). Naturally, Díaz moved against these antagonists, imprisoning them several times until in 1903, they sought refuge in the United States. From San Antonio, St. Louis, and later Los Angeles they published *Regeneración* and smuggled thousands of copies into Mexico, where that radical newspaper contributed to the growing anti-Díaz movement.

In July, 1906, the Liberal Party junta in St. Louis issued its Plan, or *Manifiesto.* Abandoning hope of a peaceful electoral change, the group now advocated revolution. Their Plan espoused typical labor demands of that era: an eight-hour work day, a minimum wage, and prohibition of child labor. Provisions to aid the peasants were more radical: creation of an agricultural bank to make low-interest loans to small farmers; cancellation of all debts owed by workers to their employers, the state to confiscate all lands not in production and give them to anyone who applied for them, and "on the triumph of the revolution, confiscation of property acquired by government employees during the dictatorship." Other provisions included abolition of the death penalty, except for treason, and a requirement that foreigners who acquired property in Mexico become citizens. Clearly, some of the demands were in the interest of social justice, but others reflected the radical ideas of the exiled leaders.

After Mexico's ambassador to the United States requested that the Flores Magón coterie be apprehended, the leader, Ricardo, and others were arrested in August, 1907, and imprisoned in Arizona for three years. About the same time, dozens of suspected Mexican revolutionaries in the United States were accused of violation of the neutrality laws and deported across the border. Meanwhile, the impact of *Regeneración* and the work of opponents of the regime led to an escalation of labor unrest and a few abortive uprisings in Mexico.

In the late spring of 1906, agitators at Cananea, Sonora, forty miles south of the Arizona border, distributed copies of *Regeneración* and helped organize a strike at the American-owned copper company. Mexican workers there, paid in pesos rather than dollars as were their American co-workers, saw their real earnings crushed by the 1905 currency devaluation—especially since commodities were imported from Arizona. Two other complaints were that Mexicans were paid less than Americans for doing the same job, and that technical and managerial posts were all filled by aliens even though qualified Mexicans were available and on the payroll in menial positions. On June 1, when unarmed strikers forced their way into locked company property, they were fired on by soldiers; in the melee twenty-three miners and two American managers lost their lives. The strike was broken, the ringleaders were dealt with by the *rurales,* and the miners returned to work.

In January, 1907, the toll was even higher when an army unit opened fire on strikers and their families at the European-owned Río Blanco Textile Mills near Orizaba. Because of press censorship the exact number of victims is unknown — estimates range from one hundred to double that figure. The regime's violent repression of labor protests created further hostility toward Díaz and contributed to his eventual fall.

In many ways Díaz himself paved the way for the collapse of the dictatorship by maintaining a "geriarchy" where the key positions were held by old men. It appeared that Don Porfirio intended to govern for life, but as he grew older, the question of succession caused uneasiness. In 1906, when he picked Ramón Corral, the unpopular former governor of Sonora, as his vice-president, it disappointed the *científicos,* even though Corral was allied with them, because they wanted their leader, Limantour, to be the heir apparent. The choice also thwarted the hopes of General Bernardo Reyes, the stern governor of Nuevo León and former secretary of war. Then in February, 1908, the seventy-eight-year-old president granted an interview to James Creelman, an American reporter, in which Díaz stated that since Mexico was now ready for democracy, he would retire in 1910. He also said that he would welcome an opposition party.

The Creelman interview became a political embarassment for Díaz, who had no intention of retiring. His remarks had been intended for foreign consumption, but when republished in a Mexico City newspaper, they caused a sensation. Hopes for reform were rekindled, there was renewed political activity, opposition forces restructured their plans, and ambitious individuals began to groom themselves for the executive office, or at least for the vice-presidency. The National Democratic Party supported the re-election of Díaz but wanted General Reyes as vice-president (until he was banished in 1909 on a mission to Europe). The Reelectionist Party favored the incumbents for yet another term. From exile the Liberal Party junta rejected elections and made plans for armed attacks, and the Anti-Reelectionist Party, founded by Francisco Madero and his friends, called for an end to *continuismo* by permitting only one term for the president and state governors.

Inside the Rio Blanco textile mill at Orizaba. Courtesy The Bancroft Library.

Soon after the Creelman interview, Francisco Madero (1873–1913), a rich cotton planter from the state of Coahuila who had become interested in politics, began to write a book entitled *La sucesión presidencial en 1910* (The Presidential Succession in 1910). Distributed early in 1909, the book had a profound influence in Mexico; its ideas even filtered down to the illiterate masses, where it contributed to their rising discontent. Although full of praise for much that Díaz had done, Madero's book criticized his unconstitutional methods and urged that at least the vice-presidency and governorships should be filled by the choice of voters. Ignoring the proletariat's working conditions and the peasants' hunger for land, Madero's panacea was political freedom. In carefully chosen words he suggested that the president should retire:

General Díaz knows perfectly well that his retirement from the presidency would be a benefit to the country. But there are powerful forces that retain him: his inveterate custom of commanding, his habit of directing the nation according to his will, and also the pressure that is brought to bear on him by a great many who call themselves his friends and who are the beneficiaries of all the concessions, of all the lucrative contracts, of all the public posts where they can satisfy their vanity and their covetousness, and who fear that a change in the government will deprive them of the favors which they enjoy and so ably exploit. . . .

If the nation will become aroused in the next electoral campaign, if the partisans of democracy unite firmly and form a powerful party, it is possible that a change may yet be made in the purpose of General Díaz, for the rude accent of an agitated country may move the hero of the Intervention and perhaps cause pure patriotism to dominate him so that he will follow its guidance and put to one side the trifles, the meannesses, that might prevent him from rendering his country the greatest service he can ever render: that of leaving it free to form a new government in accordance with its aspirations and its needs.*

By challenging the dictator, Madero became a popular hero and in 1910 was chosen as presidential candidate of the

*Francisco I. Madero, *La sucesión presidencial en 1910*, 3rd ed. (Mexico: Viuda de C. Bouret, 1911), 22–25.

Anti-Reelectionist Party. His running mate was Francisco Vásquez Gómez, a physician who taught in the medical school of the University. For two months Madero campaigned extensively, using the railroads to visit twenty-two of the states. His speeches were well attended—often from ten to twenty thousand people gathered to hear this mild-mannered, bearded man who became known as "the apostle of democracy."

Madero's popularity was a threat to the incumbents, so in June he was arrested and imprisoned, accused of fomenting a rebellion and insulting authorities including the president. By election day at least five thousand of Madero's supporters were in jail. After the election Madero was released on bail under the condition that he remain in the city of San Luis Potosí. Claiming that the elections had been fraudulent, he and leaders of his party petitioned the Chamber of Deputies to declare them invalid, but that appeal was rejected. Early in October it was officially announced that Díaz and Corral had been elected for another six years and that Madero had received only 196 votes. Madero said that he had more relatives than that who had voted for him!

Meanwhile, great fiestas were scheduled for the entire month of September, which had been designated as a national holiday to celebrate the hundredth anniversary of Mexico's independence. Coincidentally, the national centennial was also the eightieth birthday of Porfirio Díaz. Distinguished guests from all over the world came to Mexico City bearing gifts for the nation and praise for Don Porfirio, who had presided over the great advances made in Mexico. There were parades, pageants, fireworks displays, banquets, and balls. The lavish entertainment cost twenty million pesos, an amount that was more than the country's annual appropriation for education. But while the elite lifted their glasses of French champagne to toast Mexico's prosperity and stability, the smouldering discontent of the poor masses was being fanned into the fire of rebellion. Within a few months the regime of Porfirio Díaz would be toppled in a revolution that ultimately transformed the whole fabric of Mexican society.

CHAPTER 10

The Great Revolution

OF THE MANY REVOLUTIONS in their national history, Mexicans spell only one with a capital "R"—the Revolution that began in 1910. It was the bloodiest civil war in Mexico's history. During the military phase, 1910–20, about a million people out of a total population of fifteen million lost their lives; there were battles in almost every major city; a number of rebel chieftains were assassinated; and there was a tremendous amount of economic and social dislocation. Although it started simply as a political movement to overthrow the dictator, once the fighting began it became a complex social upheaval as men and women expressed serious grievances and popular leaders championed specific reforms. Some revolutionaries called for land redistribution, while others wanted protective labor laws, or massive expansion of public education, nationalization of utilities, restrictions on foreign businesses, limitation of Church power, and other changes. Eventually many of these ideas were incorporated into the new Constitution of 1917, and during the subsequent two decades Mexico's government was concerned with implementing the goals that had emerged in the ferment of rebellion.

During the military phase of the Great Revolution a large number of Mexicans supported the revolutionaries, and a wide cross section of people participated actively as rebels. There were peasant villagers who fought to regain lost ancestral lands; hacienda peons who hoped to improve their conditions; dissatisfied factory workers and miners; unemployed ranch, farm, and town workers; middle class representatives — teachers, students, newspapermen, intellectuals, small entrepreneurs, professionals — who opposed the politico-economic control exercised by national and local *caudillos;* aggrieved

Indians such as remnants of the Yaqui in Sonora; anarchists
and radicals who had their own goals; soldiers who defected
from the Mexican army; a few American soldiers of fortune;
and there were even some wealthy northern *hacendados* who
pledged their lives and fortunes to the Revolution. Although
members of all these groups opposed the oligarchy and its
federal army, that does not mean that they always worked
together; indeed, sometimes they fought against each other.
Thus the Revolution was a confusing series of civil wars,
conspiracies, and changing coalitions of rebel leaders whose
goals, methods, and programs differed.

For many noncombatants, particularly the great number of
illiterate inhabitants of villages and cities, the Revolution
was bewildering and sometimes calamitous. They could not
even tell one faction from another, for the revolutionaries
often wore parts of uniforms seized from the *federales.* One
day a guerrilla band or a full regiment would arrive in town,
seize supplies, compel able-bodied men to join them, and
force women to give them "favors." A few days later a similar
force from an opposing group or the federal army would
appear and repeat the procedure, inflicting additional punishment for those who so recently had "cooperated with the
enemy." Financial and monetary chaos added to the confusion as various state governments, revolutionary groups,
and industrial concerns issued their own paper money, the
value of which fluctuated wildly, especially in foreign exchange.

Several major foreign governments were involved in the
Mexican Revolution through munitions sales, actual or projected military intervention, diplomatic maneuvering, and
economic or financial pressure. Representatives of Great
Britain and Germany tried to protect the lives and investments of their countrymen in Mexico while countering moves
of American diplomats and business interests. Uniformed
troops of the United States moved into Mexico twice, in
1914 and again in 1916. As the Revolution progressed and
became more nationalistic, many foreign residents—Chinese
and Spaniards as well as Yankees, Germans, and English-

men—were harassed by revolutionaries. A few were killed outright. Others were obliged to give protection bribes, and many left the country. Records show that foreign companies paid high taxes, tribute, or forced loans to one faction or another in order to keep operating or to avoid confiscation. Territory north of the Rio Grande served as a sanctuary for many revolutionary leaders, and it was a source of financial aid and military equipment as well as a market for confiscated cattle, cotton, or other products.

The Great Revolution began in the fall of 1910, when the civilian spearhead Francisco I. Madero called for a national uprising to oust Porfirio Díaz. Born in 1873, Madero was from a wealthy family whose properties in the northern border state of Coahuila included haciendas, cotton plantations, distilleries, and smelters. As a young man he studied in Paris for five years, then spent a year at the University of California before returning home in 1893 to become administrator of one of the family's cotton plantations. During the next fifteen years he devoted himself to agriculture. He introduced mechanization, hybrid seeds, and, along with his wife, Sara Pérez de Madero, tried to improve living conditions of the *peones*. In many ways Madero was an eccentric person, especially for an *hacendado*—he was a vegetarian, an avid spiritualist, and he studied homeopathic medicine. With a high-pitched voice, diminutive stature, and mild manners, he seemed an unlikely political leader. Yet, when he challenged Díaz for the presidency in 1910, he attracted thousands of followers. Jailed in San Luis Potosí, precluded from winning the election, then released on bail, Madero fled north to Texas, where he hoped to stage a comeback.

In San Antonio, Texas, Madero conferred with other Mexican exiles and published his call to arms, the Plan of San Luis Potosí, which was dated October 5, 1910, the last day he had been in that city. This manifesto declared the recent elections null; it announced that Madero had assumed the provisional presidency of Mexico "until the people should choose its government according to law;" and it called for a national uprising to begin on Sunday, November 20. No-

Francisco I. Madero, "the apostle." Engraving by José G. Posada. Courtesy The Bancroft Library.

where in Madero's Plan were there any provisions to improve proletarian labor conditions, and the only reference to agrarian problems was a proposal to return lands to owners who had lost them through abuse of Díaz's land laws. There was no mention of expropriation or confiscation of property, nor recognition of popular opposition to the political influence wielded by the Catholic Church and by foreign capital. Madero's solution was purely political—remove the dictator and have free elections. Yet the Plan did become a rallying point for disaffected Mexicans; perhaps they anticipated or hoped that widespread reforms would be enacted by a new government.

Madero's agents smuggled copies of the Plan into Mexico along with arms, money, and instructions to trusted individuals. A number of Madero's relatives joined him in San Antonio, but his younger brother Gustavo was arrested in Mexico City in October and imprisoned on charges of trying to subvert military officers. His release came when the government of France protested the action; it seems that he was connected with a number of companies in which the majority of stockholders were French. Significantly, the dictator's trusted advisor, José Limantour, was then in Paris trying to negotiate a loan for Mexico. Following his release, Gustavo worked hard for the revolutionary cause and became its financial agent.

In the first part of November the Díaz government intercepted correspondence that revealed Francisco Madero's tactics and compromised his network of local rebel leaders. Subsequently, hundreds of suspects were charged with sedition and jailed in six states and the capital. On November 18, when police visited the house of Aquiles Serdán, one of the conspirators in Puebla who had armed five hundred persons throughout the city, Serdán opened fire, and the resultant engagement left him and fifteen supporters dead—the first martyrs for the cause. Two days later, the date set for the general uprising, there were a few armed movements in various states, but they were soon suppressed. And Francisco Madero, who had moved to the Rio Grande, was forced to abandon his plan to cross the river and seize the town of Porfirio Díaz (later renamed Piedras Negras) because his anticipated Mexican force failed to materialize on the right bank. It appeared that the revolutionary fire had sputtered out, whereupon Madero went to New Orleans to contemplate the future.

The spark of revolution was slow to ignite, but it soon caught fire in the northern border state of Chihuahua. There, one of the rebel chieftains was Pascual Orozco, Jr., a twenty-eight-year-old muleteer who had several grievances against the state government, especially its policy of awarding transport concessions only to friends of Luis Terrazas, the regional *caudillo* and largest landowner. In Chihuahua City, Orozco joined the Anti-Reelectionist movement headed by Abraham González, who had been educated at the University of Notre Dame in Indiana. Another member of that political group was Silvestre Terrazas, a renegade member of the powerful Terrazas-Creel clan, who published the state's only opposition newspaper, *El Correo de Chihuahua,* and who had been jailed twice because of his anti-establishment editorials. Persuaded by these men to heed Madero's call, Orozco raised an armed band of peasants, miners, and unemployed workers that attacked government forces in Ciudad Guerrero, Cerro Prieto, and other settlements. Madero later conferred the rank of general on Orozco, the first revolutionary to be so honored.

Francisco "Pancho" Villa was another insurgent leader recruited and tutored by Abraham González. Myth and mystery surround Villa's early life; some say he was born in Durango in 1878, that his real name was Doroteo Arango, and that after he shot an *hacendado* who had raped his sister, he fled to the mountains where he changed his name and joined a gang of bandits. Later, in Chihuahua, Francisco Villa had various occupations: miner, peddler, construction worker, and cattle rustler. When he decided to join the Madero revolt, he recruited an armed following of cowboys and roustabouts, plus a few ranch foremen. By the end of 1910, guerrilla bands under Villa and Orozco had attacked federal forces, cut railroad connections, and captured towns and territory in Chihuahua.

Heartened by the progress of events in Chihuahua, Madero slipped across the border in February, 1911, and joined the rebels. Meanwhile, he had sent his brother Gustavo to New York to secure financial assistance, while his 1910 vice presidential candidate, Dr. Vásquez Gómez, was in Washington as a "confidential agent." In March these two representatives and Madero's father met in New York with the Mexican ambassador and José Limantour, who had been recalled by Díaz from his financial mission to Europe. The conference resulted in the following proposals for negotiation: announcement of peace talks; suspension of hostilities; amnesty for the revolutionaries; resignation of Vice-president Corral; retirement of four cabinet ministers and ten governors to be replaced by Anti-Reelectionists; and establishment of the principle of no re-election. When he learned of the terms, Madero said that he was willing to compromise, but that any agreement would have to include the resignation of Díaz.

During the spring of 1911, revolts erupted in scattered parts of the country from Baja California to Morelos, the old sugar plantation region south of Mexico's capital. The chief revolutionary leader in Morelos was Emiliano Zapata, a thirty-one-year-old horse trader, small farmer, and elected municipal official. He headed a group of armed peasant villagers, mostly of Indian descent, who took over ancestral lands, destroyed sugar haciendas, and pounced on several towns. Zapata's guerrilla forces captured the cities of Cuautla and Cuernavaca in May, the same month that Villa and Orozco took the important northern border city of Juárez. When uprisings continued and the federal army proved unable to establish order, President Díaz capitulated. On May 21, Madero and a representative of Díaz signed the Treaty of Ciudad Juárez, which provided for removal of the president and vice-president and called for new elections. It also left intact most elements of the old regime, including the federal army, yet it called for disbanding the revolutionary armies. At the end of the month Díaz departed for

Emiliano Zapata, "the peasant messiah." Courtesy Organization of American States.

exile in France. Before leaving he said, "Madero has un-
leashed a tiger, now let us see if he can control it."

When Díaz resigned, his minister of foreign relations, Francisco León de la Barra, became provisional president and
held that office for five and a half months. With the exception of three revolutionaries, all the cabinet posts were held
by Díaz holdovers. After receiving a triumphal welcome in
Mexico City in June, Madero devoted himself to organizing
his campaign to be elected president. Dropping his former
running-mate, he chose José Pino Suárez, a journalist from
Yucatán, as his vice-presidential candidate. Together they
campaigned, were elected, and took office the first week in
November, 1911. It then appeared that the Revolution was
over, but it was just beginning.

Madero, whom one writer termed "a dove fluttering in a
sky filled with hawks," soon had his hands full. The utopian
president ruled in accordance with the law, maintained freedom of speech and the press, left many Porfiristas entrenched
in the cabinet and in government positions, and did little
in the way of reform. His conciliatory attitudes permitted
enemies to undermine him. As an atheist, he did not enjoy
clerical support; his nepotism and dependence on family
members—three were appointed to cabinet posts—offended
many supporters; he could not count on the loyalty of high-
ranking federal army officers; nor could he secure the cooperation of many politicians. Madero did not recognize that
the country needed and wanted substantial economic and
social changes, and he tried to stop the illegal seizures of
land. Almost immediately he was beset by conspiracies and
open opposition; even those who had fought for him turned
against him.

Emiliano Zapata, who had supported Madero because his
Plan of San Luis had promised return of land to the villages, soon broke with "the apostle." Zapata and thousands
like him expected immediate action, but the interim government and that of Madero proceeded in a slow, orderly way
by appointing committees "to study the agrarian situation."
Zapata then re-formed his peasant army, and on November

25, 1911, proclaimed his own agrarian program, the Plan of Ayala, which disavowed Madero as president and called for his overthrow. It also contained the following key points:

Villages or citizens unjustly deprived of lands to which they had held title should immediately reoccupy those lands and defend them to the utmost with arms. . . . Since the great majority of Mexican villages and citizens do not own land and are powerless to improve their social condition or engage in industry or agriculture because the lands, woods, and waters are monopolized in a few hands, one-third of these monopolies of the powerful property owners will be expropriated, with indemnity. . . . *Hacendados, científicos,* or *caciques* who directly or indirectly oppose this Plan will have their property nationalized and two-thirds of it will be set aside for war indemnity and pensions for widows and orphans of the victims who die fighting for this Plan.*

Zapata, the peasant messiah whose slogan became *"Tierra y Libertad!"* (Land and Liberty!), brought to light one of the deepest and most enduring aspects of the Great Revolution: land hunger. That central issue, which appealed to millions of peons, small farmers, and ranchers, as well as to communal agriculturalists, gave unity of purpose to spontaneous uprisings throughout the country. Zapata's movement spread from Morelos to the neighboring states of Guerrero, Puebla, Tlaxcala, and Mexico, where peasants burned haciendas and seized land. They fought in bands of thirty to three hundred, obtained guns from the enemy, and counted *soldadas* (women soldiers) among their leaders. Unarmed women who cooked for the soldiers, shared their beds, and nursed the wounded and ill were called *soldaderas* (camp followers). They formed part of most guerrilla bands and part of the regular Mexican army as well.

In addition to the depredations of Zapatistas, Madero's government was faced with rebellions in the north. From the state of Coahuila in December, 1911, General Bernardo

---

*Jesús Silva Herzog, *Breve historia de la Revolución mexicana,* 2 vols. (Mexico: Fondo de la Cultura Económica, 1960), 1:243–44.

evolutionaries and soldaderas. *Courtesy Foto Archivo Casasola.*

Reyes, who had returned from Europe and campaigned against Madero's election, issued a *pronunciamiento* against the president. However, when his call to arms was only feebly answered, he surrendered and was sent to the military prison in Mexico City. In Chihuahua the Vásquez Gómez clan, angry about being snubbed by the president, disavowed Madero and formed a revolutionary junta in Ciudad Juárez. And in March, 1912, Pascual Orozco, one of Madero's earliest backers, turned against him.

Orozco was disgusted with Madero, who had refused to support his candidacy for governor of Chihuahua and whose regime he considered far too conservative. Issuing the inevitable "plan," his socially advanced program called for improved industrial working conditions (ten hour maximum work day, etc.), nationalization of all railroads, distribution of government land, and expropriation of all land not regularly cultivated. Orozco's ragtag army initially achieved success in defeating regular government troops—after one engagement the humiliated federal general committed suicide. Finally, Madero sent an army north under General Victoriano Huerta, a professional soldier with a reputation for ruthlessness and a craving for brandy. Huerta got Pancho Villa, who had rounded up his followers again, to join him, and in a series of battles they dispersed the Orozquistas and forced their leader into exile in the United States. By June, 1912, the Orozco rebellion was ended.

During the northern campaign there was a dispute between Huerta and Villa, whereupon the guerrilla leader was arrested and sent under guard to the military prison in Mexico City. Villa soon escaped and made his way back to the northern border. In September when Huerta returned to the capital, he was removed from his command by Madero, who had reasons to doubt his loyalty. Not only had he disobeyed orders earlier while pursuing Zapata, but he had arrested Villa and also had tried to oust Madero's governor of Chihuahua, the prominent revolutionary Abraham González.

Madero was opposed not only by radicals such as Zapata, Orozco, and the *renovadores* (reformers) within his own party, but also by reactionaries who wanted to regain the power they had lost. Several conspiracies were hatched by ranking army officers who hoped to overthrow what they considered to be "a liberal and ineffectual government." In October, 1912, the Veracruz garrison rebelled, led by General Félix Díaz, a nephew of the deposed dictator. Other army officers failed to support Díaz, probably because they could not predict success for his poorly-planned movement. Díaz was captured and condemned to death, but the soft-hearted president commuted his sentence to imprisonment in the penitentiary. And nearby in the military prison was his longtime friend, General Reyes.

From their cells the jailed generals, Díaz and Reyes, planned a new coup d'etat and suborned a number of army officers in the federal district. On the morning of February 9, 1913, the two conspirators were released from prison by military accomplices; Reyes then took command of a unit that moved to the *zócalo* expecting the army guards to open the National Palace. But a recently-appointed commander who was loyal to Madero ordered the guards to fire, thereby killing several attackers, including Reyes. In the exchange of gunfire the commander of the palace guards was seriously wounded, and there were civilian casualties as well. Under Félix Díaz the rebel soldiers retreated to a military fort called the *Ciudadela* (Citadel) about fifteen blocks away. Madero, having been advised of the insurrection and needing an experienced officer to head those troops still loyal, recalled General Huerta to take supreme command. It was a fateful step.

There followed a period known as the Tragic Ten Days (*la Decena Trágica*), during which troops from the palace and soldiers from the *Ciudadela* bombarded each other. Considerable damage was done in the main business section between the two positions, and hundreds of civilians were killed or injured. In spite of orders "to observe the strictest impartiality," United States Ambassador Henry Lane Wilson for some time had opposed Madero's presidency and brazenly meddled in Mexico's internal problems, justifying his actions by claiming to protect foreign business interests. During this crisis he met with Huerta, Díaz, and Madero, as well as with other ambassadors. At his urging a group of foreign diplomats suggested to Madero that he and the vice-president should resign, but Madero indignantly rejected the suggestion, along with a similar one signed by twenty-five Mexican senators. Meanwhile, the traitorous Huerta secretly negotiated with the military rebels, indicating that he would join with them at the proper moment.

The denouement came on February 18 when General Huerta ordered the arrest of President Madero and the vice-president. That evening the American ambassador invited Huerta and Díaz to his office to negotiate an end to hostilities. Under the aegis of Wilson the two Mexican generals signed the Pact of the Embassy, which provided that Madero would no longer be recognized as chief executive, Huerta would become provisional president, and Félix Díaz would be the principal candidate for the highest office as soon as elections could be scheduled.

Madero's administration ended swiftly and tragically. First, he and the vice-president were "induced" to resign, whereupon the presidency fell to the minister of foreign relations, Pedro Lascuráin, who immediately appointed Huerta as his foreign minister. Then Lascuráin resigned, making Huerta legally president. This exercise in constitutional form during a military coup d'etat seemed comic, but it became tragic when Madero and Pino Suárez were fatally shot. The official report said that "while they were being transported to the penitentiary, an armed force attempted to rescue them, and in the confusion they were killed accidentally." Although "the apostle" was dead the Revolution was destined to continue.

As provisional president, General Victoriano Huerta relied on force "to restore order." Son of a Huichol Indian mother and a *mestizo* father, he had been in the army since his teens. In his long military career he had fought Indians in Sonora and Yucatán, opposed Zapatistas in Morelos, arrested Villa in Durango, bested Orozco in Chihuahua, and stunned the nation with his seizure of the presidency from Madero. After cowing the bewildered and frightened Congress into approving his takeover, he proceeded to rule despotically and silence his opponents. Gustavo Madero was assassinated, presumably on orders from Huerta; a like fate befell Abraham González, the governor of Chihuahua. A senator from Chiapas who referred to the chief executive as "Madero's assassin" was found murdered; when other congressmen protested the murder, Huerta sent eighty-four legislators to the penitentiary and dissolved Congress.

Huerta also filled government posts with military cronies, sent Félix Díaz on a mission to Japan to keep him from claiming the presidency, and quintupled the size of the federal army. When the number of enlistees lagged, the government relied on the *leva* (forced conscription), under which indigents were picked off the streets, men leaving a bullfight or a bar were often pressed into service, and petty criminals were transferred from jails into the army. As a result the quality of the army declined sharply, and the *federales* were loathed and feared by the general public.

A broadly-based movement to avenge the murder of Madero and oust General Huerta arose in three northern Mexican states. The leader was a bewhiskered civilian *hacendado* named Venustiano Carranza who had been a senator in the Díaz era and Madero's governor of Coahuila. He announced his Plan of Guadalupe on March 26, 1913. A purely political program, it proclaimed a national uprising against Huerta and demanded reestablishment of the Constitution of 1857. Calling himself First Chief and his forces the Constitutionalist Army, Carranza had the support of three principal generals: Pablo González in the northeast; Francisco Villa, who had escaped from prison, for the north central region; and in the northwest, Álvaro Obregón, a rancher from the state of Sonora whose troops included many fierce Yaqui and Mayo Indians. While these irregular forces harassed federal troops and gradually pushed south toward Mexico City, Zapata, who distrusted both Carranza and Huerta, led his peasants on the warpath in the south.

Pancho Villa's success against Huerta's *federales* was partly because of the intense loyalty and bravery of his men and

Generals Álvaro Obregón (left) *and Francisco Villa, 1914. Photograph by Otis Aultman. Courtesy El Paso Public Library.*

Yaqui Indian soldada *from Sonora, 1915. Courtesy The Bancroft Library.*

partly because of his innovative military tactics. Considering *soldaderas* to be an encumbrance to his highly mobile cavalry units, Villa expelled a great number of them. He also favored night attacks, lightning raids on military bases, and the use of railroad trains to move troops, horses, and supplies. An American correspondent who accompanied Villa during his attack on Torreón in 1914 described the unique field hospital:

It consisted of forty box-cars enameled inside, fitted with operating tables and all the latest appliances of surgery, and manned by more than sixty doctors and nurses. Every day during the battle shuttle trains full of the desperately wounded ran from the front to the base hospitals at Parral, Jimenez and Chihuahua. He took care of the Federal wounded as carefully as of his own men.*

Villa's charisma and early military victories made him an idol of the masses. His deeds, shrouded in myth, were perpetuated by *corridos,* those popular ballads sung by the common people to commemorate events or glorify individuals. The following verses are from a ballad about Villa:

> *Fly; fly away little dove*
> *Fly all over the mesas,*
> *And say that Villa has come*
> *To chase them off their bases.*
>
> *Get ready now,* federales,
> *Be prepared for very hard rides,*
> *For Villa and his soldiers*
> *Will soon take off your hides!*

Impelled by his primitive concept of justice, Villa frequently set up "people's courts," where cruelties or injustices were denounced and the accused perpetrators summarily dealt with on the spot. Perhaps just as often he displayed the qualities of vengeance and violence — for example, ordering his men to shoot prisoners or pillage towns. A Mexican

*John Reed, *Insurgent Mexico* (New York: D. Appleton and Company, 1914), 144.

saying of the time sums up his popularity: "Villa was hated by thousands, but beloved by millions."

Besides mobilizing army units to fight Villa and other revolutionaries, President Huerta waged a diplomatic campaign for American recognition of his government. By early summer, Great Britain and forty-nine other nations had extended recognition, but the new occupant of the White House, Woodrow Wilson, remained opposed—he disliked the way the regime had come to power. In the summer of 1913, Wilson recalled the American ambassador and sent John Lind as a special commissioner with the promise of recognition and financial assistance to Mexico if Huerta would declare an armistice, hold free elections, and not present himself as a candidate. Spurning the offer, Huerta then arranged for his own election in the fall. About the same time, the United States imposed an arms embargo that cut off munitions shipments to Huerta's forces. Then in April, 1914, a seemingly small event in Tampico led to American armed intervention in Mexico.

One historian aptly termed the Tampico incident and its sequel "An Affair of Honor." It began when some American sailors, who had inadvertently entered a restricted wharf area, were arrested briefly then released with an apology. But their Yankee admiral demanded that the Mexican authorities hoist the Stars and Stripes and give it a twenty-one gun salute. When that was not done, and, further, when President Wilson received news that the German ship *Ypiranga* was scheduled to arrive in Veracruz with an arms shipment for Huerta, Wilson ordered the seizure of that primary port. Unfortunately, the American bombardment of Veracruz resulted in hundreds of Mexican casualties. It also generated violent anti-American demonstrations in several cities, the seven-month occupation did not prevent Huerta from getting the arms, and the United States never received the controversial flag salute.

Even had there been no trouble with the United States, Huerta's regime was doomed because of the victories gained by insurgent forces against his federal troops. After Villa

took Zacatecas in June, 1914, and Obregón entered Guadalajara early in July, Huerta resigned and fled to Spain. Later
he went to Texas, where a plot for his return to Mexico was
cut short by his arrest and subsequent death from natural
causes. Meanwhile, Obregón's army occupied Mexico City,
paving the way for Carranza to assume the presidency in
August, 1914. Carranza, like Madero, was a wealthy landowner from Coahuila, and like him, he favored a deliberate,
legal approach to Mexico's problems.

The chaotic period following Huerta's overthrow has been
called "near anarchy"—it was highlighted by armed struggles
between former Constitutionalists allies. Villa, who had expropriated large estates, quarreled with the cautious Carranza over this issue and finally withdrew his support of the
First Chief. Then Zapata and twenty-seven of his generals
issued a manifesto which opposed "putting authority into the
hands of a traditional Señor of the old regime" (Carranza)
and called for immediate confiscation and division of land.
In October, 1914, a convention at Aguascalientes attended by
representatives of the revolutionary factions resulted in further splits. The Conventionalists disavowed Carranza and
chose a new provisional president, Eulalio Gutiérrez, who,
aided by Villa's army, moved into Mexico's capital, while
Carranza's Constitutionalists, championed by Obregón, transferred their headquarters to Veracruz.

Once again Mexico had two governments at war with each
other, a situation that divided families and devastated much
of the country. Although Gutiérrez was nominally in control
of Mexico City for a few months, actually the capital was
held and terrorized by the undisciplined troops of Villa or
Zapata, sometimes acting together, sometimes separately.
Despite their military prowess and the support of rural
countrymen, neither leader could maintain a stable government or cooperate to complete a reform program. The Revolution seemed to be disintegrating. Finally, Gutiérrez and
some of his associates, unable to tolerate the excesses, fled
to San Luis Potosí and ultimately to the United States.

The Constitutionalists eventually triumphed because of

the military victories of General Obregón. First he contained Zapata in his homeland of Morelos; then, using artillery, machine guns, and barbed-wire barricades, he defeated Villa's cavalry in two fierce battles near Celaya in April, 1915. Obregón had eleven thousand men in that engagement and Villa commanded perhaps double that number. The victors later claimed that they had killed or wounded nine thousand Villistas and taken six thousand as prisoners. By the end of the year Villa was back in Chihuahua with a much reduced army that resorted to guerrilla tactics.

Villa's actions in 1916 are puzzling—only he knew the reasons for them. In January his men stopped a train in Chihuahua and murdered fifteen American mining engineers. Apparently this was a reprisal against the United States for having recognized Carranza's government and for stopping arms shipments to Villa and other anti-Carranza revolutionaries. Or was it an attempt to draw the American army into the Mexican Revolution? Two months later about 360 Villistas crossed the border and shot up the town of Columbus, New Mexico, killing seventeen Americans. Their immediate goal was to secure arms from an adjacent military base. The United States then sent to Mexico a punitive military expedition of about six thousand troops led by General John J. Pershing, but the clever Villa eluded his pursuers, and Carranza ordered the Americans to withdraw. The ten-month invasion stirred up further anti-Yankee sentiment in Mexico.

Meanwhile, in 1915 Carranza reestablished his government in Mexico City and ruled from there for the next five years. His administration soon received diplomatic recognition by the United States and other governments. One of the First Chief's priorities was to suppress the continuing rebellions in several states, notably Chihuahua, Morelos, and Yucatán. Armies sent to those areas eventually quelled the uprisings. He also had to deal with runaway inflation, black markets, high unemployment, and a series of labor strikes orchestrated by the Casa del Obrero Mundial (Workers' Hall), an anarchosyndicalist organization that was opposed to capitalism. Although thousands of trade union workers, organized into six

Venustiano Carranza, the First Chief. Courtesy The Bancroft Library.

Red Battalions, enlisted in 1915 to fight for the Constitutionalists against Villistas and Zapatistas, Carranza disbanded
them nine months later. Then he moved to crush the radical
labor movement. After two general strikes called by the Casa
in mid-1916, government agents raided the movement's offices throughout the country, arrested its leaders, and outlawed the organization.

Carranza is a controversial figure in Mexican history—was
he a revolutionary or a conservative? He did not favor expropriation of large estates, and on this issue he was opposed
by Zapata, Villa, and others. Zapata, whose primary focus
was on land redistribution, carried out extensive direct restoration of land to peasant villages—there were no delaying or
expensive court proceedings. Pancho Villa confiscated some
large haciendas in Chihuahua and Durango, but he did not
divide them among resident peons or peasant villagers;
instead, he transferred them to state ownership or gave them
to his revolutionary cronies. Carranza, a wealthy *hacendado,*
wanted to restore the confiscated estates to their pre-revolutionary owners. His major concession to agrarian reform
was a decree that set up a centralized national bureau to
oversee the return to villages of lands that had been taken
illegally. Eventually forty-four thousand communal farmers
(a very small percentage of the total) benefitted from this
decree. Carranza also issued decrees that legalized divorce
and abolished debt peonage, reforms later incorporated into
the fundamental law of the land.

Convinced by his advisors that he should institutionalize
some of the revolutionary actions and decrees, Carranza reluctantly convoked a congress that would meet in Querétaro
to draft a new constitution. Election of delegates was strictly
controlled—all who had aided with arms or served public
office under factions hostile to the Constitutionalists (Huer-
tistas, Villistas, Zapatistas) were excluded. Completed in six
weeks, the new Constitution of 1917 (which with later amend-
ments is still in force) was promulgated in February as the
supreme law of the land. Influenced by Obregón and General
Francisco Mújica, as well as by Andrés Molina Enríquez, a

promoter of agrarian reform who was not a delegate, the drafters came up with a revolutionary document that did not please Carranza. He generally ignored the new charter, interpreting it as a statement of ideals and goals yet to be achieved. Although the new Constitution preserved many features of the old one of 1857, it also contained some innovative and controversial sections, especially those dealing with land, labor, and religion.

Article 27 of the new Constitution addressed the ancient problem of land. It stated that all property was subject to the public welfare; it affirmed that all water and subsoil riches belonged to the nation, which could grant concessions for their exploitation; and it declared that *ejidos* were inalienable. Foreigners were not permitted to own land or to obtain concessions unless they agreed to be considered Mexicans and not invoke the protection of their government; and foreigners were prohibited from acquiring direct ownership of land within one hundred kilometers (sixty-two miles) of the frontiers or fifty kilometers (thirty-one miles) from the seacoast. The article directed Congress and the state legislatures to enact laws dividing the large estates and establishing a maximum area that individuals or corporations could own.

Perhaps the most startling provision of Article 27 was the prohibition of religious institutions from owning, acquiring, or administering real property—the article clearly stated that "places of public worship are the property of the nation." Legal justification for assuming title to all Church property was found in the peace treaty between Spain and Mexico wherein the former mother country ceded all royal property to the newly independent nation. Mexican lawyers maintained that the Spanish state, not the Roman Catholic Church, had financed construction of the religious buildings in Mexico; thus they were government buildings.

Not only did the Catholic Church lose title to all of its real estate, without compensation, but in addition other constitutional provisions severely curtailed its activities. Article 3, which made all elementary education free, compulsory, and secular, prohibited churches or ministers of any creed from establishing or directing schools of primary instruction. Article 5 outlawed monastic orders, and Article 130 restricted priests and ministers: they were required to register with the government; each state was authorized to limit the number within its borders; foreign priests were to be expelled; no minister was to criticize the fundamental laws of the country, the authorities in particular, or the government in general; and priests were ineligible for public office and denied the vote. The Constitution attacked the clergy and the great landowners, as had the document of 1857, but the new one also targeted foreign investors and employers of labor.

The new constitutional provisions for the benefit of organized labor marked Mexico as an advanced nation in this field. Article 123 gave workers the right to organize, to bargain collectively, and to strike; it set a maximum eight-hour work day, required one day of rest each week, ordained a minimum wage, and required double pay for overtime "which in no case shall exceed three hours nor continue for more than three days." Women were entitled to receive the same compensation as men for doing the same job, they were precluded from unhealthy or dangerous occupations, and they were to be given one month's leave with pay after bearing a child. Employers were made liable for on-the-job accidents or occupational diseases; and agricultural, mining, or industrial employers were to provide schools, dispensaries, and "comfortable and sanitary housing at a monthly rental not exceeding one-half of one percent of the assessed value of the property." The article also called for establishment of government insurance plans to cover unemployment, sickness, old age, and death. Liberal as it seems, this article was seen by its Constitutionalist framers as a way to circumvent more radical labor demands by members of the recently disbanded *Casa del Obrero Mundial.*

Although he was elected president in 1917 and served the next three years, Carranza was either unwilling or unable to enforce the constitutional reforms. He had distractions stemming from World War I and Germany's bid for Mexican support against American belligerency (the Zimmerman Telegram of February 1917), but most of all he had domestic problems. The country was suffering from years of civil war, uprisings continued to disrupt the peace, and Carranza resorted to suppression and martial law to maintain his waning power. Opposition by organized labor and continued strikes led to the arrest of Luis Morones, the principal labor organizer, who had founded the nation's first large labor association, the Regional Confederation of Mexican Workers, known by its acronym, CROM. In 1919 the labor secretary, Plutarco Elías Calles, resigned to protest the government's hostility toward organized labor.

Carranza also had problems with several heroes of the Revolution. Zapata still demanded that one-third of hacienda land be redistributed among landless peons, but the president was not in favor of confiscation. When agrarian protesters criticized the president and took matters into their own hands, Carranza sent an army unit after them. Finally, Zapata was treacherously assassinated in April, 1919, and his head was displayed at Cuautla for some time to convince his followers that their messiah was dead and to dissuade them from continuing their illegal seizures of land.

Most serious of all was the threat from Obregón, who had returned to Sonora where his loyalty cooled while his presidential ambition warmed. In April, 1920, when it became apparent that Carranza intended to control the election so that a puppet would succeed him, armed uprisings occurred. Obregón "pronounced" against the government; the governor of Sonora, Adolfo de la Huerta, declared his state an independent republic; and General Calles gathered an army of Obregonistas who marched toward Mexico City, picking up adherents along the way. On May 5, Carranza packed his bags (some say with five million pesos from the treasury) and boarded a train for Veracruz, hoping to take a ship to exile. The First Chief only made it partway to the coast—his train was attacked, and while fleeing his pursuers, he was murdered. Mexico's government was taken over by de la Huerta, who served as provisional president until the end of November, 1920, when Obregón took over as the duly-elected president. Thus ended the first decade of the Revolution, the military phase; the next period would be one of postwar reconstruction.

As president of Mexico for the first four years of the 1920s Álvaro Obregón enforced domestic peace on the war-wracked country, resumed payments of the foreign debt, and gradually began implementation of the revolutionary goals. This one-armed man from the Northwest—he had lost his right arm in a battle against Villa—was a moderate whose practical nature permitted him to compromise on issues. To aid reconstruction he proclaimed an amnesty, invited exiled enemies of the Revolution to return home, and brought Villistas and Zapatistas into government. Peace was made with Villa, who was awarded the hacienda of Canutillo in Durango, where he lived quietly with some of his soldiers until his mysterious assassination in 1923. One of his self-proclaimed assassins stated that "it was a belated act of justice for Villa's countless unpunished crimes."

Aware of continuing discontent among peasants and proletarians, Obregón began to fulfill revolutionary promises made to them. To assuage land hunger he established a special agrarian commission that did not inaugurate a general confiscation or division of haciendas. Instead, it methodically granted titles to Indian communities that had regained their land by force or that showed proof of prior ownership of property that had been taken from them illegally. During Obregón's presidency almost a million hectares of land were redistributed in that way. The president also supported labor legislation, encouraged the formation of trade unions, and favored Luis Morones, whose confederation of workers (CROM) increased its membership from 50,000 to 1,200,000. Besides consolidating the working sectors, Obregón was sympathetic to the revolutionary demand for an expansion of educational opportunities.

José Vasconcelos, a philosopher and lawyer who served as minister of education between 1921 and 1924, abandoned the elitist policies of the *científicos* and initiated a vast effort to combat illiteracy and awaken the common people. Under this great man, who inspired young men and women to devote their lives to teaching even at very low salaries, the federal government pursued an active role. More than a thousand rural schools were constructed; teacher training facilities were expanded; 671 public libraries were established; the Classics and other books were printed by the government in inexpensive editions and distributed nationwide; and "cultural missions"—mobile units composed of teachers, public health workers, and agricultural specialists—were sent to rural areas. In some remote places Spanish was introduced for the first time, and everywhere teachers spread the new gospel of nationalism.

Vasconcelos also supported folk or popular arts, and he encouraged Manuel Ponce, Carlos Chávez, and other composers to write ballet and symphonic music based on indigenous themes and rhythms. A nativist musical movement had begun during the Revolution when Mexican songs like "Adelita," "La Cucaracha," and "Estrellita" were written and became popular throughout the nation.

Out of this period also came a great renaissance of Mexican art, stimulated by government commissions for artists to decorate public buildings. Following the pre-Columbian and Spanish colonial traditions of fresco paintings on walls, dozens of artists created magnificent murals in postoffices, city halls, schools, hospitals, and other government buildings. These frescoes and mosaics became "textbooks" for the illiterate, because they portrayed Mexico's past, the goals of the Revolution, and showed heroes and villains of national history, often in caricature. Glorifying Indians and *mestizos,* the nationalistic artists at the same time denigrated foreigners—from the *gachupín* Hernán Cortés, depicted as whipping Indian slaves, to the *yanqui* John D. Rockefeller, whose Standard Oil Company was accused of profiteering from Mexico's "black gold." Three muralists who achieved international fame were José Clemente Orozco, Diego Rivera, and David Siqueiros. Because the last two were Marxists,

Sugar Cane Harvest. *Mural by Diego Rivera, Cortés's Palace, Cuernavaca.*

their paintings often included a red star, hammer and sickle, or a clenched fist.

The Revolution also inspired a nationalistic literary flowering. Vasconcelos himself wrote *The Cosmic Race* (1925), in which he exalted Mexicans (and Latin Americans) and predicted a brilliant destiny for them because of their multicultural heritage stemming from a blend of blood and traditions from the New World, Europe, and Africa. Dozens of novels about the Great Revolution were published, beginning in 1916 with Mariano Azuela's *Los de abajo* (*The Underdogs*). Azuela, who had been a physician with Pancho Villa's army, revealed the haphazardness and violence of the civil war. One of his characters remarked that the Revolution was like a volcano in eruption; another observed, "it is like a hurricane which carries you along as if you were a dead leaf." Martín Luis Guzmán, a journalist and one-time secretary to Villa, titled his revolutionary-era novel *The Eagle and the Serpent;* he also compiled documents and reminiscences into an account called *Memoirs of Pancho Villa.* For a generation, Mexican writers focused almost exclusively on the Revolution. Perhaps that was natural, since the upheaval had touched virtually every family, and during three decades government leaders constantly referred to the Revolution as they tried to implement the program that had evolved between 1910 and 1920.

Obregón's reform measures were overshadowed by fiscal and political problems. Mexico's economy and transportation had been severely disrupted. The worldwide recession following World War I caused a slump in silver and copper prices, and the United States government refused to recognize Obregón's government—partly because of pressure from American mining and petroleum companies whose officers feared nationalization of sub-soil riches. Finally, in August, 1923, a compromise was reached in the Bucareli Agreement. Mexico conceded that Article 27 would not be retroactive—lands acquired before 1917 would not be affected—whereupon the United States opened its embassy again. That support came at an opportune time, because Obregón was being challenged in the domestic political arena.

When Obregón proposed General Calles as his presidential successor, it touched off a revolt led by his former treasury secretary, Adolfo de la Huerta, who enlisted the support of ultra-conservatives as well as military commanders in Jalisco, Oaxaca, and Veracruz. Beginning in December, 1923, the fighting continued for three months, but the rebels were defeated. De la Huerta escaped to California, his military champions were executed, and Calles took office.

Plutarco Elías Calles proved to be a ruthless and fearless president who was determined to carry out the aims of the Revolution and to enforce the Constitution. Although he served only one four-year term, he continued behind the scenes to manage puppets in the executive office for another six years; thus, he "ruled" Mexico for a decade. Calles was a self-made man who had been a teacher, newspaperman, and hotel manager before he organized a brigade to aid Carranza in the Revolution. His military service brought him the governorship of Sonora and subsequently the cabinet post of minister of interior (*gobernación*) under Obregón, from which he rose to the presidency.

As chief executive Calles launched an ambitious program of social improvement. His administration initiated a public health campaign against infectious diseases; began large irrigation and highway projects; continued the expansion of educational opportunities; established agricultural schools; and redistributed more than 3,000,000 hectares (7,413,000 acres) of land, triple the amount under Obregón. He also supported trade unions and named union boss Luis Morones as his minister of industry, commerce, and labor. Faced with a bare treasury and a huge government debt of $54 million pesos, Calles adopted a rigid fiscal policy that balanced the budget and consolidated the debt, and in addition he established a national bank and an agricultural credit bank. He also must be given credit for attempting to reform the army by subjecting it to civilian control, reducing its share of the national budget to 25 percent, modernizing the military college curriculum, and establishing schools in the barracks to raise the level of literacy among common soldiers.

Unfortunately, the *Jefe Máximo* (Supreme Chief), a title

Calles preferred, became less reform-minded and more dicta-
torial as the years passed. Hundreds of his enemies were
jailed, others were dispatched by the army, and a large number were reported to have "committed suicide." Moreover, he
and his close associates became corrupted by power and were
transformed into millionaires. Their lavish estates in the
Lomas district of the capital and their weekend houses in
Cuernavaca were referred to as "palaces of Ali Baba and the
Forty Thieves."

Calles is often remembered for his controversy with the
Catholic Church. In 1926, when Archbishop José Mora y
del Río publicly reaffirmed the hierarchy's opposition to
the anticlerical articles of the Constitution, the president
moved to enforce those provisions. His administration ordered all priests to register with the government, deported
about two hundred alien priests and nuns, secularized all
primary education, and closed seventy-three monasteries
and convents. Church leaders countered with nationwide
protests and then with a papal-approved interdiction under
which they closed all Catholic churches and the clergy abstained from administering the sacraments—even baptism
and marriage. Although this church lockout and clerical
strike lasted for three years, it failed to achieve a change
in official policy. Indeed, the government took a harder line
by taking possession of all religious buildings and Church
property. Later the government converted many church edi-
fices to libraries, schools, museums, health clinics, or other
public functions.

The Cristero rebellion, which caused at least fifty thousand
deaths, flamed up during these years; its name was derived
from the rebels' rallying cry, *Viva Cristo Rey!* (Long Live
Christ the King!) This armed movement by fanatic Catholics
occurred primarily in the northern and western states of
Jalisco, Colima, Guanajuato, Durango, Zacatecas and Michoacán. There the guerrilla forces destroyed schools and
other government property, murdered teachers, dynamited a
train, killing a hundred innocent passengers, and committed

other hostile acts. In suppressing the rebellion federal soldiers murdered priests and took brutal revenge on suspected Cristeros or their families. Government agents harassed prominent Catholic laymen and deported the archbishop and five other prelates accused of aiding the Cristeros. Calles refused to soften his anticlerical position despite the pressure of rising public opinion at home and abroad.

Strained relations with the United States resulted from the determination of Calles to enforce the Constitution — the religious articles as well as those dealing with land. When he ordered owners of petroleum properties to exchange their titles for fifty-year leases dating from the time of acquisition, his decree was denounced by foreign powers as a violation of the earlier Bucareli Agreement. Finally, in 1928, a Mexican Supreme Court decision pointing to non-confiscatory interpretation of the legislation, and mediation by Dwight Morrow, the newly-appointed American ambassador, temporarily settled the oil controversy. Morrow, an able diplomat who loved Mexico and its culture, met secretly with Calles and several Catholic representatives in an attempt to reach a compromise on the Church-state issue. These talks ultimately led to reopening the churches in June, 1929, and the Cristero revolt died out, but the outcome was a victory for the government because its laws regulating the Church were not rescinded. (They still are in effect, though not totally enforced.)

While Calles was embroiled in the Church controversy, the question of presidential succession arose. The former president, Obregón, sought the position and became eligible after Congress amended the Constitution to permit one non-immediate re-election. (This violation of the no-reelection principle was later annulled.) At the same time Congress lengthened the presidential term to six years. Clearly Obregón would win the election, but two "anti-reelectionist" candidates, Generals Francisco Serrano and Arnulfo R. Gómez, were executed "for plotting a revolt." Then in mid-July, 1928, two weeks after Obregón's election but before his inauguration, he was assassinated by an artist who had been painting his portrait in an outdoor restaurant. The murder stunned the nation and exacerbated the Church problem, because the assassin was a fanatic Catholic.

For the next six years the *Jefe Máximo* dominated national politics through puppet presidents and by his control of the official revolutionary political party, the *Partido Nacional Revolucionario (PNR)*, which he organized in 1929. One reason it was called the official party was that all civil servants were obliged to contribute a small percentage of their salary. (With two reorganizations and name changes, this party has continued to govern Mexico to the present.) Emilio Portes Gil was the first interim president; he served for two years, until the election of Pascual Ortiz Rubio, who fell out of favor in 1932 and was replaced by another Calles henchman, General Abelardo Rodríguez. During the latter's term the public schools introduced sex education, and in 1934 they were obliged by a constitutional amendment to make all education "socialistic and nonreligious." Catholic and conservative leaders opposed these programs, but most Mexicans were more concerned about economic conditions than school curriculum.

Between 1929 and 1934, the world economic depression hit Mexico very hard. Foreign trade, a key source of public revenue, fell by one-half; unemployment rose dramatically; and tens of thousands of destitute Mexicans returned home from the United States. Mexican radicals, some of them Marxists, pointed to the economic crisis and demanded a restructuring of society. The PNR responded with a Six-Year Plan to coincide with the next presidential term. It called for a new economic system under state control and direction, which would reform agriculture, give wider benefits to organized labor, diminish if not vanquish illiteracy, and free Mexico from foreign economic domination. To carry out this program the PNR backed General Lázaro Cárdenas, the presidential candidate designated by the *Jefe Máximo*.

Although he was a darkhorse candidate, Cárdenas was no political novice. Born in 1895 in a village of Michoacán, he left school at the age of fourteen when his father died, became a printer, then in 1913 joined the Revolution and fought in the brigades of Obregón and Calles. By 1920 he was a general. During the next dozen years he served as military commander of Tampico, governor of Michoacán, head of the PNR, and secretary of war. His record as a progressive governor made him acceptable to the radicals, and his honesty, sincerity, and dreams for the nation won other backers. In 1934 he campaigned extensively throughout the nation, expounding the Six-Year Plan to peasants and workers and listening to their complaints. After his election to the presidency he consolidated the support of various sectors including the military forces. His entry into national politics had been facilitated by the *Jefe Máximo,* but Cárdenas soon proved that he was no puppet.

In the first months of his administration Cárdenas resolved a conflict of authority with Calles by publicly condemning his interference and by taking direct action. He eliminated Calles's men from the cabinet and gradually forced Callistas out of key positions in the PNR, governorships, and other offices. Cárdenas, who had a puritanical temperament, closed gambling casinos and brothels, many of them operated by Calles's friends, and he refused to live in the sumptuous Chapultepec Castle, converting it to a museum. When the former president continued political intrigues, he was hustled aboard an airplane and sent to the United States in April, 1936. Deported along with Calles was the corrupt labor boss Luis Morones.

Organized labor underwent a revival under Cárdenas's patronage. The old CROM group of unions was in disarray and out of favor with the government and with many workers as well. Backed by the chief executive, a radical labor leader named Vicente Lombardo Toledano organized a new confederation of Mexican workers, the *Confederación de Trabajadores de México* (CTM), which received occasional subsidies from the government. Lombardo Toledano was a professor of law, a brilliant orator, and an intellectual with strong Marxist leanings. Under his leadership the labor movement expanded

Lázaro Cárdenas, the president who nationalized petroleum. Courtesy Organization of American States.

rapidly and secured many gains. In the Cárdenas years there were more than twenty-eight hundred labor strikes—seven times the total of the previous ten years, and more than during any other presidential term. Cárdenas also helped unite disparate peasant organizations into a powerful and officially sponsored confederation, the *Confederación Nacional de Campesinos* (CNC). However, when Lombardo Toledano attempted to merge the peasant and proletarian unions, the president blocked that move, because he feared it would create a political force that neither he nor the PNR could control. (A decade later Lombardo Toledano was a cofounder of such an organization, the *Unión General de Obreros y Campesinos Mexicanos.*)

Cárdenas, who was fully committed to agricultural reform, favored the system of collective land tenure rather than private ownership. His administration distributed 17,889,792 hectares (44,000,000) of land, which was double the cumulative total since 1920 and more than any administration which followed him. For the first time, entire haciendas were nationalized and divided. Very early in his regime Cárdenas personally attended a ceremony in the cotton-growing Laguna region near Torreón where 356,000 hectares, which had belonged to 332 owners, were expropriated and turned over to collective ownership of 31,000 families numbering 150,000 people. The government organized other collective *ejidos* on hundreds of former haciendas in states from Baja California to Yucatán. To help these new groups of peasant owners, a National Bank of Ejidal Credit, established in 1935, extended farm loans for the purchase of seeds, fertilizer, tools, tractors, and other equipment. And the government constructed twelve dams to provide irrigation water for the collective farms. Although the granting of land to communities had great psychological value to the peasants, unfortunately *ejidos* proved to be inefficient agricultural units— partly because of their small size—and crop yields have been disappointing.

Cárdenas's collectivist principles applied to industry as well as farming. He sponsored a nationalization law that authorized expropriation and conversion to workers' cooperatives of businesses that did not comply with the labor legislation of Article 123 of the Constitution. Under this law the labor courts ordered a number of private enterprises to be given to the employees. A notable example of collectivization was the national railway system, *FF. CC. Nacional de México,* most of which had been under government ownership since the Díaz era. In June, 1937, Cárdenas reorganized the system and transferred its administration to the railroad workers. The results were disastrous: efficiency, safety, and service declined until December, 1940, when the government took back ownership and management of the railroads.

The most dramatic event of his administration occurred in March, 1938, when Cárdenas announced the nationalization of all foreign petroleum companies. This bold act culminated a two-year dispute over wages for oilfield workers. The seventeen British and North American firms had refused to pay the amount set by arbitration and confirmed by a Supreme Court order, thus the expropriation was based on Article 123, the labor code, rather than Article 27, which declared subsoil wealth to be the property of the nation. Citizens of all sectors enthusiastically supported their president's assertion of the revolutionary promise, "Mexico for the Mexicans," and the action was a boost for the nation's honor, since the foreign oil companies had a long history of operating as if they were above the law.

In the president's March 18 radio message to the nation he summarized the dispute and briefly traced the spectacular history of the oil companies' economic success in Mexico. Then Cárdenas, who had been based in the petroleum zone for several years, castigated the firms for their lack of social responsibility:

Let us now examine the social contributions of the companies. In how many of the villages bordering on the oil fields is there a hospital, or school or social center, or a sanitary water supply, or an athletic field, or even an electric plant fed by the millions of cubic meters of natural gas allowed to go to waste?

What center of oil production, on the other hand, does not have its company police force for the protection of private, selfish, and often illegal interests? These organizations, whether authorized by the Government or not, are charged with innumerable outrages, abuses, and murders, always on behalf of the companies that employ them.

Who is not aware of the irritating discrimination governing construction of the company camps? Comfort for the foreign personnel; misery, drabness, and insalubrity for the Mexicans. Refrigeration and protection against tropical insects for the former; indifference and neglect, medical service and supplies always grudgingly provided, for the latter; lower wages and harder, more exhausting labor for our people. . . .

Another inevitable consequence of the presence of the oil companies, strongly characterized by their antisocial tendencies, and even more harmful than all those already mentioned has been their persistent and improper intervention in national affairs. . . .*

Even though Mexico agreed to compensate the former owners, nationalization of the oil properties caused some unfavorable international reaction. Diplomatic relations with Great Britain were severed for three years, but the Good Neighbor Policy of the United States kept channels open in that direction. For a few years oil production declined under the new government monopoly called Petróleos Mexicanos, or Pemex, and most foreign oil companies boycotted and refused to transport Mexican oil or sell the nation vital petroleum equipment. Upon the outbreak of World War II and a subsequent financial settlement with the companies (British firms received $81 million and American companies $24 million, plus interest), Mexico's petroleum industry boomed again.

Offsetting the anti-foreign feelings that accompanied Mexico's property expropriations was the government's vigorous effort to promote tourist trade, particularly from the United States. In April, 1936, Cárdenas established a Department of Tourism that launched an advertising campaign heralding

---

Mexico's Oil; A Compilation of Official Documents (Mexico: Gobierno de México, 1940), 878–79.

Mexico's architectural treasures, folk arts, Indian cultures, unique cuisine, and scenic wonders. The Pan-American highway from Laredo, Texas, to Mexico City was completed; so were all-weather roads from the capital to Acapulco and Guadalajara. Thousands of Americans drove by automobile to Mexico, where they not only contributed significantly to the economy, but also created a new bond between the people of Mexico and the United States. The influx of foreigners in those years included many Spanish refugees who became permanent residents.

During the Spanish Civil War (1936–39), Mexico supported the Republic through diplomacy in the League of Nations and by furnishing arms and munitions to the beleagured republican Loyalists. When Francisco Franco triumphed, Mexico never recognized his government nor exchanged diplomats with his regime until after Franco's death forty years later. The greatest impact of that struggle on Mexico was the arrival of thousands of anti-Franco Spanish refugees (estimates vary from sixteen to forty thousand) who were offered Mexican citizenship. Many of these Spaniards were intellectuals, professionals, or highly-skilled technicians; some were Communists, but that did not dismay Cárdenas, who, while he was not himself a Marxist, sympathized with the goals of socialism. Cárdenas also granted asylum to the Russian revolutionary, Leon Trotsky, who was brutally murdered there in 1940 by a Stalinist agent.

Maneuverings of Communists and Fascists in Europe had repercussions in Mexico, where Nazi and Spanish Falangist agents recruited followers. A number of ultra-conservative Mexicans became members of a right-wing organization founded in 1937 and known as the *Unión Nacional Sinarquista* (UNS). The ideology of this organization was based on the trinity of God, church, and family under an authoritarian government; members were obliged to obey without question orders from their leaders. At first Mexican Marxists opposed this group, but during the Soviet Russian–Nazi German rapprochement of August, 1939, to June, 1941, they followed orders from Moscow to cooperate with the Fascists and to oppose the democratic countries.

The outbreak of World War II in September, 1939, influenced Mexico's choice of a president to succeed Cárdenas. Radical members of the official party, which had been reorganized in 1938 and re-named the *Partido Revolucionario Mexicano* (PRM), favored General Francisco Mújica, author of key articles of the Constitution of 1917 and the oil expropriation document of 1938, but Cárdenas preferred his moderate secretary of defense, General Manuel Ávila Camacho, who became the official candidate. His principal opponent was General Juan Andreau Almazán, candidate of a new conservative party called the *Partido de Acción Nacional* (PAN). After a lively campaign, the official party candidate won by the usual overwhelming majority.

Ávila Camacho's election marked a watershed in Mexico's history — government policy abruptly became more conservative. The emphasis on acute radical nationalism and rights of peasants and proletarians was replaced by a focus on modernizing the nation through economic development, especially by industrialization. Because of this change many historians have concluded that the Great Revolution ended in 1940.

CHAPTER 11

The Modern Era

BEGINNING in 1940, Mexico entered a new phase of its history. One author termed the transition "from Revolution to evolution;" another said the Revolution had not ended, it merely had been "institutionalized." Although revolutionary rhetoric continued to be used, there was a move to the right, evidenced by a shift from radical socialism to industrial capitalism. The government played a major role in converting the economy from a backward agrarian type to one with a modern industrial base.

In the modern era, important trends have been: a high rate of population increase; vast expansion of healthcare facilities; rapid urbanization; doubling of the middle class; curtailment of military influence in government; continued political stability; expanded participation of women in business and politics; encouragement of foreign investments; increased tourism; accelerated industrial expansion; a sixteenfold rise in crude oil production; and augmented agricultural output. These factors radically transformed Mexican society.

General Manuel Ávila Camacho, the last military president of Mexico, presided over the transitional phase from 1940 to 1946. (His successors would all be civilian technocrats with experience in national government.) Although he had been in the army for thirty-two years and had participated in the Great Revolution, Ávila Camacho's career was not marked by heroic exploits—indeed, his detractors called him "the Unknown Soldier"—but his competence and administrative ability led to promotion to the highest rank. As president he promised to govern for all Mexicans, and he stressed evolution rather than revolution.

Ávila Camacho was a moderate conservative whose policy of "national unity" terminated persecution of the clergy, *hacendados,* and foreigners. By declaring publicly, *"Soy creente,"* which meant that he was a Roman Catholic, the president conciliated the Church. He placated landowners when he announced that private property would be respected. The one major pro-labor program inaugurated by Ávila Camacho was a new social security system, *Instituto Mexicano de Seguro Social* (IMSS), which, beginning in 1943, paid benefits to a limited number of blue and white collar workers and their dependents for illness, disability, maternity, old age, and death. (By 1946, insured workers totaled 246,000.) In general, the president showed little patience with organized labor; he removed the National Railroads from union control, sponsored labor legislation to prohibit "illegal strikes," and maneuvered to have the radical CTM labor leader Lombardo Toledano replaced by the more moderate Fidel Velásquez (who remained the labor czar for four decades).

Radicals were purged from the education ministry by the new secretary, the noted scholar-poet Jaime Torres Bodet. He phased out socialist and anticlerical policies and greatly expanded the number of teachers, schoolhouses, libraries, and museums. To reduce adult illiteracy he initiated a national program that achieved notably better results than previous *alfabetismo* (literacy) campaigns. During the 1940s Mexico's illiteracy declined from 58 percent to 42.5 percent of the population. (Torres Bodet later became a delegate to the United Nations and Director-General of UNESCO.)

The 1940s marked a rapid growth of Mexico's movie industry, spurred by the unavailability of European films because of World War II and the unsuitability of many Hollywood wartime propaganda pictures. Two modern studios, Churubusco and Tepeyac, were built; many new theaters were opened; and Mexican companies were established to finance and distribute motion pictures. Mexico soon surpassed Spain and Argentina as the leading producer of Spanish-language films, and the best ones received international acclaim. At the first Cannes Film Festival in 1946 *María Candelaria* (1943),

Modern States and Capitals

directed by Emilio Fernández and starring Dolores del Río and Pedro Armendáriz, won first prize; the next year at Venice another film by Fernández, John Steinbeck's *The Pearl,* won three awards. But soon after World War II ended, the film industry began to decline, partly because of the internecine struggles of cinema labor unions.

World War II, which roughly coincided with Ávila Camacho's presidency, projected Mexico into an active role in international relations. Within a few days after the Japanese attack on Pearl Harbor in December, 1941, Mexico broke diplomatic relations with Japan, Germany, and Italy, and the following month at the Pan American Conference, Ezequiel Padilla, foreign minister in Ávila Camacho's cabinet, became a spokesman for the Allied powers by declaring, "The Japanese attack on the United States is an aggression by the totalitarian states on the world's democracies. . . ."

The Mexican Congress declared war on the Axis powers on May 28, 1942, after German submarines in the Caribbean torpedoed two Mexican tankers, with the loss of twenty-three Mexican lives. The government seized German-held property including ships, coffee plantations, and retail stores; it arrested dozens of enemy agents and interned them in a fortress in Perote for the duration of the war; it instituted compulsory military service for able-bodied men over eighteen; and it recalled former president Cárdenas, who became secretary of defense. One Mexican air squadron of three hundred men participated in active combat in the Philippine Islands. (About fifteen thousand Mexican citizens who resided in the United States served in that country's armed forces during the war.)

Mexico's close cooperation with its northern neighbor during the war was an abrupt change from its traditional xenophobic attitude. The new *amigo* policy was highlighted when Ávila Camacho and Franklin Roosevelt met in Monterrey, Mexico, in April, 1943. That was the first time a United States president had entered Mexico (Taft met with Díaz on the border in 1909). An agreement between the two executives initiated the important *bracero* (hired hand) program of contract paid laborers who went north to alleviate the wartime manpower shortage in the United States. About 200,000 Mexican *braceros* worked in railroad maintenance and agriculture during World War II. (Although the program was terminated in 1964, it continued to fulfill contracts until 1967. During the quarter-century this program was in effect, 4,712,866 Mexicans participated, and bank records show they sent back home $749,900,000 through official channels, plus an unknown amount through the mails.)

Mexico's chief contribution to the Allied war effort was supplying strategic materials. During those years, production of the following was rapidly increased: copper, antimony, cadmium, graphite, lead, zinc, mercury, petroleum, rubber, agricultural products, and pharmaceutical drugs. A reciprocal trade treaty in 1942 lowered duties on raw materials sent north across the border and on a long list of manufactured goods exported south.

Because many formerly imported items were unavailable to Mexicans, new businesses were established and others expanded to fill the domestic need for such things as cement, steel, textiles, glass, and processed foods. This wartime expansion dovetailed with the administration's policy of fomenting industrialization. The government gave tax concessions to new industries and created a state development bank, the Nacional Financiera, which successfully channeled private funds to industry—by 1946 it had invested more than 830 million pesos in industrial plants and was organizing a dozen new manufacturing enterprises. To augment funds for the ambitious program, a law of July, 1944, permitted foreign capital participation as long as Mexican interests owned the controlling stock of any joint venture. Beginning in 1941 the government itself built (and continues to operate) the Altos Hornos steel mill at Monclova, Coahuila, which was Mexico's second integrated steel complex. The first one had been built with private Mexican and French capital at Monterrey in 1900.

World War II stimulated Mexico's economic development, but it also produced economic dislocation. High profits to certain producers, amplified by profiteering and corruption in some cases, accentuated the unequal distribution of wealth. Soaring inflation — the cost of living more than doubled during the war — complicated matters for workers, as did wartime government regulations. Because the population increase outpaced the growth of agricultural production, there were food shortages that resulted in food riots in 1943 and 1944.

Ávila Camacho's agrarian program concentrated less on the distribution of land and more on its utilization. The number of land grants declined to one-third of the previous administration, and the new policy required that land titles be given to individuals rather than to villages or *ejidos.* In order to increase food supplies, the government guaranteed moderate-sized estates against expropriation. Higher yields were obtained by introducing mechanization, commercial fertilizers, and hybrid seeds. The Rockefeller Institute established a food production project in Mexico in 1944; its scientific research greatly benefited Mexican agriculture.

During the presidential term of Miguel Alemán (1946–52) Mexican agriculture continued to expand. Candidate of the official party, renamed the *Partido Revolucionario Institucional* (PRI), Alemán had been governor of Veracruz, a national senator, and Ávila Camacho's secretary of the interior. He promised to eliminate corruption in the state and local party organizations, but as time went on his own national regime became tarnished by extravagance and graft. Doubtless some of the corruption resulted from the government's inexperience in supporting a number of massive construction schemes.

Vast irrigation projects involving government-financed dams brought hundreds of thousands of hectares of land into cultivation and tripled the output of electrical energy. Morelos Dam on the Colorado River near Mexicali, Baja California, made the desert bloom. Álvaro Obregón Dam in northern Sonora had the same effect for its region, and there were other new water reservoirs in Nayarit and Michoacán. The most ambitious project was on the Papaloapan River in the states of Veracruz and Oaxaca, where four dams were built to control flooding, provide electricity, and reclaim agricultural land.

Alemán's government also focused new attention on the subsoil industries of mining and petroleum exploitation. The management of Pemex was reorganized; new refineries, pipelines, and wells were completed; and production of crude oil doubled. In 1947, Alemán became the first Mexican president to visit the United States as head of state. During that visit he arranged loans from the Export-Import Bank and invited American investment capital to participate in the offshore petroleum explorations of Veracruz and Tabasco—their pay would be in oil rather than cash.

The regime allocated considerable funds for improvements in transportation. The mileage of paved roads quadrupled, the final link in the Pan-American Highway to Guatemala was completed in 1951, a new freeway connected Mexico City and Acapulco, and a highway across the Isthmus of Tehuantepec was built. The government also acquired the last foreign-owned railroad, the Southern Pacific of Mexico, thereby extending its national rail network. New airports were constructed and older ones modernized to allow expansion of air service, which was vital in attracting the important tourist dollars. In 1953 more than half a million foreigners visited Mexico (84 percent of them were from the United States); they spent $313 million for goods and services.

One of the tourist attractions was the new campus of the National University of Mexico (UNAM) dedicated in 1952. Built on a lava bed at the southern edge of the capital, the University City boasted some of the finest examples of modern architecture in the world; furthermore the exterior surfaces of many of the buildings were decorated with mosaics and frescoes by Mexico's eminent artists—Siqueiros, Rivera, O'Gorman, Chávez Morado, and others. This distinguished intellectual facility, built for a student population of 25,000, soon served quadruple that number, justifying the great outlay of funds and energies. A large statue of Alemán on the campus was for some time the focus of protestors who ob-

Library, National University of Mexico. Mosaic mural by Juan O'Gorman. Photograph by Paul Quyle.

jected to having the president memorialize himself so openly.

Adolfo Ruiz Cortines, a fellow Veracruzano and protégé of Alemán, became the PRI candidate for the presidency in 1952. After his military service during the Great Revolution he had become a functionary in the federal bureaucracy; then he served as governor of Veracruz from 1944 to 1948, when he was appointed secretary of the interior in Áleman's cabinet. In the 1952 election he easily defeated his principal challenger for the presidency.

Almost immediately the new president, who had a long-standing reputation for honesty, sought to eliminate corruption that had crept into the central government. He instituted a complete audit of the previous administration and warned civil servants that the public expected and deserved an honest government. Concurrently the Congress passed a law against "illegal enrichment," according to which all federal officials were required to file a declaration of their own and spouse's wealth at the time they took office and to be liable to an accounting on leaving their posts. However, only modest headway was made against the well-established custom of the *mordida* ("bite" or bribe) demanded by minor bureaucrats and the larger payoffs expected by those officials who awarded lucrative government contracts.

Another "clean-up campaign" involved the coastal areas, where the government launched a vast program to drain the swamps and eradicate malaria. Focusing attention on the nation's maritime resources, the president's "March to the Sea" project embraced improvements in port facilities for seventy Gulf and Pacific harbors, new interoceanic communications, creation of additional links between the highlands and littoral, and a program to resettle families in newly-developed areas of the lowlands.

Additional land area was brought into fruitful productivity through irrigation and flood control measures that cost more than 3 billion pesos. During the six years of the Ruiz Cortines regime, a million formerly arid hectares (almost two and a half million acres) were put under irrigation. The Falcón Dam on the lower Río Bravo (Rio Grande) was a joint ven-

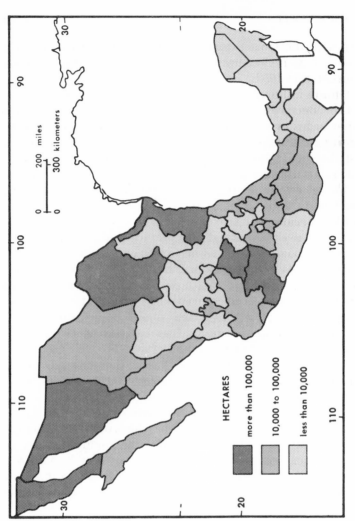

HECTARES

more than 100,000

10,000 to 100,000

less than 10,000

Area Under Irrigation, 1980

ture with the United States; the presidents of both nations attended its dedication in October, 1953. The project was completed in 1957.

Although the total amount of land granted to peasants, 3.5 million hectares (8.65 million acres), was lower than under either of his two immediate predecessors, Ruiz Cortines did continue that revolutionary program. The most notable redistributions followed expropriation (with compensation) of three latifundia located in northern Mexico and owned by foreigners; these haciendas were named: Cananea, San José Cloete, and Babícora (the latter belonged to the Hearst family). Because of the regime's measures, agricultural production showed improved results. In 1954 the nation did not have to import maize or wheat, and sugar became an export commodity. When set alongside the rapidly increasing population—it doubled between 1934 and 1958—the progress appeared to be significant.

Agricultural production was outmatched by industrial output, which rose at an annual rate of 8 percent in the 1950s. The dozen automobile assembly plants were a major component of the manufacturing sector, and in 1952 the government helped to establish a new factory at Sahagún, Hidalgo, to build railroad cars. Labor unrest was at a minimum during these years. Hundreds of disputes were settled by arbitration or by mediation of the secretary of labor; there were only thirteen industrial strikes in the Ruiz Cortines years. A general strike was narrowly averted in April, 1954, when the government devalued the peso; it went from 8.65 to 12.50 to the American dollar.

Culminating years of protest and hard work by many people, in 1953 the president pushed through a constitutional change that gave women the right to vote and to hold elective offices. Like men, they were enfranchised at age eighteen if married, or age twenty-one if not. Within the next two years five women legislators had been elected; others were appointed as ambassadors, magistrates, and high-level bureaucrats.

In 1958, when women voted for the first time in a presi-

dential election, it was conjectured that they might support
the Church-endorsed PAN conservative candidate, but the
results showed an overwhelming preference for the PRI
nominee, Adolfo López Mateos. Comparatively young and
energetic, he became one of the most popular Mexican presidents both at home and abroad. His modest family background—orphaned at five, he had worked his way through
school—and his previous experience as a professor, senator,
diplomat, and secretary of labor, gave him broad training
for the difficult position as chief executive.

Describing his program as "extreme left within the Constitution," López Mateos continued to implement his nation's
revolutionary goals. Land distribution was revived on a large
scale: the administration allotted sixteen million hectares
(almost forty million acres) of land, which was more than the
total of the previous eighteen years and almost as much as
under Cárdenas. In 1961 the administration initiated rural
colonization projects for sparsely-settled Quintana Roo and
the Isthmus of Tehuantepec. For urban workers the government entered the housing business and built large-scale low-
rent projects in many cities; one *vecindad* in Mexico City
accommodated one hundred thousand persons. To meet the
nutritional needs of lower-income people and ensure a stable
market for basic farm products, in 1961 the government established a discount food distribution system called the National
Company of Popular Subsistence (CONASUPO). Although
competing with private retailers, CONASUPO sales never
amounted to more than 10 percent of the total market.

State control of the nation's economy increased in the
1960s. Early in that decade the government nationalized all
foreign power companies and touted the new slogan, *"La
electricidad es nuestra"* (The electricity is ours). Intervention
in the automobile industry took the form of an executive
decree of 1962 that required car and truck manufacturers to
use at least 60 percent Mexican-made components. The decree also restricted motor vehicle imports, regulated the price
of vehicles and fixed annual production quotas for each firm
on the basis of prior sales and the amount of Mexican capital

participation in each company. The Mexican government itself owned 60 percent of two of the principal firms: Diesel Nacional (Renault), and Vehículos Automotores Mexicanos (American Motors).

Labor unrest in 1959 and 1960 resulted in a series of strikes by workers who protested the inflationary rise of prices. When the National Railroad employees joined the strike, the president ordered the arrest of Demetrio Vallejo, head of that Communist-dominated union, and used the army to end the walkout. He also expelled two members of the Soviet embassy for their alleged role in the strike and arrested a former secretary of the Mexican Communist Party, the famous painter David Siqueiros, who was imprisoned on the charge of "social dissolution" (equated with subversion). As a benefit to labor the government expanded social security coverage and instituted a profit-sharing plan for Mexican industrial workers.

Education was also emphasized by the López Mateos regime, which allocated more for it than any other component of the national budget. Jaime Torres Bodet, who had served Ávila Camacho as secretary of education, was recalled to that post, where he launched a series of programs to build schools, train additional teachers, and provide teaching materials. During just one year, 1963, a dozen new classrooms were constructed each day, and 82 million free textbooks were distributed.

Partly as an extension of popular education, the government commissioned architects to design and build a number of museums throughout the country. Heading that list was the National Museum of Anthropology designed by Pedro Ramírez Vásquez and opened in 1964. Fittingly located in Chapultepec Park where the Aztecs first established a settlement, the museum displays and interprets pre-Columbian Indian artifacts as well as contemporary ethnographic materials. The innovative architecture and splendid contents of this and other cultural centers has made a deep impression on Mexicans and foreign visitors.

Eighteen heads of state visited Mexico during the presidency of López Mateos. Especially enthusiastic receptions were given to Eisenhower and Kennedy of the United States, de Gaulle of France, Nehru of India, and Tito of Yugoslavia. Traveling abroad more than any of his predecessors, the Mexican president visited sixteen countries in Asia, Europe, and the Western Hemisphere. During these travels he proclaimed Mexico's non-alignment with the superpowers and his country's adherence to the policies of self-determination and non-intervention.

Fidel Castro's takeover of Cuba in 1959 and the subsequent imposition of Marxian socialism in that island presented a challenge to Mexico's policy. There were public demonstrations for and against Castro and angry debates in Congress. Mexico's highest officials denounced the United States' abortive invasion of the Bay of Pigs in 1961, refused to follow the American recommendation for economic sanctions against Castro's regime, abstained from voting for Cuba's expulsion from the Organization of American States (OAS), and never broke diplomatic or commercial ties with Cuba, as did all the other Latin-American nations. In 1962, when the Soviet Union placed long-range missiles on the island and Fidelista propaganda and munitions were slipped into neighboring countries, the Mexican attitude toward Cuba cooled somewhat.

Except for the Cuban issue, relations between Mexico and the United States were congenial. In 1963, executives of the two countries settled a boundary dispute over 244 hectares (600 acres) of land known as *El Chamizal.* The problem originated a century earlier when the Rio Grande *(Río Bravo)* shifted its course near the city of El Paso, thereby casting a section of Mexican land into Texas. In 1911 an international commission proposed dividing the territory between the two neighbors, but the United States balked; it countered with offers to purchase the land. By terms of the 1963 treaty the United States agreed to transfer the land to Mexico, to reimburse the former owners, and to share the cost of a concrete river bed and a new international bridge between the cities of El Paso and Cuidad Juárez. The Mexican press lauded López Mateos for his role in the return of the Chamizal, calling it "the greatest diplomatic triumph in Mexican history."

In a familiar pattern the outgoing president nominated his secretary of the interior, Gustavo Díaz Ordaz, as his successor, and when the PRI concurred, it assured his victory in the election of 1964. But PRI candidates did not win all the congressional posts, because a constitutional amendment of 1964 guaranteed minority parties representation based on their percentage of the national vote. Thus in 1964 the *Partido de Acción National* (PAN) received twenty congressional seats and the *Partido Popular Socialista* (PPS) got ten out of the total of 210 seats. This revision only partially alleviated criticism of the official party's monopoly of government.

Díaz Ordaz had been a judge, professor of law, vice-rector of the University of Puebla, federal deputy, senator, and cabinet officer before being elected president. He described himself as a conservative; he was an active Catholic, opposed Communism, and took a stern position regarding labor strikes. His dour personality matched some of his actions—he quarreled with and dismissed several officials, notably the reform-minded head of the PRI, Carlos Madrazo.

The president's severe attitude was most evident during the demonstrations that erupted in Mexico City in 1968 on the eve of the Olympic Games held there. Preparatory and National University (UNAM) students clashed with police and security forces in a series of escalating confrontations beginning in July. Thousands were arrested. Students and professors marched and issued a series of demands, including freedom for the jailed students, abolition of the riot police, and annulment of the law of "social dissolution." In September the army occupied UNAM, but the climax came on the night of October 2 in the heart of the capital at Tlatelolco— the Plaza of the Three Cultures—where students were holding a rally. Security forces ordered the demonstrators to disperse but were unheeded; then, claiming that they had been fired on first by snipers, they opened fire with automatic rifles. Later, the Mexican government announced that 32 students had been killed, but *The* [Manchester, England]

Postage stamp commemorating the 1968 Olympic Games in Mexico. Courtesy Dirección General de Correos.

Guardian reported the number at 325, and many Mexicans swear it exceeded 300. In the melee at least 500 students were wounded and 2,000 arrested.

Although this student unrest paralleled outbreaks in Europe and the United States, Mexico's bloodbath was by far the worst. Mexican poet Octavio Paz suggested that this episode was an instinctive return to the Aztec ritual of sacrifice, and he noted the coincidence that it had occurred on the site of the great pyramid of Tlatelolco.

That same historical plaza also was the site of an international meeting in 1967, when a number of nations signed the Treaty of Tlatelolco. This agreement, which prohibited the development or acquisition of nuclear weapons by Latin American states, was eventually endorsed by twenty-two Caribbean and Latin American nations. Only Argentina, Brazil, Chile, and Cuba did not ratify it.

Relations with Central America were improved when Díaz Ordaz became the first Mexican president to visit that neighboring region. Problems had developed — Central Americans were agitating against Mexican commercial imperialism and were referring to Mexico, not the United States, as the "Colossus of the North." Furthermore, Mexico's relative prosperity had attracted illegal or undocumented immigrants; 30,000

Guatemalan *braceros* crossed the border each year to compete with Mexican workers, and others arrived from countries farther south. The president's diplomatic tour alleviated friction and opened avenues of communication to resolve regional controversies.

Interrelations with the United States were very cordial under Díaz Ordaz. An enthusiastic welcome was given to President Lyndon Johnson when he visited Mexico City in 1966 to attend the unveiling of a statue of Abraham Lincoln. A year later the Mexican president traveled to Washington, where he spoke before the Organization of American States and conferred with President Johnson; and in 1970 he met with President Richard Nixon at Puerto Vallarta. During those visits two issues were of special concern: illicit drug traffic across the border and high unemployment along the Mexican side of the frontier. The executives pledged to cooperate in seeking solutions to the problems.

After bilateral negotiations the Mexican government established the Border Industrialization Program in 1965. A twenty-kilometer (12.4-mile) strip south of the boundary was designated as a special zone where American (or any foreign) companies could import parts and components, have them assembled by Mexican labor, and then export the finished items without payment of duties on either side except for the value-added tax. Within ten years these assembly plants, called *maquiladoras,* which produced chiefly television sets, electronic devices, and toys, employed about a hundred thousand people in the nine Mexican border cities where they were located.

Between 1965 and 1970, Mexico's federal government spent 120 billion pesos, of which 66 percent was for industrialization and economic infrastructure. One of the major outlays was for a huge steel complex on the Pacific Coast north of Acapulco at the mouth of the Balsas River. First called Las Truchas, the state enterprise was later renamed for former president Lázaro Cárdenas and is generally known by its corporate acronym, SICARTSA. Construction began in 1968; the plant was dedicated eight years later. A railroad was built

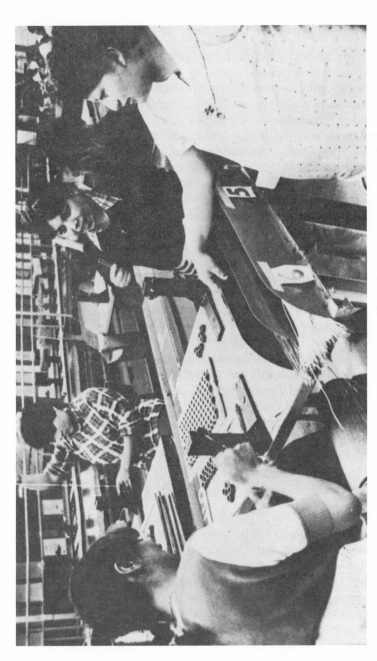

Women workers in border assembly plant (maquiladora). Photograph by Mitchell Denburg.

Steel mill at Lázaro Cárdenas on the Pacific Coast. Courtesy Altos Hornos de México.

to the site, a deepwater port was dredged, and an entire new city was built, complete with public housing projects. SI-CARTSA's output has been lower and its costs higher than anticipated, but the plant has provided many jobs and lessened dependence on imported steel.

Economic growth was stimulated by other government projects for industry, agriculture, and public works. State financing helped modernize mineral refineries and expand more than fifty airports, and it also was responsible for construction of petrochemical factories, dams, a seawater distillation plant, and electrical lines to carry power to more than two million new consumers. In Mexico City, the Museum of Modern Art was opened, several sports arenas were built in time for the 1968 summer Olympic Games, and a $3 billion subway system was inaugurated in 1969. The economy was booming in 1970 as Díaz Ordaz and the voting public chose Luis Echeverría Álvarez as the next president.

When Luis Echeverría won the 1970 presidential election, it was the first time he had ever run for office, despite a political career of twenty-eight years. Born in Mexico City, he had studied at UNAM where he received a law degree, and he married into a politically prominent family from Jalisco. He then served as press secretary and head of the official party (PRI), and subsequently he held various appointive positions in the federal bureaucracy, the last being secretary of the interior. Upon becoming president, Echeverría gave innumerable speeches full of revolutionary rhetoric that made him sound like a radical, even though most of his actions were conventional. One example was his declaration that Mexico's policy would be "revolutionary nationalism," which he defined as "an alliance of classes for social change and distributive economic progress."

Proclaiming that Mexico followed a path between capitalism and socialism, Echeverría hoped to establish his country as a leader of the Third World with himself as chief spokesman. He said that Mexico was a developing country with problems of international commerce, balance of payments, technological backwardness, and strong social contrasts similar to the other hundred *tercermundista* (Third World) nations. In various world forums the Mexican president deplored the growing imbalance between rich and poor nations, and he asked for a new international economic order. In 1976, Echeverría proposed, and the legislature approved, a constitutional amendment that extended Mexico's maritime claim over an economic zone two hundred miles (322 kilometers) offshore. This action greatly increased the nation's fishing and petroleum potential, but it conflicted with United States policy.

Echeverría tried to lessen Mexico's economic and cultural dependence on the United States and asked his countrymen to stop emulating Yankee styles, customs, and business endeavors. "We ought to be profoundly independent in economy, in technology, in spirit, in the education of our children," he said. Concerned that three-fourths of the foreign investment in Mexico was American and two-thirds of his nation's foreign trade was with its northern neighbor, the president sought alternate sources of financing and commerce. His success was minimal, though he attracted a few Japanese investors.

This Mexican president traveled widely: he visited the Far East, the Soviet Union, Western Europe, Arab nations in the Middle East, black African republics, Chile, the United States, and Canada. Addressing the United Nations in 1971, he supported the admission of the People's Republic of China and the following year Mexico established diplomatic relations with mainland China (a year before the United States opened an embassy there). One of Echeverría's ploys had unexpected repercussions at home—when he instructed the Mexican UN delegate to vote for a resolution equating Zionism with racism, that position angered American Jews, who boycotted Mexican tourist spots. The president's critics claimed that he devoted too much time to world affairs and accused him of trying to secure some international post. Indeed, in October, 1976, Echeverría announced his candidacy for the secretary-generalship of the United Nations, but he failed to secure that position.

At home the chief executive lambasted transnational corporations and private enterprise, which he charged with "betrayal of Mexico's national needs." To curb foreign or multinational companies a landmark law of 1971 required all new business ventures to have a majority of Mexican ownership and local management control. Increased regulation of licensing and patent agreements was another aspect of this Mexicanization of business. At the same time, the government expanded its role in business—it provided more than half of the new investment capital, and state-owned corporations increased from 86 to 740. During Echeverría's tenure, Mexico more than doubled its production of petroleum, electrical energy, and steel—but this was accomplished through heavy government borrowing.

After thirty years of sustained economic growth, sometimes called "the Mexican Miracle," the economy cooled in the early 1970s, and the nation was in serious financial difficulty. The foreign debt had doubled to more than $20 billion; government expenditures—triple those of the previous administration—greatly exceeded income, and the shortfall required further borrowing. To offset huge budget deficits the government increased taxes and fees; it raised prices for gasoline, electric and telephone services; and it increased the amount of money in circulation. These factors contributed to an inflation rate of 20 to 30 percent a year. Finally, Mexico's economic problems resulted in devaluation of the peso in 1976, the first time the dollar-peso relationship had changed in twenty-two years. The peso fell from 12.5 to more than 20 to the dollar. This was a blow to national pride but more important, it caused an outflow of Mexican capital.

Domestic problems escalated in the last half of 1976. At least a quarter of the working-age population was unemployed and another quarter under-employed. This was one reason for the growing number of emigrants who illegally crossed to the United States—most estimates exceed a hundred thousand a year. In various parts of the country, scattered instances of violence erupted: anti-government guerilla forces under Luis Cabañas ambushed politicians in the state of Guerrero, some tourists were murdered along the West Coast, and terrorist bands harassed individuals in several states. Kidnap victims included Monterrey industrialist Eugenio Garza Sada; the rector of the University of Guerrero, Dr. Jaime Castrejón Díez; the United States Consul in Guadalajara, Terrence Leonhardy; and President Echeverría's father-in-law, José Guadalupe Zuno. Garza Sada was assassinated, but the others were released after payment of ransom. In mid-November, when peasant squatters (*paracaidistas*) seized land in the Northwest, the president expropriated more than a hundred thousand hectares (almost a quarter-million acres) of privately-held farm land, which was then given to collective *ejidos.* The former owners were outraged, but the president claimed their holdings exceeded constitutional limits. With that dramatic action President Echeverría ended his term and turned over the office to his successor.

José López Portillo, who had been secretary of the treasury, was inaugurated as president on December 1, 1976. His election had been unopposed. The leftist parties supported him and the conservative party, PAN, declined to nominate a candidate, charging that the PRI did not permit free campaigns and elections. Like his predecessor, the new president had been born in Mexico City, studied at UNAM, where he received a law degree, taught courses there, and held appointive positions in the federal bureaucracy. A cultivated and witty man, López Portillo was the author of a scholarly book, *Genesis and Theory of the Modern State,* and two novels, *Quetzalcoatl* and *Don Q.* As president he initiated a number of governmental reforms.

Based on his recent experience with monetary matters and international financing, López Portillo reorganized the administration of the federal bureaucracy. Some secretariats were consolidated, centralized control of the budget was instituted, and the position of the proliferated government agencies and institutes was clarified. After consultation with the governors, the president transferred to the states certain responsibilities including maintenance of local highways, provision of potable water, improvement of housing, and establishment of regional cultural centers. His appointees to high-level positions represented a broad cross-section of society: labor chiefs, scholars, peasant leaders, businessmen, and politicians. One appointee, Rosa Luz Alegría, minister of tourism, became Mexico's first female cabinet officer.

To aid the nation's economy the administration offered tax credits to entrepreneurs who would create jobs by starting new businesses or expanding older ones. Four family-linked holding companies based in the industrial city of Monterrey took maximum advantage of the tax credits and cheap energy provided by the government. A business reporter who visited the plants and interviewed several managers in 1979 published the following account:

The Monterrey Group is controlled—and largely owned—by two branches of the interrelated Garza and Sada families, and they are

fabulously rich in the way that people are rich in a relatively poor
country, where services that are a luxury in the U.S. are still
quite cheap. . . .

The four big companies controlled and managed by the Garza
and Sada families—with combined assets of $3 billion at present—
plan investments totaling almost $7 billion in the next four years
in support of Mexico's National Development Plan. One company
of the four—Grupo Industrial Alfa, S.A.—has been diversifying
for the last five years from its base in steel into petrochemicals,
fibers, television sets, capital machinery, tourism and, recently,
farm equipment. . . .

Alfa Group is headquartered in a squat, bunker-like building
inside the heavily guarded gates of the company's main steel mill
on Avenida Los Angeles in Monterrey. An impressive collection of
contemporary Mexican art gives one the first hint that these are
something more than a steel mill's offices. Then there are the top
management people, schooled at Wharton and Harvard and the
Massachusetts Institute of Technology. Chairman Bernardo Garza
Sada, 48, is a graduate of MIT. Of stocky build and aquiline features, he collects the art that lines his office walls and even covers
its floor, in the form of a Picasso-like snow-white-and-dove-gray
carpet.

Like any good businessman, Bernardo Garza Sada wants to make
money and live well, but . . . he also wants to use his wealth and
power and brains to help transform Mexico and preserve its culture
in a modern setting. . . . "The government," says he, "is trying to
do the same thing we are, produce cheaper goods for the Mexican
market and for export."*

While industrial growth was notable, the agricultural sector
performed poorly, with the consequent need to import food.
Grain imports from the United States in 1980 totaled 8.2 million tons, and sugar, formerly an export product, was purchased from Cuba. Drought and climatic conditions only
partially explained the lagging farm productivity; other
factors were low prices, inadequate credit, lack of storage
facilities, and poor transportation. Hoping to increase food
production, the administration launched the Mexican Food

*James Flanigan, "Mexico's Drive to Industrialize," *Forbes* 124 (Oct. 29,
1979): 44–45.

System (SAM) in 1980. It was a program of government subsidies to producers, processors, and consumers—growers were given a boost in price guarantees, and the government agreed to compensate farmers in case of crop failure. Although the government "mulched the plants with 1,000 peso notes," the program fell far short of its goal, to make Mexico self-sufficient in agriculture. Grain imports continued to be paid for with petrodollars.

After the discovery of vast new oil fields in the southeastern states of Tabasco and Campeche, petroleum was perceived as a panacea for all of Mexico's problems. Between 1977 and 1980 the nation's estimated petroleum reserves tripled from 20 to 60 billion barrels. (Four years later the government decreased the estimates by half.) Although not a member of the Organization of Petroleum Exporting Countries (OPEC), Mexico benefitted when the tactics of that cartel increased the world price of crude oil. By 1980, Mexico, with an output of 2,300,000 barrels a day, was the world's fifth largest oil producer.

Capitalizing on the oil gushers, the government built new refineries, pipelines, railroad sidings, tanker facilities, and petrochemical plants. In the private sector factories converted from coal to diesel fuel or natural gas supplied by the government at very low rates. After two years of negotiations, Mexico agreed in 1979 to sell natural gas to the United States— 300 million cubic feet a day. Contracts to sell oil were signed with the United States and a number of countries, several of which bartered goods or services for "black gold." But there were serious problems with the oil bonanza. It created a scant number of jobs compared with other industries; careless drilling and escaping gases caused ecological problems; a blowout of the Ixtoc well fouled Gulf waters for ten months in 1979–80; and in order to exploit the offshore oil, Mexico had to import machinery and technology and borrow billions of dollars from international lenders.

During visits abroad, López Portillo and his staff negotiated loans, arranged petroleum sales, and discussed other topics. Addressing a joint session of the United States Con-

Pemex petrochemical plant in Minatitlán. Courtesy Petróleos Mexicanos.

gress in February, 1977, the Mexican president said that
additional American aid to his country would help stem the
flow of poor immigrants across the border. The following
year he studied socialist agricultural systems in the Soviet
Union, Bulgaria, and the People's Republic of China. Tourism was the chief topic broached with Fidel Castro in Havana
in 1980 and later at Cancún, Mexico. López Portillo also
visited Central America, Brazil, Venezuela, Canada, Japan,
France and Sweden.

Meanwhile, Mexico hosted a number of notable visitors.
The sojourn of King Juan Carlos and Queen Sophia of Spain
in November, 1978, marked the resumption of good relations
between the two countries after forty years of estrangement.
The deposed Shah of Iran spent four months in Cuernavaca

in 1979, and Sweden's monarchs paid a state visit early in 1982. When Pope John Paul II journeyed to Mexico—the world's second largest Roman Catholic nation (after Brazil)—in January, 1979, millions of people thronged the streets to pay homage to the first Vatican leader ever to set foot in the country. In contrast, two weeks later thousands of anti-American demonstrators jeered President Jimmy Carter when he arrived in Mexico City to discuss petroleum purchases, trade controls, drug smuggling, and illegal Mexican emigration. Although relations were strained over these issues and Mexico's friendly policy toward Castro's Cuba and the Sandinista government of Nicaragua, the interdependence of Mexico and the United States transcended their quarrels.

During López Portillo's final year as president, Mexico experienced one of the most severe economic crises of its history, the worst in fifty years. It began in 1981 when a worldwide oil glut forced Mexico to curtail production of crude oil and cut its price, which resulted in a fall of revenue that triggered spending cutbacks. To keep its many enterprises going, the government borrowed billions of dollars at high interest rates until finally, in 1982, it announced that it would have to postpone payments on its foreign debt, which had risen to $80 billion (dollars), one-fourth of which was private—one of the highest in the world. The crisis had international implications that caused major world banks to tremble as they reconsidered their indulgent policy of making loans to developing countries. Behind Mexico's troubles was a legacy of government mismanagement, over-extended spending, padded budgets, gross overstaffing, excessive political patronage, and massive corruption.

Economic news in 1982 overshadowed such earthshaking events as the eruption of the volcano El Chichón. Inflation soared to 99 percent. In an attempt to control inflation the government froze prices on 5,000 items. Nervous investors withdrew billions of dollars, economic growth went from 8 percent to zero, and Mexico's largest private enterprise, Alpha Group, suspended payment on $2.3 billion of debt, most of it owed to foreign banks. The government imposed foreign exchange controls and devalued the peso, then let it float. Its ordinary rate went from 26.5 to 150 for a dollar, and a controlled preferential exchange rate was established for crucial imports and to pay foreign debts. In September the president announced that he had nationalized all Mexican banks because they had been funneling badly needed foreign exchange out of the country. Because of the crisis the government cancelled grandiose plans to install eighteen additional nuclear reactors. A nuclear power facility under construction at Laguna Verde in the state of Veracruz was expected to be completed by 1984; like the automated petrochemical plants, it would employ very few people.

López Portillo's popularity plummeted in 1982—he called himself "a devalued president,"—but the alienation seemed not to affect his hand-picked presidential candidate, Miguel de la Madrid Hurtado, who won the July election with 74 percent of the vote. PRI candidates also won a great majority of seats in the Senate and Chamber of Deputies. Señor de la Madrid, who received a law degree from the University of Mexico and a master's degree in public administration from Harvard University, had served in the cabinet as secretary of budget and planning. Although he had designed Mexico's long-range Global Development Plan, that plan had to be shelved as Mexico sought to remedy the economic crisis. On taking office in December, 1982, the new president acknowledged that Mexico was in serious trouble, but he expressed confidence in the nation's ability to recover.

Part of the prescription for economic recovery was dictated by the International Monetary Fund (IMF) which offered a bailout loan of $4 billion provided the government would slash public spending, raise taxes, and curb imports. Besides accepting the IMF conditions, President de la Madrid initiated a strong campaign against government graft and corruption. Jailed and charged with fraud were several officials including Senator Jorge Díaz Serrano, head of Pemex from 1976 to 1981. The new administration also raised prices for public goods and services (utilities, gasoline, permits); doubled the value-added tax (IVA); lifted subsidies for food and transportation; abolished price controls on 4,700 items; began phasing out free-trade zones along the border (to curb luxury imports); offered to sell more than three hundred government-controlled companies; and inaugurated a program to create 700,000 jobs in road construction and public works. The new direction had positive results: inflation in 1983 was reduced to 80 percent, and the trade balance showed a surplus of approximately 12 billion dollars. Like his predecessor, the new president was a technocrat rather than a politician, and some observers suggested that Mexico's problems required a politician's skills.

The oil boom and subsequent economic crisis caused many Mexicans to question the strategy of modernizing the nation through capital-intensive industries. They saw that heavy industrialization required deficit financing to import the machinery and technology; it resulted in more urbanization and environmental pollution; it weakened rural communities; it led to heightened income disparity between rich and poor; and it further split Mexico into a cosmopolitan, modern sector versus a traditional (backward), rural one. Some economists suggested that Mexico should shift its pattern to imitate Hong Kong or Taiwan, where labor-intensive industries such as clothing or toy manufacturing have proved successful. Others recommended intermediate technology, or the model of Switzerland and Denmark, where small communities prosper by combining their native skills with modern techniques. Another ideal was expressed a generation ago by a Mexican who wanted a nation "modest but balanced, healthy and happy, that would live by thirds on its agriculture, its industry, and its mining."

Decisions about the future direction of Mexico's economic development will be made by federal bureaucrats, not private businessmen. Mexico's economy is dominated by the state, which owns or controls many of the basic industries: steel, petroleum, petrochemicals, railroads, airlines, electric utilities, communications, automobile plants, shipbuilding, paper, sugar mills, hotels, and banks. In the mid-1980s, government-owned enterprises accounted for three-fourths of the nation's output of goods and services.

Because the government's role is so pervasive and the bureaucracy is run from the top by members of the official Revolutionary Institutional Party (PRI), elite control of the government apparatus becomes another problem. Some analysts have called the Mexican political system "one-party democracy," others term it "democratic dictatorship," and a few have spoken of a "New Porfiriato," likening it to the era of Porfirio Díaz. The PRI is closely intertwined with the government, and it has been an instrument of control as well as one of representation. Its organization is based on delegates from three sectors: agrarian, labor, and popular (mostly civil servants), who are linked to regional and national units. The party's hierarchical structure and the Mexican Constitution give the chief executive a considerable amount of power. He controls key appointments, his proposed laws are enacted by the PRI-dominated legislature, and in reality he determines his successor.

The constitutional provision barring reelection is the chief limitation to the presidency, but for other government officers and for PRI officials the practice of *continuismo* (continuously staying in office) is widespread. Naturally, this practice of extended tenure has been denounced by younger political aspirants. Beginning in 1972, the party tried to include the names of one person under twenty-six years of age and one woman on lists of nominees for office. This is an example of how the PRI stays supreme—it permits gradual, minor changes to meet criticism from within the party or outside it. By maintaining that it is the party of the Revolution and by using socialist rhetoric the PRI co-opts and defuses challengers such as Marxists, who themselves are splintered into a dozen antagonistic parties. Clearly, the government party dominates politics and intends to keep the preeminent position it has held for half a century.

One problem facing Mexican politicians is the government position regarding Indians. Since the Great Revolution there has been a dichotomous policy of trying to integrate the natives into national life while at the same time preserving their culture. But by actions such as teaching them Spanish, vaccinating their children, and obliging the young men to do military training, the government diverts natives from their traditional ways. Although many social workers and scholars have dedicated their lives to helping Indians, many Mexicans scorn the natives and use *"indio"* as a term of reprobation. The question of defining who is an Indian is a difficult one; often it means one who speaks an Indian language, wears native clothing, and follows a native pattern of life. Based on that definition, in 1980 there were about four million Indians in Mexico who represented more than sixty ethnic groups and spoke more than forty distinct languages. Through acculturation and the growth of the non-Indian population, the percentage of Indians has declined from 29 percent in 1920 to 6 percent in 1980, yet this persistent and colorful segment of the populace is still a significant factor.

Mexico's rapid population increase is an overriding problem that dramatically affects other issues as well as the nation's future. For decades, while the mortality rate was falling and life-expectancy increasing, the growth rate was more than 3 percent, compared to a world rate of 1.9 and the United States average of 1.5 percent. In the 1970s Mexico's growth rate declined, and by 1982 was 2.5 percent. Part of this decline was attributed to a national family-planning program initiated by the government in 1972. Featuring a slogan of "responsible parenthood," announcements appeared in periodicals and on radio and television shows; new mothers were given family planning counseling before leaving social security hospitals; and health centers disseminated birth control information and devices. Yet, even with the lower rate, the population continues to grow faster than the nation can feed and employ the expanding numbers. And there is an ominous bulge—half the population is under fifteen years of age—which presages stress in the decades ahead.

Several factors account for the doubling of Mexico's population in the past twenty years and its projected doubling again by the end of the century. A major determinant was the reduction of the mortality rate as a result of expanded public health care. The Catholic Church's position against artificial birth control probably has had some influence; so has the peasant view of the necessity for many children to help with the work and to care for aged parents. Abetting these causes is the prevalent attitude of *machismo* (exaggerated maleness) by which Mexican men demonstrate their manhood through fathering numerous offspring, and the female counterpart, Marianism, wherein women idolize the Virgin Mary and see motherhood as a way they can follow her example. Other reasons for the high birth rate include the fact that Mexicans marry at an early age, illiteracy prevents many couples from understanding the issue, many rural and poor mothers have their babies at home and thus receive no family-size counseling, and abortion is illegal.

Mexico's burgeoning population compounds the difficulty of educating the young and finding employment for them. Although the government builds more schools, trains additional teachers, and allocates ever-larger sums to education each year, it can not keep up with the growing numbers. Since 1940, the percentage of illiteracy has been reduced from 58 to 19, but because of the rise in population, the actual number of illiterate persons has risen from 11.3 million to 12.8 million. Some Mexican children never enter a school, frequently because there is no room for them. Only 30 percent of those who begin *primaria* (elementary school) complete the six grades, even though it is free and compulsory. One-fifth of those who finish *primaria* drop out of school at that point, and only one-third of those who begin *secondaria* (secondary school) finish that level. This means that only about 8 percent of the children who begin the first grade make it through secondary school. A few of those who finish go on to higher education but the majority join the school dropouts looking for employment. Eight hundred thousand young people come into the job market each year.

Seeking work, education, or hoping for improvement, thousands of peasants and villagers continue to move to the already overcrowded cities or migrate north of the border. Sixteen Mexican cities have over a quarter of a million inhabitants, and the metropolitan area of the capital contains 14 million people, almost a fifth of the total national population. Every day more than a thousand newcomers arrive in Mexico City to stay, even though they face serious vexations: air pollution, horrendous street traffic, water and power shortages, scarcity of affordable housing, intense competition for jobs, and the cultural shock of city life. Many of those who migrate to the capital or other cities can not find employment and live in pitiful slums or shanty towns. Recently, at least a hundred thousand Mexicans have crossed to the United States each year looking for work. Of course, not all of them stay there, so a large number return home annually. Estimates of the number of Mexican nationals living in the United States range from two to six million.

Migrants have been leaving small settlements and rural areas because of lack of opportunities. There is a vast difference between country and city life in Mexico. Many rural areas are isolated and lack electricity, potable water, flush toilets, schooling beyond the fourth grade, physicians, hospitals, libraries, and other amenities found in cities. Furthermore, most available jobs are for low-paid, unskilled agricultural or ranch hands. Although 40 percent of Mexico's workers are in agriculture or livestock, only two percent of these are covered by the government social security system (IMSS), which provides workers with family health care as well as old-age and death benefits.

The agrarian reform program that evolved out of the Great Revolution did destroy the semi-feudalism which existed before 1910, and it redistributed the great majority of the land, but in other ways it has been disappointing. One problem involves clouded land titles—in June, 1984, President de la Madrid acknowledged that "about half the land in Mexico is in a vague legal status with no clear ownership titles." Another problem is Malthusian: because Mexico's population has been rising faster than its ability to increase food production, the nation has been obliged to import basic foodstuffs such as wheat and maize. In effect, Mexico is now trading oil for grain. A curious anomoly exists—Mexico imports cereals, but one-third of its exports are farm products such as tomatoes, sugar, cacao, and coffee.

Mexico's multiple agrarian problems are not fully understood because there are few detailed maps of land and water use; not enough studies of land tenure, farm management, rural credit, or marketing; and a lack of reliable agricultural statistics upon which to formulate policies. A basic limitation is the scarcity of good farmland; only 12 percent of the total land area is under permanent or temporary cultivation, compared to the United States figure of more than 20 percent and India's 55 percent. In the recent generation, Mexico's agricultural area has been expanded through irrigation. Possibilities for the future include reclamation, greater utilization of public domain lands, and conversion of pasturelands or idle tropical regions into productive agricultural zones.

For many reasons, the productivity of Mexican fields is meager. In 1978 the United States yield of maize (a native Mexican cereal) was almost five times the Mexican figure, the American potato yield was double, and the tobacco leaf yield was half again as much as that of its southern neighbor. One factor is the small size of many Mexican farms, which precludes the use of machinery. Two-thirds of the landholdings are smaller than five hectares (12 acres). Greater use of hybrid seeds, commercial fertilizers, and insecticides would also make a difference; so would an expansion of agricultural education at all levels.

Ejidos, the communal land holdings that comprise about one-fourth of the agricultural land, are a special problem. Long supported by the government, they were considered a panacea, but most of them are inefficient in terms of production. Their value is psychological and historical. In 95 percent of the *ejidos,* land is assigned to an individual who has the use of it but does not own it; thus he has no real property collateral for obtaining loans to purchase seeds, fertilizers, or equipment. And like a renter, he has little

Peasant with oxen and wooden plow, Oaxaca.

incentive to make long-term improvements to the property. Furthermore, the size of the *ejidal* plots is too small for machinery; they are limited to a maximum of twelve hectares (thirty acres), or half that if the land is irrigated. A few of the *ejidos,* such as the Laguna complex, are very large, operate like cooperatives, have modern equipment, are managed efficiently, and show high yields.

It is the very large privately-held farms that are the showpieces of Mexican production, providing more and more foodstuffs, export crops, and jobs—not necessarily in the fields, but in packing plants, machine repair shops, transportation, and related endeavors. Commercial growers in the northwestern states of Sinaloa and Sonora annually ship across the northern border more than a million dollars worth of tomatoes; in other states the principal farm surpluses are coffee, cotton, and beef. Agricultural products vie with minerals and petroleum as primary exports. Mexico's chief trading partner is the United States, which accounts for two-thirds of all exports and imports; no other country's share is more than 8 percent.

Metaphorically, Mexico might be likened to a huge cornucopia, its open end fronting upon the United States, into which it pours a wealth of agricultural products, minerals, and workers. Through this funnel it receives manufactured goods, technology, capital, and tourists. The southward flow includes a host of cultural influences: music, films, television, periodicals, books, clothing fads, and words like "okay" or "laser." The Americanization of Mexico, aided by satellite transmissions of sports events, movies, and television programs, has proceeded rapidly during the past generation. Indeed, many Mexican intellectuals are concerned about *"yanqui* cultural imperialism."

Proximity to the United States has been a vital factor in shaping Mexico's foreign policy. During the first century of its independence the struggling republic lived in fear of intervention and actually experienced aggression from its northern neighbor. But since the Great Revolution there has been no security threat from across the frontier; thus Mexico, unlike most of the Latin American republics, has been able to reduce its military establishment. Today, less than 2 percent of the federal budget is allocated to the armed forces. With a relatively small defense force and no overseas territories or interests to protect, Mexico relies on international law, various treaties, and regional and world organizations to which it belongs.

Beginning about 1940, Mexico abandoned its isolationist stance and gradually became more involved in international affairs. Part of that outward movement was related to securing modern technology, financial backing, and markets for its surplus goods. Examples of the internationalism are: presidential visits to foreign countries around the globe; initiating the regional nuclear arms limitation agreement (Treaty of

Tlatelolco); hosting the 1968 Summer Olympic Games; holding an International Women's Congress in 1974; and joining with Venezuela, Colombia, and Panama in 1983 in the Contadora initiative to achieve peace in Central America through negotiations and removal of all foreign military forces.

In regional and international organizations, Mexico's voting record has followed its twin principles of self-determination and non-intervention. According to this policy each country has the right to determine its own form of government as well as its economic pattern, and no nation should interfere in the internal affairs of another country. Mexico also has adhered to a policy of non-alignment, refusing to become a satellite or lackey of any superpower. Another basis of its foreign policy is the Estrada Doctrine, formulated in 1930 by the foreign minister, Genaro Estrada, which calls for recognition of any government regardless of the way it came to power, its ideology, or its domestic policies. (Mexico's refusal to recognize Franco's government in Spain was a notable exception to this policy.)

In deliberations of the Organization of American States (OAS), set up in 1948 as a successor to the Pan American Union, Mexico has played an important role. It is the most populous of the Spanish-speaking countries, and its success in having eliminated military coups and feudalism, plus greatly reducing foreign economic domination, has given the nation prestige among its Latin neighbors. It also serves as a geographical and cultural buffer or bridge between Anglo America and Latin America. Mexico has sometimes taken a contrary position on proposals sponsored by the United States and endorsed by a majority of OAS members. These differences usually involved measures to combat international communism (Guatemala, 1954; Cuba, 1962; Dominican Republic, 1965). Voting with the majority of OAS members in October, 1983, Mexico protested American military intervention in Grenada. In hemispheric meetings Mexico has promoted extension of maritime economic zones and restrictions on certain activities of transnational corporations, and it has backed regional trade groups such as the Latin American Free Trade Association (LAFTA) and the Latin American Economic System (SELA).

Mexico was a charter member of the United Nations, founded in 1945, and its delegates have served on important committees since that date. It has been a non-permanent member of the Security Council, and in the 1950s the distinguished Mexican diplomat Luis Padilla Nervo was president of the General Assembly. Not voting consistently with the Latin American bloc or any other group, Mexico generally has supported proposals for disarmament, for ending colonialism, and opposing imperialism. Mexico never has contributed a contingent to the various UN peace-keeping forces, because it views such action as a violation of the sovereignty of the nation where those troops are stationed. Based on its former experience with domination by foreign capitalists, and wanting to curtail the impact of transnational corporations on the economies of small countries, Mexico introduced the Charter of the Rights and Economic Obligations of States, which was approved by the UN General Assembly in 1974. Other problem areas in which Mexico has special interest and expertise are: underdevelopment, public health, and human rights.

Internationalism and a world outlook are also evident in Mexico's cultural life. No longer are artists, musicians, and writers content to focus solely on national themes; indeed, many have publicly rejected the narrowness of the past, especially the worship of the Great Revolution and its heroes. That is not to say that they have abandoned their *mexicanidad* (Mexican-ness), or even their country as a setting for a literary, visual, or musical piece, but rather, they now envision Mexico as a part of the world and Mexican problems as universal ones.

Contemporary writers Octavio Paz and Carlos Fuentes are exemplars of the new worldly view. Both have taught at Cambridge University and at universities in the United States, and both were Mexican ambassadors—Paz in India, and Fuentes in France. In Fuentes's novel, *Una familia lejana*

(A Distant Family), published in 1980, his characters search for their family history and connections on both sides of the Atlantic—in a sense it is a search for the essence of the Mexican personality. Paz, one of Mexico's greatest poets, observed that his compatriots now realize that their past and destiny are intertwined with the whole human race. He explained it in the following way:

Despite certain differences in degree, in methods and in "historical time," our situation is much like that of many other countries in Latin America, Africa and the Orient. We have freed ourselves from feudalism, military bosses and the Church, but our problems are essentially the same. They are immense problems, difficult to resolve. We are surrounded by many dangers, and also by many temptations, from "government by the bankers" (that is, the intermediaries) to Caesarism, along with nationalistic demagoguery and other spasmodic political forms. Our material resources are few and we have still not learned how to use them effectively. Our intellectual instruments are even poorer. We have done very little thinking on our own account; most of our ideas have been borrowed from the United States or Europe....

We have forgotten that many others are as isolated as ourselves. We Mexicans must acquire a new awareness of Latin America.... Our nationalism, to be more than a mental illness or self-adulation, must search the whole world. We must recognize that our alienation is not unique, that it is shared by a majority of the world's peoples.... For the first time in our history we are contemporaries of all mankind.*

Taking up this theme, many young Mexican painters abandoned the socialist-message mural tradition and looked abroad for inspiration. The result was a wave of paintings and exhibits representing abstract expressionist, non-objective, op art, pop art, and other Western world vogues. The inspired drawings of José Luis Cuevas, who had his first show in Washington, D.C., in 1957, were as popular in Paris or New York as Mexico City, and he won the International

*Octavio Paz, *The Labyrinth of Solitude; Life and Thought in Mexico*, trans. Lysander Kemp (New York: Grove Press, 1961), 192–94.

Museum of Modern Art, Mexico City.

Prize at the São Paulo Biennial. About the same time, Juan Soriano's painting titled *El Pez* (The Fish) won first prize in a Mexican exhibit, the first time a Mexican jury had awarded a prize to an abstract painting. A decade earlier Rufino Tamayo, whom one art critic labeled a "primitive modern" painter, had become internationally established as a major artist. Although his inspirations were Mexican, his paintings have a universal quality and appeal. In the 1960s a group of avant-garde artists founded a publication and exhibited together under the name *Nueva Presencia* (New Image). One of the most recent artists to achieve world recognition was Pedro Coronel, whose paintings vibrate with color and dynamic shapes.

The world acclaim accorded Mexican artists was also reflected in their home country. The new Museum of Modern Art—its building resembling a huge glass serpent—was opened

Undeveloped Mexico: thatched shacks near Oaxaca.

in Mexico City in 1964. Since then the number of museums and galleries in various cities has multiplied, art sales to wealthy Mexicans have soared, famous collectors have journeyed to Mexico on purchasing trips, and Mexican exhibits have traveled around the world. Examples from related fields show the scope of Mexico's cultural impact. Architect Pedro Ramírez Vásquez, who was project director for the stunning National Museum of Anthropology, also designed buildings in Africa, South America, and the United States; and the noted sculptor Federico Cannessi had commissions from Belgium, France, and India. Before 1950, virtually all of Mexico's statues portrayed national figures; since then, new monuments have been unveiled honoring foreigners: Salvador Allende, Simón Bolívar, Miguel Cervantes, Winston Churchill, Mahatma Gandhi, Abraham Lincoln, and Sun Yat-sen.

Developed Mexico: view of modern Mexico City.

Internationalism in the arts is just one aspect of Mexico's transformation during the last generation. Because it is larger in area and population than any Western European nation and because it has vast resources and potential, Mexico has long interested world bankers, industrialists, and investors. In the past three decades, these foreign interests have helped Mexicans transform their country from a rural, agricultural base to one that is now 65 percent urban, with a fifth of the working population employed in industry and a growing middle class that dominates business and government. Along the way the nation acquired a huge foreign debt that is a major current problem, but through international financial restructuring and domestic austerity measures, it appears that the debt can be managed.

Although Mexico's progress has been notable, especially when compared with her southern neighbors, the unequal distribution of wealth is strikingly apparent everywhere. Unlike the pyramidal structure of pre-Revolutionary society, where a very small elite at the top monopolized the principal sources of wealth and power, denying upward mobility to the bulk of the peasant population at the bottom, today's division is less rigid and more balanced numerically. Yet, one can see immediately two Mexicos: the world of the well-dressed versus the threadbare; fine houses in one section, shanties elsewhere; well-educated people and illiterates; those with good jobs or incomes alongside the jobless or underemployed. In sum, one group has benefitted from modernization; the other has not. This inequality is the most serious challenge facing Mexico today.

Demographic and Economic Tables

A-1. Population Statistics, 1520–1980

Year	Total population	Year	Total population
1520	25,200,000	1850	7,660,000
1532	16,800,000	1860	8,210,000
1548	6,300,000	1870	9,100,000
1570	3,380,000	1880	9,580,000
1595	1,375,000	1890	11,500,000
1605	1,075,000	1900	13,607,000
1646	1,713,000	1910	15,160,000
1742	2,477,000	1921	14,334,000
1793	3,800,000	1930	16,553,000
1800	4,500,000	1940	19,654,000
1810	6,122,000	1950	25,791,000
1820	6,204,000	1960	34,923,000
1830	6,382,000	1970	48,225,000
1840	7,016,000	1980	67,406,000

SOURCES: Since 1950, *Statistical Abstract of Latin America* and *UNESCO Statistical Yearbooks;* 1800–1950 in Mexico, Dirección General de Estadística, *Séptimo censo general de población, 1950,* p. 734; pre-1800, various printed estimates.

A-2. Rural-Urban Population Distribution, 1900–1980

Year	Percent rural	Percent urban
1900	80.0	20.0
1910	70.7	29.3
1920	75.0	25.0
1930	66.5	33.5
1940	65.0	35.0
1950	57.0	43.0
1960	49.3	50.7
1970	41.4	58.6
1980	34.0	66.0

SOURCES: *Statistical Abstract of Latin America; Mexico: Facts, Figures and Trends*, Mexico, 1968.

A-3. Literacy, 1810–1980

Year	Percent literate	Year	Percent literate
1810	5	1921	29
1850	6	1930	33
1860	7	1940	42
1880	10	1950	57
1895	17	1960	62
1900	18	1970	71
1910	23	1980	81

SOURCES: 1980, *UNESCO Statistical Yearbook, 1981;* 1895–1970, Mexican census reports; pre-1895, estimates.

A-4. Average Life Expectancy, 1930–1980

Year	Male	Female
1930	36.1	37.5
1940	40.4	42.5
1950	48.1	51.0
1960	57.6	60.3
1970	59.0	62.0
1980	63.5	66.5

SOURCES: American Universities Field Staff, *Fieldstaff Reports, North America Series*, vol. 2, no. 1 (July 1974), p. 16; 1980 estimated.

A-5. Landholdings by Size, 1960

	Under 5 hectares	% of total	5–100 hectares	% of total	100–1,000 hectares	% of total	Above 1,000 hectares	% of total
No.	899,108	65.9	365,015	26.0	87,438	6.4	22,600	1.7
Ha.	1,328,000	.8	9,523,000	5.6	25,774,000	15.2	132,540,000	78.4

SOURCE: *Statistical Abstract of Latin America* 21 (1981): 58.

A-6. Land Tenure Systems and Operators, 1960

	Owners	%	Renters	%	Collectives	%	Other	%
No.	1,289,979	94.5	36,759	2.4	18,699	1.4	6,003	1.7
Ha.	96,958,475	57.3	7,451,561	4.4	44,497,076	26.3	20,177,195	12.0

SOURCE: *Statistical Abstract of Latin America* 16 (1972): 219.

A-7. Production of Selected Crops, 1907–1980
(thousands of metric tons)

Year	Maize	Wheat	Dry Beans	Rice	Coffee	Cotton	Sugar cane
1907	1,088	312	63	33	50	34	1,885
1920	2,349	280	116	31	36	32	2,873
1930	1,377	370	83	75	49	38	3,293
1940	1,640	464	97	108	52	65	4,973
1950	3,122	587	250	187	66	260	9,419
1960	5,386	1,190	528	328	124	470	19,542
1970	8,997	2,047	811	367	440	398	32,550
1980	11,081	2,645	1,130	463	222	340	34,500

SOURCES: *The Europa Year Book,* 1982; *Statistical Abstract of Latin America;* United Nations, *FAO Production Yearbook;* Mexico, *Anuario estadístico,* various years.

A-8. Production of Iron and Steel (tons), 1906–1980

Year	Pig iron	Steel
1906	31,000	33,463
1910	55,000	67,944
1921	34,000	43,263
1930	107,000	102,859
1940	111,000	149,655
1950	286,000	332,631
1960	939,000	1,491,778
1970	3,450,000	3,881,201
1980	4,738,000 (1979)	7,300,000

SOURCES: *The Europa Year Book; Enciclopedia de México.*

A-9. Production of Non-Ferrous Metals (metric tons), 1900–1980

Year	Gold	Silver	Copper	Lead	Zinc
1900	13	1,766	22,500	63,800	1,100
1910	37	2,305	52,000	120,000	1,833
1920	22	2,069	49,192	82,518	15,651
1930	20	3,272	73,412	232,931	124,084
1940	27	2,570	37,602	196,253	114,955
1950	12	1,528	61,698	238,078	223,510
1960	9	1,385	60,330	190,670	262,425
1970	6	1,332	61,012	176,597	266,400
1980	6	1,477	174,008	145,620	236,050

SOURCES: *The Europa Year Book,* 1982; Banco Nacional de México, *Yearbook of Industrial Statistics.*

A-10. Production of Crude Oil, 1901–1980

Year	Cubic meters	Barrels
1901	1,643	10,334
1910	577,455	3,632,192
1920	24,971,173	157,068,678
1930	6,284,563	39,529,901
1940	7,066,485	44,448,191
1950	11,745,862	73,881,472
1960	17,292,779	108,771,583
1970	28,235,143	177,599,055
1980	112,709,375	708,942,000

SOURCES: U.S. Department of Energy, *International Energy Statistical Review; Anuario Estadístico de PEMEX; Enciclopedia de México.*

A-11. Principal Exports, 1980

Product	Value (millions U.S.$)	Percent of total
Petroleum & derivatives	10,305	67.3
Agricultural	1,424	9.3
Processed foods & beverages	773	5.0
Minerals	750	4.9
Machinery & equipment	524	3.4
Chemicals & petrochemicals	507	3.3
Automotive	425	2.8
Textiles & clothing	201	1.3
Wood & printed paper	144	1.0
Livestock	77	.5
Plastics & miscellaneous	73	.5
Steel	61	.4
Fish, game & honey	43	.3
Total	15,307	100.0

SOURCE: *Anuario Estadístico de los Estados Unidos Mexicanos,* 1980.

A-12. Principal Imports, 1980

Product	Value (millions U.S.$)	Percent of total
Machinery & Equipment	8,912	48.0
Steel & metals	2,209	11.9
Agricultural	1,871	10.1
Chemicals	1,485	8.0
Processed foods & beverages	1,175	6.3
Petrochemicals & derivatives	827	4.4
Wood & paper	705	3.8
Plastics, rubber & clay	412	2.2
Textiles & clothing	262	1.4
Minerals & petroleum	256	1.4
Unclassified	216	1.2
Livestock, fish & game	141	.8
Other manufactures	102	.5
Total	18,572	100.0

SOURCE: *Anuario Estadístico de los Estados Unidos Mexicanos,* 1980.

A-13. Tourism, 1930–1980

Year	Foreign Tourists	Expenditures (U.S.$)
1930	23,769	(not available)
1940	125,569	50,300,000
1950	384,297	232,784,000
1960	690,693	521,255,000
1970	1,984,307	1,333,000,000
1980	4,100,000	3,000,000,000

SOURCES: *Enciclopedia de México;* 1980 figures from *Wall Street Journal,* Sept. 8, 1981.

A-14. Rates of Exchange, Pesos to U.S. Dollars, 1821-84

Year	Pesos for $1	Dollar equivalent
1821	0.97	1.03
1850	0.96	1.04
1877	1.04	.96
1894	1.98	.51
1900	2.06	.49
1910	2.01	.50
1917	1.91	.52
1925	2.03	.49
1931	2.65	.38
1933	3.50	.29
1939	5.19	.19
1945	4.85	.21
1950	8.65	.12
1955	12.50	.08
1977	26.50	.04
1983	95.00 (preferential)	.01
1983	150.00 (floating)	.007
1984	195.00 (floating)	.005

SOURCES: *Anuario Estadístico de los Estados Unidos Mexicanos,* 1943, p. 934; since 1950, IMF, *International Financial Statistics Yearbook.*

Glossary

Acordada. A colonial tribunal and police force to combat banditry.
Adelantado. A frontier governor or leader of an expedition.
Alcabala. A sales or excise tax.
Alcalde. A mayor or municipal judge.
Alcalde mayor. The chief magistrate of a district.
Almojarifazgo. A colonial export and import tax.
Arroba. A measure of weight, about twenty-five pounds.
Asiento. A royal contract to import black slaves into the colonies.
Audiencia. An administrative-judicial court; a supreme court.
Auto de fe. A public ceremony of those condemned by the Inquisition.
Ayuntamiento. The city council or building where it meets. Cf. *cabildo.*
Bachiller. Holder of a bachelor's degree, the lowest academic degree.
Bracero. A field hand or farm worker.
Caballero. A mounted horseman, hence a Spanish knight or gentleman.
Cabecera. The head town of an Indian district.
Cabildo. A town council; alternate words: *ayuntamiento* or *regimiento.*
Cacique. An Indian chieftain or leader; a local or political boss.
Cálmecac. An Aztec school or seminary for children of dignitaries.
Calpixqui. An Aztec tax collector or overseer.
Calpulli. An Aztec territorial unit akin to a ward or clan.
Camino Real. The royal highway.
Campesino. A farm worker; one who lives in a rural area.
Carga. A load; Indian bearers carried two *arrobas,* or fifty pounds.
Casa de Contratación. The Spanish royal board of colonial trade.
Caudillo. A military chieftain, political leader, or dictator.
Cédula. A royal decree or order.
Cenote. A natural well in Yucatán.
Chacmool. A Toltec statue of a reclining figure with knees raised.
Chinampa. An artificial island, often called a "floating garden."
Científicos. A name applied to Positivist advisers of Porfirio Díaz.
Cimarrón. A runaway Negro slave, or a wild or fugitive animal.

Colegio. A secondary school or college preparatory facility.

Congregación. A concentration of Indian families into a town.

Consulado. A merchant's guild or "chamber of commerce."

Contador. An accountant, one of the royal treasury officials.

Continuismo. A prolonged extension of tenure in political office.

Corregidor. A royal officer who governed an Indian district.

Corrido. A ballad or folk song.

Cortes. Spain's parliament or congress.

Criollo. A person of European ancestry who was born in the New World.

Cristeros. Members of a fanatic armed Catholic movement in the 1920s.

Cruzada. A tax or offering originally levied to finance the Crusades.

Cuartelazo. A military revolt or barracks uprising.

Curandero. A folk medicine healer.

Diezmo. A tenth part or Church tithe.

Ejido. A communal or village landholding; a cooperative farm.

Encomendero. A Spaniard who was granted Indian tribute from an area.

Encomienda. An allotment of Indian tribute to principal conquistadors.

Entrada. An expedition or military campaign into hostile territory.

Estancia. A ranch or grazing rights for livestock.

Factor. A colonial royal disburser or treasury agent.

Fanega. A dry measure of 1.6 bushels or one hundred pounds.

Fiesta. A celebration of a public or religious holiday.

Fiscal. A crown or government prosecuting attorney.

Flota. The regular merchant fleet crossing between Cadiz and Veracruz.

Fraile (Fray). A friar or member of a mendicant religious order.

Fuero. The right of the clergy and army to be tried in their own courts.

Gachupín. A derogatory term applied to peninsular Spaniards.

Gente de razón. People of reason; colonial term for whites and *mestizos.*

Gremio. A craft guild for skilled artisans.

Gringo. A term, usually derogatory, applied to a foreigner.

Grito. A cry, especially the *Grito de Dolores* heralding independence.

Hacendado. An owner of an *hacienda* or large estate.

Hacienda. A large landed estate; also the government treasury.

Hidalgo. A nobleman; he was called *Don* and his womenfolk *Doña.*

Intendencia. An administrative department headed by an intendant.

Latifundio. A great rural estate, often with primitive agriculture.

Léparo. A beggar, renegade, or vagabond.

Ley fuga. Fugitive law; a pretext for shooting prisoners.

Licenciado. A licentiate, the academic degree ranking below doctor.

Macehual. An Aztec commoner or peasant.

Machismo. An exaggerated sense of virility or maleness.

Maguey. An *Agave* plant used for fiber and to obtain *pulque.*

Mayeque. An Aztec serf who tilled land belonging to clergy or nobles.

Mayorazco. An entail of property, usually to the eldest son.

Media anata. Payment of half of first year's salary by an appointee.

Mesada. A month's income paid by newly appointed Church officials.

Mestizo. A person of mixed ancestry, usually Spanish and Indian.

Milpa. A small plot of agricultural land; an Indian's cornfield.

Mordida. A "bite"; slang word for a bribe to an official.

Noche triste. The "Sad Night" when Cortés's men fled Tenochtitlán.

Obraje. A workshop or sweatshop, usually of textiles.

Oidor. A judge of the colonial *audiencia* court.

Patronato Real. Papal grants giving the crown some control over the church.

Pemex. Petróleos Mexicanos, the nationally-owned petroleum industry.

Peninsulares. Spaniards born in Spain, or the Iberian Peninsula.

Peones. Manual laborers or daily wage workers, especially farm workers.

Peso. A colonial silver coin; Mexico's monetary unit.

Pilli. An Aztec hereditary nobleman.

Plan. A manifesto or political program of a leader or group.

Pochteca. Aztec merchants or long distance traders.

Presidio. A garrison or fort, especially on the frontier.

Pronunciamiento. A declaration of revolt by a revolutionary leader.

Pueblo. A town or people; also a group of New Mexico Indians.

Pulque. A mildly alcoholic beverage made from *Agave* plants.

Puro. A member of the radical political faction, 1822–50.

Quinto. The royal "fifth," a tax on precious metals mined.

Reales. Spanish coins valued eight to a peso; "pieces of eight."

Real de minas. A colonial community.

Regidor. A member of the *cabildo* or town council.

Repartimiento. A levy of Indian paid labor for public projects.

Residencia. Review of an official's conduct at the end of his term.

Rurales. A rural police force created to suppress highwaymen and bandits.

Sacbeob. The causeways or artificial roads built by Maya Indians.

Telpóchcalli. An Aztec school for boys operated by each *calpulli.*

Teuctli. An Aztec knight or elite warrior.

Tezontle. A brown volcanic lava stone used for building.

Tienda de raya. A company store at a hacienda or industrial plant.

Tlacotli. An Aztec slave.

Tlalmaitl. An Aztec day laborer or farm worker.

Tlatoani. An Aztec sovereign or prince.

Tonalámatl. The Aztec almanac or book of fates.

Tortilla. A thin unleavened cake of cornmeal, the Mexican bread.

Uei tlatoani. The Aztec Chief Speaker or emperor.

UNAM. Acronym for the National University of Mexico.

Vaquero. A cowboy or herdsman.

Vecindad. A housing development, tenement, or neighborhood.

Visita. An official visit by a royal inspector, the *visitador.*

Xochiyaoyotl. Periodic wars arranged by the Aztecs with neighbors.

Zambo. An offspring of Negro and Indian parentage.

Zócalo. A marketplace; the central plaza of Mexico City.

Selected Bibliography

There is a vast literature on Mexico with historical works in many languages embracing subjects from anthropology to zoology. Because this book was written for undergraduate students and general readers, the list of recommended titles has been limited to books in English. Most of the books are readily available in college or public libraries.

Chapter 1. Early Indian Cultures

Anawalt, Patricia R. *Indian Clothing Before Cortés: Mesoamerican Costumes from the Codices.* Norman,, 1981.

Andrews, George F. *Maya Cities; Placemaking and Urbanization.* Norman, 1975.

Anton, Ferdinand. *Woman in Pre-Columbian America.* Translated by Marianne Herzfeld. New York, 1973.

Augur, Helen. *Zapotec.* New York, 1954.

Bernal, Ignacio. *The Olmec World.* Translated by Doris Heyden and Fernando Horcasitas. Berkeley, 1969.

Coe, Michael D. *America's First Civilization: Discovering the Olmecs.* New York, 1968.

———. *The Maya.* New York, 1956.

———. *Mexico.* 2nd. ed. New York, 1977.

Coe, Michael D., and Richard A. Diehl. *In the Land of the Olmec.* 2 vols. Austin, 1980.

Cornyn, John H., ed. and trans. *The Song of Quetzalcoatl.* Antioch, 1930.

Craine, Eugene R., and Reginald C. Reindorp, eds. *The Chronicles of Michoacán.* Norman, 1970.

Culbert, Patrick, ed. *The Classic Maya Collapse.* Albuquerque, 1972.

Davies, Nigel. *The Toltecs: Until the Fall of Tula.* Norman, 1977.

Diehl, Richard A. *Tula: The Toltec Capital of Ancient Mexico.* London and New York, 1983.

Gallenkamp, Charles. *Maya: The Riddle and Rediscovery of a Lost Civilization.* New York, 1976.

Hammond, Norman. *Ancient Maya Civilization.* New Brunswick, 1982.

Hardoy, Jorge. *Pre-Columbian Cities.* New York, 1973.

Henderson, John S. *The World of the Ancient Maya.* Ithaca, 1981.

Huddleston, Lee E. *Origins of the American Indians: European Concepts.* Austin, 1967.

Jennings, Jesse D., and Edward Norbeck, eds. *Prehistoric Man in the New World.* Chicago, 1964.

Katz, Friedrich. *The Ancient American Civilizations.* New York, 1974.

Landa, Diego de. *Landa's Relación de las cosas de Yucatán.* Edited and translated by Alfred M. Tozzer. Cambridge, Mass., 1941 (Peabody Museum Papers, vol. 18).

León-Portilla, Miguel. *Pre-Columbian Literatures of Mexico.* Translated by Grace Lobanov, and the author. Norman, 1969.

Meyer, Karl E. *Teotihuacán: First City in the Americas.* New York, 1973.

Millon, René. *Urbanization at Teotihuacán.* Austin, 1973.

Morley, Sylvanus G., and George W. Brainerd. *The Ancient Maya.* 4th ed. rev. by Robert J. Sharer. Stanford, 1983.

Paddock, John, ed. *Ancient Oaxaca: Discoveries in Mexican Archeology and History.* Stanford, 1966.

Peterson, Frederick A. *Ancient Mexico: An Introduction to the Pre-Hispanic Cultures.* New York, 1962.

Proskouriakoff, Tatiana A. *An Album of Maya Architecture.* Norman, 1963.

Ramírez Vásquez, Pedro, et al. *Mexico: The National Museum of Anthropology: Art, Architecture, Archaeology, Anthropology.* Translated by Mary Jean Labadie and Aza Zatz. Mexico, 1968.

Reed, Alma. *The Ancient Past of Mexico.* New York, [1966].

Robicsek, Francis, and Donald Hales. *The Maya Book of the Dead: The Ceramic Codex.* Norman, 1983.

Roys, Ralph L. *The Indian Background of Colonial Yucatán.* Norman, 1972.

Sanders, William T., and Barbara J. Price. *Mesoamerica: The Evolution of a Civilization.* New York, 1968.

Smith, Mary Elizabeth. *Picture Writing from Ancient Southern Mexico: Mixtec Place Signs and Maps.* Norman, 1973.

Soustelle, Jacques. *The Olmecs: The Oldest Civilization in Mexico.* Trans. R. Lane. New York, 1984.

Spores, Ronald. *The Mixtec Kings and their People.* Norman, 1967.

———. *The Mixtecs in Ancient and Colonial Times.* Norman, 1984.

Stierlin, Henri. *Art of the Maya: From the Olmecs to the Toltec-Maya.* Translated by Peter Graham. New York, 1981.

Thompson, J. Eric S. *Maya History and Religion.* Norman, 1970.

———. *The Rise and Fall of Maya Civilization.* 2nd ed. Norman, 1966.

Tompkins, Peter. *Mysteries of the Mexican Pyramids.* New York, 1976.

Von Hagen, Victor W. *World of the Maya.* New York, 1960.

Von Winning, Hasso. *Pre-Columbian Art of Mexico and Central America.* New York, 1978.

Wauchope, Robert. *The Indian Background of Latin American History: The Maya, Aztec, Inca and Their Predecessors.* New York, 1970.

Whitecotton, Joseph W. *The Zapotecs: Princes, Priests and Peasants.* Norman, 1977.

Wolf, Eric R. *Sons of the Shaking Earth: The People of Mexico and Guatemala—Their Land, History, and Culture.* Chicago, 1974.

Chapter 2. The Aztec Civilization

Barlow, Robert H. *The Extent of the Empire of the Culhua Mexica.* Berkeley, 1949 (Ibero-Americana, 28).

Bernal, Ignacio. *Mexico Before Cortez: Art, History and Legend.* Translated by Willis Barnstone. Garden City, 1975.

Borah, Woodrow, and Sherburne F. Cook. *The Aboriginal Population of Central Mexico on the Eve of the Spanish Conquest.* Berkeley, 1963 (Ibero-Americana, 45).

Brundage, Burr Cartwright. *The Fifth Sun: Aztec Gods, Aztec World.* Austin, 1979.

———. *The Phoenix of the Western World: Quetzalcoatl and the Sky Religion.* Norman, 1982.

———. *A Rain of Darts: The Mexica Aztecs.* Austin, 1972.

Carrasco, Davíd. *Quetzalcoatl and the Irony of Empire: Myth & Prophecies in the Aztec Tradition.* Chicago, 1982.

Caso, Alfonso. *The Aztecs: People of the Sun.* Translated by Lowell Dunham. Norman, 1958.

Davies, Nigel. *The Aztecs: A History.* Norman, 1980.

Durán, Diego. *The Aztecs: The History of the Indies of New Spain.* Translated by Doris Heyden and Fernando Horcasitas. New York, 1964.

———. *Book of the Gods and Rites and the Ancient Calendar.* Translated and edited by Fernando Horcasitas and Doris Heyden. Norman, 1971.

Gillmor, Frances. *Flute of the Smoking Mirror; A Portrait of Nezahual-coyotl.* Albuquerque, 1949.

———. *The King Danced in the Marketplace.* Tucson, 1964.

Keen, Benjamin. *The Aztec Image in Western Thought.* New Brunswick, 1971.

León-Portilla, Miguel. *Aztec Thought and Culture: A Study of the Ancient Nahuatl Mind.* Translated by Jack Emory Davis. Norman, 1963.

Sahagún, Bernardino de. *Florentine Codex: General History of the Things of New Spain.* Translated by Arthur J. O. Anderson and Charles E. Dibble. 13 vols. Salt Lake City, 1970–82.

Sejourné, Laurette. *Burning Water: Thought and Religion in Ancient Mexico.* Translated by Irene Nicholson. New York, 1960.

Soustelle, Jacques. *The Daily Life of the Aztecs on the Eve of the Spanish Conquest.* Translated by Patrick O'Brian. Stanford, 1970.

Stevenson, Robert M. *Music in Aztec and Inca Territory.* Berkeley, 1968.

Vaillant, George C. *Aztecs of Mexico: Origin, Rise and Fall of the Aztec Nation.* Rev. ed. Garden City, 1962.

Von Hagen, Victor W. *The Aztec: Man and Tribe.* New York, 1961.

Westheim, Paul. *The Sculpture of Ancient Mexico.* Garden City, 1963.

Zurita, Alonso de. *Life and Labor in Ancient Mexico: The Brief and Summary Relation of the Lords of New Spain.* Translated by Benjamin Keen. New Brunswick, 1963.

Chapter 3. The Spanish Conquest

Blacker, Irwin, and Harry M. Rosen, eds. *The Golden Conquistadores.* Indianapolis, 1960.

Cerwin, Herbert. *Bernal Díaz: Historian of the Conquest.* Norman, 1963.

Collis, Maurice. *Cortés and Montezuma.* London, 1954.

Cortés, Hernán. *Hernán Cortés: Letters from Mexico.* Edited and translated by A. R. Pagden. New York, 1971.

Díaz del Castillo, Bernal. *The Bernal Díaz Chronicles: The True Story of the Conquest of Mexico.* Translated and edited by Albert Idell. Garden City, 1956.

Elliot, John H. *Imperial Spain, 1469–1716.* New York, 1964.

Fuentes, Patricia de, ed. *The Conquistadors; First-Person Accounts of the Conquest of Mexico.* New York, 1963.

Gardiner, C. Harvey. *The Constant Captain: Gonzalo de Sandoval.* Carbondale, 1961.

———. *Martín López, Conquistador Citizen of Mexico.* Lexington, 1958.

———. *Naval Power in the Conquest of Mexico.* Austin, 1956.

Iglesia, Ramón. *Columbus, Cortés and Other Essays.* Translated and edited by Lesley B. Simpson. Berkeley, 1969.

Johnson, Harold B., ed. *From Reconquest to Empire: The Iberian Background to Latin American History.* New York, 1970.

Kelly, John E. *Pedro de Alvarado, Conquistador.* Princeton, 1932.

Kirkpatrick, F. A. *The Spanish Conquistadors.* New York, 1962.

León-Portilla, Miguel, ed. *The Broken Spears: The Aztec Account of the Conquest of Mexico.* Translated by Lysander Kemp. Boston, 1962.

López de Gómara, Francisco. *Cortés: The Life of the Conqueror by His Secretary.* Translated and edited by Lesley B. Simpson. Berkeley, 1964.

Lynch, John. *Spain under the Hapsburgs.* New York, 1964.

Madariaga, Salvador de. *Hernán Cortés: Conqueror of Mexico.* Coral Gables, 1967.

Padden, Robert. *The Hummingbird and the Hawk: Conquest and Sovereignty in the Valley of Mexico, 1503-1541.* Columbus, 1967.

Prescott, William H. *History of the Conquest of Mexico.* New York, 1967.

Wagner, Henry R. *The Rise of Fernando Cortés.* Los Angeles, 1944.

Warren, J. Benedict. *The Conquest of Michoacan; The Spanish Domination of the Tarascan Kingdom in Western Mexico, 1521-1530.* Norman, 1985.

White, Jon Manchip. *Cortés and the Downfall of the Aztec Empire.* New York, 1971.

Wilkes, John. *Hernán Cortés, Conquistador of Mexico.* Cambridge, UK, 1974.

Chapter 4. New Spain Established

Aiton, Arthur S. *Antonio de Mendoza: First Viceroy of New Spain.* Durham, 1927.

Bannon, John F. *The Spanish Borderlands Frontier, 1513-1821.* New York, 1970.

Barrett, Ward J. *The Sugar Hacienda of the Marqueses del Valle.* Minneapolis, 1970.

Benítez, Fernando. *The Century After Cortés.* Translated by Joan

MacLean. Chicago, 1965.

Blom, Frans F. *The Conquest of Yucatán.* Boston, 1936.

Bolton, Herbert E. *Coronado on the Turquoise Trail: Knight of Pueblos and Plains.* Albuquerque, 1949.

Borah, Woodrow. *Early Colonial Trade and Navigation between Mexico and Peru.* Berkeley, 1954 (Ibero-Americana, 38).

Borah, Woodrow, and Sherburne F. Cook. *The Population of Central Mexico in 1548; An Analysis of the Suma de Visitas de Pueblos.* Berkeley, 1960 (Ibero-Americana, 43).

Braden, Charles S. *Religious Aspects of the Conquest of Mexico.* Durham, 1930.

Brinckerhoff, Sidney B., and Odie B. Faulk. *Lancers for the King; A Study of the Frontier Military System of Northern New Spain.* Phoenix, 1965.

Chamberlain Robert S. *The Conquest and Colonization of Yucatán, 1517-1550.* Washington, 1948.

Chipman, Donald E. *Nuño de Guzmán and the Province of Pánuco in New Spain, 1518-1533.* Glendale, Calif., 1966.

Crosby, Alfred W., Jr. *The Columbian Exchange: Biological Consequence of 1492.* Westport, 1972.

Day, A. Grove. *Coronado's Quest.* Berkeley, 1940.

Gibson, Charles. *Tlaxcala in the Sixteenth Century.* New Haven, 1952.

Hallenbeck, Cleve. *Alvar Nuñez Cabeza de Vaca.* Glendale, Calif., 1940.

Hammond, George P., and Agapito Rey. *Don Juan de Oñate, Colonizer of New Mexico, 1595-1628.* 2 vols. Albuquerque, 1953.

——. Trans. and eds. *Narratives of the Coronado Expedition, 1540-1542.* Albuquerque, 1940.

Hanke, Lewis. *The Spanish Struggle for Justice in the Conquest of America.* Philadelphia, 1949.

Holmes, Maurice G. *From New Spain by Sea to the Californias, 1519-1668.* Glendale, Calif., 1963.

Kubler, George. *Mexican Architecture of the Sixteenth Century.* 2 vols. New Haven, 1948.

Leonard, Irving A. *Books of the Brave.* Cambridge, Mass., 1949.

Liss, Peggy K. *Mexico Under Spain, 1521-1556: Society and the Origins of Nationality.* Chicago, 1975.

McAndrew, John. *The Open-Air Churches of Sixteenth-Century Mexico.* Cambridge, Mass., 1965.

Mecham, J. Lloyd. *Francisco de Ibarra and Nueva Vizcaya.* Durham, 1927.

Parry, John H. *The Audiencia of New Galicia in the Sixteenth Cen-*

tury; A Study in Spanish Colonial Government. Cambridge, UK, 1948.

Powell, Philip W. *Soldiers, Indians & Silver; The Northward Advance of New Spain, 1550-1600.* Berkeley, 1952.

Ricard, Robert. *The Spiritual Conquest of Mexico.* Translated by Lesley B. Simpson. Berkeley, 1966.

Riley, G. Michael. *Fernando Cortés and the Marquesado in Morelos, 1522-1547.* Albuquerque, 1973.

Ruiz de Alarcón, Hernando. *Treatise on the Heathen Superstitions That Today Live Among the Indians Native to This New Spain, 1629.* Translated and edited by J. Richard Andrews and Ross Hassig. Norman, 1984.

Schurz, William L. *The Manila Galleon.* New York, 1939.

Simpson, Lesley B. *The Encomienda in New Spain.* Berkeley, 1950.

Wagner, Henry R. *Spanish Voyages to the Northwest Coast of America in the Sixteenth Century.* San Francisco, 1929.

Chapter 5. Colonial Institutions and Life

Altman, Ida, and James Lockhart, eds. *Provinces of Early Mexico: Variants of Spanish-American Regional Evolution.* Los Angeles, 1976.

Bacigalupo, Marvyn H. *A Changing Perspective: Attitudes Toward Creole Society in New Spain (1521-1610).* London, 1981.

Baird, Joseph A., Jr. *The Churches of Mexico, 1530-1810.* Berkeley, 1962.

Bakewell, Peter J. *Silver Mining and Society in Colonial Mexico: Zacatecas, 1546-1700.* Cambridge, UK, 1971.

Barth, Pius J. *Franciscan Education and the Social Order in Spanish North America (1502-1821).* Chicago, 1945.

Borah, Woodrow. *Silk Raising in Colonial Mexico.* Berkeley, 1943 (Ibero-Americana, 20).

———. *Justice by Insurance; The General Indian Court of Colonial Mexico and the Legal Aides of the Half Real.* Berkeley, 1983.

Brading, David A. *Haciendas and Ranchos in the Mexican Bajío: León, 1700-1860.* Cambridge, UK, 1978.

Cervantes de Salazar, Francisco. *Life in the Imperial and Loyal City of Mexico in New Spain and the Royal and Pontifical University of Mexico.* Translated by Minnie L. Shepard. Austin, 1953.

Chance, John K. *Race and Class in Colonial Oaxaca.* Stanford, 1978.

Chevalier, François. *Land and Society in Colonial Mexico: The Great Hacienda.* Translated by Alvin Eustis, edited by Lesley B. Simpson. Berkeley, 1963.

Cook, Sherburne F., and Woodrow Borah. *Essays in Population History; Mexico and the Caribbean.* Berkeley, 1971.

Cooper, Donald B. *Epidemic Disease in Mexico City, 1761-1813; An Administrative, Social, and Medical Study.* Austin, 1965.

Cruz, Sor Juana Inés de la. *A Woman of Genius; The Intellectual Autobiography of Sor Juana Inés de la Cruz.* Translated by Margaret Sayers Peden. Salisbury, Conn., 1982.

Dunne, Peter M. *Pioneer Jesuits in Northern Mexico.* Berkeley, 1944.

Dusenberry, William H. *The Mexican Mesta: The Administration of Ranching in Colonial Mexico.* Urbana, 1963.

Farriss, Nancy M. *Crown and Clergy in Colonial Mexico, 1759-1821; The Crisis of Ecclesiastical Privilege.* London, 1968.

Fisher, Lillian E. *Viceregal Administration in the Spanish-American Colonies.* Berkeley, 1926.

Flynn, Gerard. *Sor Juana Inés de la Cruz.* New York, 1971.

Friede, Juan, and Benjamin Keen, eds. *Bartolomé de Las Casas in History: Toward an Understanding of the Man and his Work.* DeKalb, Ill., 1971.

Gage, Thomas. *Thomas Gage's Travels in the New World.* Edited by J. Eric S. Thompson. Norman, 1958.

Gerhard, Peter. *Pirates on the West Coast of New Spain, 1575-1742.* Glendale, Calif., 1960.

Gibson, Charles. *The Aztecs Under Spanish Rule; A History of the Indians of the Valley of Mexico, 1519-1810.* Stanford, 1964.

———. *Spain in America.* New York, 1967.

———. *Tlaxcala in the Sixteenth Century.* New Haven, 1952.

Greenleaf, Richard E. *The Mexican Inquisition of the Sixteenth Century.* Albuquerque, 1969.

———. *Zumárraga and the Mexican Inquisition, 1536-1543.* Washington, 1961.

Hanke, Lewis. *Bartolomé de Las Casas: Bookman, Scholar, and Propagandist.* Philadelphia, 1952.

Haring, Clarence H. *The Spanish Empire in America.* New York, 1952.

———. *Trade and Navigation between Spain and the Indies in the Time of the Hapsburgs.* Cambridge, Mass., 1918.

Howard, David A. *The Royal Indian Hospital of Mexico City.* Tempe, 1980.

Hu-DeHart, Evelyn. *Missionaries, Miners and Indians; Spanish Contact with the Yaqui Nation of New Spain, 1533-1820.* Tucson, 1981.

Israel, Jonathan I. *Race, Class and Politics in Colonial Mexico, 1610-1670.* London, 1975.

Konrad, Herman W. *A Jesuit Hacienda in Colonial Mexico: Santa Lucía, 1576-1767.* Stanford, 1980.

Lafaye, Jacques. *Quetzalcoatl and Guadalupe; The Formation of Mexican National Consciousness, 1531-1813.* Translated by Benjamin Keen. Chicago, 1976.

Lanning, John T. *Academic Culture in the Spanish Colonies.* London, 1940.

——. *The University in the Kingdom of Guatemala.* Ithaca, 1955.

Leonard, Irving A. *Baroque Times in Old Mexico: Seventeenth Century Persons, Places, and Practices.* Ann Arbor, 1971.

——. *Don Carlos de Sigüenza y Góngora, a Mexican Savant of the Seventeenth Century.* Berkeley, 1929.

Liebman, Seymour B. *The Jews in New Spain: Faith, Flame, and the Inquisition.* Coral Gables, 1970.

Lockhart, James, and Enrique Otto, eds. *Letters and People of the Spanish Indies; The Sixteenth Century.* Cambridge, UK, 1976.

MacLachlan, Colin M. *Criminal Justice in Eighteenth Century Mexico; A Study of the Tribunal of the Acordada.* Berkeley, 1975.

MacLachlan, Colin, and Jaime Rodríguez O. *The Forging of the Cosmic Race: A Reinterpretation of Colonial Mexico.* Berkeley, 1980.

Morales, Francisco. *Ethnic and Social Background of the Franciscan Friars in Seventeenth Century Mexico.* Washington, 1973.

Mörner, Magnus. *Race Mixture in the History of Latin America.* Boston, 1967.

Mullen, Robert J. *Dominican Architecture in Sixteenth-Century Oaxaca.* Tempe, 1975.

Palmer, Colin A. *Slaves of the White God: Blacks in Mexico.* Cambridge, UK, 1976.

Phelan, John L. *The Millennial Kingdom of the Franciscans in the New World: A Study of the Writings of Gerónimo de Mendieta.* Berkeley, 1956.

Shiels, William E. *King and Church: The Rise and Fall of the Patronato Real.* Chicago, 1961.

Stevenson, Robert M. *Music in Mexico: A Historical Survey.* New York, 1971.

Taylor, William B. *Drinking, Homicide, and Rebellion in Colonial Mexican Villages.* Stanford, 1979.

——. *Landlord and Peasant in Colonial Oaxaca.* Stanford, 1972.

Toussaint, Manuel. *Colonial Art in Mexico.* Translated and edited by Elizabeth W. Weismann. Austin, 1967.

Van Young, Eric. *Hacienda and Market in Eighteenth-Century Mex-

ico: The Rural Economy of the Guadalajara Region, 1675-1820. Berkeley, 1981.

Vázquez de Espinosa, Antonio. *Compendium and Description of the West Indies.* Translated by Charles Upson Clark. Washington, 1942.

Wagner, Henry R., and Helen R. Parish. *The Life and Writings of Bartolomé de Las Casas.* Albuquerque, 1967.

Warren, Fintan B. [J. Benedict]. *Vasco de Quiroga and his Pueblo Hospitals of Santa Fé.* Washington, 1963.

Weismann, Elizabeth W. *Mexico in Sculpture, 1521-1821.* Cambridge, Mass., 1950.

West, Robert C. *The Mining Community in Northern New Spain: The Parral Mining District.* Berkeley, 1949 (Ibero-Americana, 30).

Chapter 6. Enlightenment and Independence

Anna, Timothy E. *The Fall of the Royal Government in Mexico City.* Lincoln, 1978.

Archer, Christon I. *The Army in Bourbon Mexico, 1760-1810.* Albuquerque, 1977.

Benson, Nettie Lee, ed. *Mexico and the Spanish Cortes, 1810-1822: Eight Essays.* Austin, 1966.

Bobb, Bernard E. *The Viceregency of Antonio María Bucareli in New Spain, 1771-1779.* Austin, 1962.

Bolton, Herbert E. *Anza's California Expeditions.* 5 vols. Berkeley, 1930.

Brading, David A. *Miners and Merchants in Bourbon Mexico, 1763-1810.* Cambridge, UK, 1971.

Caruso, John A. *The Liberators of Mexico.* New York, 1954.

Charlot, Jean. *Mexican Art and the Academy of San Carlos, 1785-1915.* Austin, 1962.

DeVolder, Arthur L. *Guadalupe Victoria: His Role in Mexican Independence.* Albuquerque, 1978.

Fireman, Janet R. *The Spanish Royal Corps of Engineers in the Western Borderlands: Instrument of Bourbon Reform, 1764-1815.* Glendale, Calif., 1977.

Fisher, Lillian E. *The Background of the Revolution for Mexican Independence.* Boston, 1934.

———. *The Intendant System in Spanish America.* Berkeley, 1929.

Flores Caballero, Romeo. *Counterrevolution: The Role of the Spaniards in the Independence of Mexico, 1804-1838.* Translated by Jaime E. Rodríguez O. Lincoln, 1974.

Floyd, Troy, ed. *The Bourbon Reforms and Spanish Civilization: Builders or Destroyers?* Boston, 1966.

Gálvez, Bernardo de. *Instructions for Governing the Interior Provinces of New Spain, 1786.* Translated and edited by Donald E. Worcester. Berkeley, 1951.

Hamill, Hugh M., Jr. *The Hidalgo Revolt: Prelude to Mexican Independence.* Gainesville, Fla., 1966.

Hamnett, Brian R. *Politics and Trade in Southern Mexico, 1750-1821.* Cambridge, UK, 1971.

Harris, Charles H., III. *A Mexican Family Empire: The Latifundio of the Sánchez Navarro, 1765-1867.* Austin, 1975.

Howe, Walter. *The Mining Guild of New Spain and Its Tribunal General, 1770-1821.* Cambridge, Mass., 1949.

Humboldt, Alexander von. *Political Essay on the Kingdom of New Spain.* Translated by John Black. 4 vols. London, 1811-22; several later editions.

Jones, Oakah L., Jr. *Los Paisanos: Spanish Settlers on the Northern Frontier of New Spain.* Norman, 1979.

Kinnaird, Lawrence, ed. *The Frontiers of New Spain: Nicolás de Lafora's Description, 1766-1768.* Berkeley, 1958.

Kicza, John E. *Colonial Entrepreneurs: Families and Business in Bourbon Mexico City.* Albuquerque, 1983.

Ladd, Doris M. *The Mexican Nobility at Independence, 1780-1826.* Austin, 1976.

Lieberman, Mark. *Hidalgo: Mexican Revolutionary.* New York, 1970.

Lindley, Richard B. *Haciendas and Economic Development: Guadalajara, Mexico at Independence.* Austin, 1983.

McAlister, Lyle N. *The "Fuero Militar" in New Spain, 1764-1800.* Gainesville, Fla., 1957.

Manfredini, James M. *The Political Role of the Count of Revillagigedo, Viceroy of New Spain, 1789-1794.* New Brunswick, 1949.

Mörner, Magnus, ed. *The Expulsion of the Jesuits from Latin America.* New York, 1965.

Motten, Clement G. *Mexican Silver and the Enlightenment.* Philadelphia, 1950.

Nunn, Charles F. *Foreign Immigrants in Early Bourbon Mexico, 1700-1760.* Cambridge, UK, 1979.

O'Crouley, Pedro Alonso. *A Description of the Kingdom of New Spain, 1774.* Translated and edited by Seán Galvin. San Francisco, 1972.

Priestly, Herbert I. *José de Gálvez, Visitor-General of New Spain,*

1765-1771. Berkeley, 1916.

Rippy, J. Fred. *Joel R. Poinsett, Versatile American.* Durham, 1935.

Robertson, William S. *Iturbide of Mexico.* Durham, 1952.

Ronan, Charles E. *Francisco Javier Clavigero, S.J. (1731-1787); Figure of the Mexican Enlightenment.* Chicago, 1977.

Rydjord, John. *Foreign Interest in the Independence of New Spain.* Durham, 1935.

Sprague, William F. *Vicente Guerrero, Mexican Liberator.* Chicago, 1939.

Thomas, Alfred B., tr. and ed. *Teodoro de Croix and the Northern Frontier of New Spain, 1776-1783.* Norman, 1941.

Timmons, Wilbert H. *Morelos: Priest, Soldier, Statesman of Mexico.* El Paso, 1963.

Chapter 7. First Empire and Early Republic

Barker, Eugene C. *Mexico and Texas, 1821-1835.* Dallas, 1928.

Bauer, K. Jack. *The Mexican War, 1846-1848.* New York, 1974.

———. *Surfboats and Horse Marines; U.S. Naval Operations in the Mexican War, 1846-48.* Annapolis, 1969.

Bill, Alfred H. *Rehearsal for Conflict: The War with Mexico, 1846-48.* New York, 1947.

Calderón de la Barca, Fanny. *Life in Mexico: The Letters of Fanny Calderón de la Barca.* Edited by Howard T. Fisher and Marion H. Fisher. Garden City, 1966.

Callcott, Wilfred H. *Church and State in Mexico, 1822-1857.* Durham, 1926.

———. *Santa Anna: The Story of an Enigma Who Once Was Mexico.* Norman, 1936.

Castañeda, Carlos E., ed. *The Mexican Side of the Texas Revolution.* Dallas, 1928.

Connor, Seymour V., and Odie B. Faulk. *North America Divided; The Mexican War, 1846-48.* New York, 1971.

Costeloe, Michael P. *Church and State in Independent Mexico: A Study of the Patronage Debate, 1821-1857.* London, 1978.

———. *Church Wealth in Mexico: A study of the 'Juzgado de Capellanias' in the Archbishopric of Mexico, 1800-1856.* Cambridge, UK, 1967.

Cotner, Thomas E. *The Military and Political Career of José Joaquín de Herrera, 1792-1854.* Austin, 1949.

Fuller, John D. *The Movement for the Acquisition of All Mexico, 1846-*

1848. Baltimore, 1936.

Garber, Paul N. *The Gadsden Treaty.* Philadelphia, 1923; reprinted Magnolia, 1959.

Hale, Charles A. *Mexican Liberalism in the Age of Mora, 1821-1853.* New Haven, 1968.

Hanighen, Frank C. *Santa Anna: The Napoleon of the West.* New York, 1934.

Harris, Charles H., III. *The Sánchez Navarros: A Socio-economic Study of a Coahuilan Latifundio, 1846-1853.* Chicago, 1964.

Jones, Oakah L., Jr. *Santa Anna.* New York, 1968.

McWhitney, Grady, and Sue McWhitney, eds. *To Mexico with Taylor and Scott, 1845-47.* Waltham, 1969.

Mayer, Brantz. *Mexico: Aztec, Spanish and Republican.* 2 vols. Hartford, 1852.

Peña, José Enrique de la. *With Santa Anna in Texas: A Personal Narrative of the Revolution.* Translated and edited by Carmen Perry. College Station, 1975.

Poinsett, Joel R. *Notes on Mexico Made in the Autumn of 1822.* Philadelphia, 1824.

Potash, Robert A. *Mexican Government and Industrial Development in the Early Republic: The Banco de Avío.* Amherst, 1983.

Price, Glenn W. *Origins of the War with Mexico: The Polk-Stockton Intrigue.* Austin, 1967.

Ramírez, José Fernando. *Mexico During the War with the United States.* Edited by Walter V. Scholes and translated by Elliot B. Scherr. Columbia, 1950.

Randall, Robert W. *Real del Monte: A British Mining Venture in Mexico.* Austin, 1972.

Reed, Nelson. *The Caste War of Yucatán.* Stanford, 1964.

Ruiz, Ramón E., ed. *The Mexican War: Was it Manifest Destiny?* New York, 1963.

Santa Anna, Antonio López de. *The Eagle: The Autobiography of Santa Anna.* Edited by Ann Fears Crawford; translated by Sam Guyler and Jaime Platón. Austin, 1967.

Singletary, Otis A. *The Mexican War.* Chicago, 1960.

Smith, George W., and Charles Judah, eds. *Chronicles of the Gringos: The U.S. Army in the Mexican War, 1846-48.* Albuquerque, 1968.

Smith, Justin H. *The War with Mexico.* 2 vols. New York, 1919; reprinted, Gloucester, 1963.

Stephens, John L. *Incidents of Travel in Central America, Chiapas, and Yucatan.* 2 vols. New York, 1841; reprinted, New Brunswick, 1949.

Thompson, Waddy. *Recollections of Mexico*. New York, 1846.
Ward, Henry G. *Mexico in 1827*. 2 vols. London, 1828.
Weber, David J. *The Mexican Frontier: The American Southwest Under Mexico, 1821-1846*. Albuquerque, 1982.
Weems, John E. *To Conquer Peace: The War Between the United States and Mexico*. Garden City, 1974.

Chapter 8. Juárez and Maximilian

Acuña, Rodolfo F. *Sonoran Strongman: Ignacio Pesqueira and his Times*. Tucson, 1974.
Barker, Nancy N. *Distaff Diplomacy: The Empress Eugénie and the Foreign Policy of the Second Empire*. Austin, 1967.
———. *French Experience in Mexico, 1821 to 1861: A History of Constant Misunderstanding*. Chapel Hill, 1979.
Bazant, Jan. *Alienation of Church Wealth: Social and Economic Aspects of the Liberal Revolution, 1856-1875*. Cambridge, UK, 1971.
Berry, Charles R. *The Reform in Oaxaca, 1856-1876: A Microhistory of the Liberal Revolution*. Lincoln, 1981.
Blumberg, Arnold. *The Diplomacy of the Mexican Empire, 1863-1867*. Philadelphia, 1971 (Transactions of the American Philosophical Society, 61, Part 8).
Cadenhead, Ivie E., Jr. *Benito Juárez*. New York, 1973.
———. *Jesús González Ortega and Mexican National Politics*. Ft. Worth, 1972.
Callcott, Wilfred H. *Liberalism in Mexico, 1857-1929*. Stanford, 1931; reprinted, Hamden, Conn., 1965.
Corti, Egon C. *Maximilian and Charlotte of Mexico*. Translated by Catherine A. Phillips. 2 vols. New York, 1929.
Dabbs, Jack A. *The French Army in Mexico, 1861-1867*. The Hague, 1962.
Evans, Albert S. *Our Sister Republic: A Gala Trip Through Tropical Mexico in 1869-70*. Hartford, 1870.
Hanna, Alfred J., and Kathryn A. Hanna. *Napoleon III and Mexico: Triumph Over Monarchy*. Chapel Hill, 1971.
Hyde, Harford M. *Mexican Empire: The History of Maximilian and Carlota of Mexico*. New York, 1946.
Johnson, Richard A. *The Mexican Revolution of Ayutla, 1854-1855*. Rock Island, 1939.
Knapp, Frank A. *The Life of Sebastián Lerdo de Tejada, 1823-1889*.

Austin, 1951.

Knowlton, Robert J. *Church Property and the Mexican Reform, 1856-1910.* DeKalb, Ill., 1976.

Miller, Robert R. *Arms Across the Border; United States Aid to Juárez of Mexico During the French Intervention.* Philadelphia, 1973 (Transactions of the American Philosophical Society, 63, Part 6).

Perry, Laurens B. *Juárez and Díaz: Machine Politics in Mexico.* DeKalb, Ill., 1977.

Roeder, Ralph. *Juárez and His Mexico.* 2 vols. New York, 1947.

Salm-Salm, Agnes [Princess Felix]. *Ten Years of My Life.* 2 vols. London, 1876.

Salm-Salm, Felix C. *My Diary in Mexico in 1867 Including the Last Days of the Emperor Maximilian.* 2 vols. London, 1868.

Scholes, Walter V. *Mexican Politics During the Juárez Regime, 1855-1872.* Columbia, 1969 (University of Missouri Studies, 30).

Sinkin, Richard N. *The Mexican Reform, 1855-1876; A Study in Liberal Nation Building.* Austin, 1979.

Smart, Charles A. *Viva Juárez!* Philadelphia, 1963.

Stevenson, Sara Y. *Maximilian in Mexico: A Woman's Reminiscences of the French Intervention, 1862-1867.* New York, 1899.

Turlington, Edgar W. *Mexico and Her Foreign Creditors.* New York, 1930.

Chapter 9. The Age of Porfirio Díaz

Anderson, Rodney D. *Outcasts in Their Own Land: Mexican Industrial Workers, 1906-1911.* DeKalb, Ill., 1976.

Arnold, Channing, and Frederick J. Frost. *The American Egypt: A Record of Travel in Yucatán.* New York, 1909.

Baerlein, Henry. *Mexico, The Land of Unrest: Being Chiefly an Account of What Produced the Outbreak of 1910.* Philadelphia, 1914.

Beals, Carleton. *Porfirio Díaz: Dictator of Mexico.* Philadelphia, 1932.

Bernstein, Marvin D. *The Mexican Mining Industry, 1890-1950.* Albany, 1965.

Coatsworth, John H. *Growth Against Development: The Economic Impact of Railroads in Porfirian Mexico.* DeKalb, Ill., 1981.

Cockcroft, James D. *Intellectual Precursors of the Mexican Revolution, 1900-1913.* Austin, 1968.

Coerver, Don M. *The Porfirian Interregnum: The Presidency of Manuel González of Mexico, 1880-1884.* Ft. Worth, 1979.

Cosío Villegas, Daniel. *The United States Versus Porfirio Díaz.* Translated by Nettie Lee Benson. Lincoln, 1963.

Creelman, James. *Díaz: Master of Mexico*. New York, 1916.

Davids, Jules. *American Political and Economic Penetration of Mexico, 1877-1920*. New York, 1976.

Flandrau, Charles M. *Viva Mexico!* New York, 1908; Urbana, 1964.

Gil, Carlos B., ed. *The Age of Porfirio Díaz: Selected Readings*. Albuquerque, 1977.

Godoy, José F. *Porfirio Díaz: President of Mexico*. New York, 1910.

Gregg, Robert D. *The Influence of Border Troubles on Relations Between the United States and Mexico, 1876-1910*. Baltimore, 1937.

Hannay, David. *Porfirio Díaz*. London, 1917; reprinted, Port Washington, 1970.

Hart, John M. *Anarchism and the Mexican Working Class, 1860-1931*. Austin, 1978.

Kroeber, Clifton B. *Man, Land, and Water: Mexico's Farmlands Irrigation Policies, 1885-1911*. Berkeley, 1984.

Perry, Laurens B. *Juárez and Díaz: Machine Politics in Mexico*. DeKalb, Ill., 1977.

Pletcher, David M. *Rails, Mines, and Progress: Seven American Promoters in Mexico, 1867-1911*. Ithaca, 1958.

Raat, William D. *Revoltosos! Mexico's Rebels in the United States, 1903-1923*. College Station, 1981.

Romero, Matías. *Mexico and the United States*. New York, 1898.

Timmons, Wilbert H., ed. *John F. Finerty Reports on Porfirian Mexico: 1879*. El Paso, 1975.

Tischendorf, Alfred. *Great Britain and Mexico in the Era of Porfirio Díaz*. Durham, 1961.

Turner, John K. *Barbarous Mexico*. Chicago, 1910; reprinted, Austin, 1969.

Tweedie, [Ethel B.] Mrs. Alec. *Mexico As I Saw It*. London, 1901.

Vanderwood, Paul J. *Disorder and Progress: Bandits, Police, and Mexican Development*. Lincoln, 1981.

Vaughan, Mary Kay. *The State, Education, and Social Class in Mexico, 1880-1928*. DeKalb, Ill., 1982.

Zea, Leopoldo. *Positivism in Mexico*. Translated by Josephine H. Schulte. Austin, 1974.

Chapter 10. The Great Revolution

Ashby, Joe C. *Organized Labor and the Mexican Revolution Under Lázaro Cárdenas*. Chapel Hill, 1967.

Atkin, Ronald. *Revolution! Mexico 1910-20.* New York, 1970.

Bailey, David C. *Viva Cristo Rey: The Cristero Rebellion and the Church-State Conflict in Mexico.* Austin, 1974.

Beezley, William H. *Insurgent Governor: Abraham González and the Mexican Revolution in Chihuahua.* Lincoln, 1973.

Blaisdell, Lowell L. *The Desert Revolution: Baja California, 1911.* Madison, 1962.

Brading, David, ed. *Caudillo and Peasant in the Mexican Revolution.* Cambridge, UK, 1980.

Brenner, Anita, and George Leighton. *The Wind that Swept Mexico; The History of the Mexican Revolution, 1910-1942.* Austin, 1971.

Charlot, Jean. *The Mexican Mural Renaissance, 1920-1925.* New Haven, 1962.

Clendenen, Clarence C. *The United States and Pancho Villa; A Study in Unconventional Diplomacy.* Ithaca, 1961.

Cline, Howard F. *The United States and Mexico.* New York, 1963.

Cumberland, Charles C. *Mexican Revolution: The Constitutionalist Years.* Austin, 1972.

———. *Mexican Revolution: Genesis under Madero.* Austin, 1952.

Dulles, John W. *Yesterday in Mexico: A Chronicle of the Revolution, 1919-1936.* Austin, 1961.

Fagen, Patricia W. *Exiles and Citizens: Spanish Republicans in Mexico.* Austin, 1973.

Gilderhus, Mark T. *Diplomacy and Revolution: U.S.-Mexican Relations Under Wilson and Carranza.* Tucson, 1977.

Grieb, Kenneth J. *The United States and Huerta.* Lincoln, 1969.

Gruening, Ernest H. *Mexico and Its Heritage.* New York, 1934.

Guzmán, Martín Luis. *Memoirs of Pancho Villa.* Translated by Virginia H. Taylor. Austin, 1965.

Haddox, John H. *Vasconcelos of Mexico.* Austin, 1967.

Hall, Linda B. *Alvaro Obregón: Power and Revolution in Mexico. 1911-1920.* College Station, 1981.

Helm, Mackinley. *Man of Fire: J. C. Orozco.* New York, 1953.

Henderson, Peter V. *Félix Díaz, the Porfirians, and the Mexican Revolution.* Lincoln, 1981.

Jacobs, Ian. *Ranchero Revolt: The Mexican Revolution in Guerrero.* Austin, 1983.

Johnson, William W. *Heroic Mexico; The Narrative History of a Twentieth-Century Revolution.* Garden City, 1968.

Katz, Friedrich. *The Secret War in Mexico: Europe the United States and the Mexican Revolution.* Chicago, 1981.

Lieuwen, Edwin. *Mexican Militarism: The Political Rise and Fall of the Revolutionary Army, 1910-1940.* Albuquerque, 1968.

Macías, Anna. *Against All Odds: The Feminist Movement in Mexico to 1940.* Westport, 1982.

Martínez, Oscar J., ed. *Fragments of the Mexican Revolution: Personal Accounts from the Border.* Albuquerque, 1983.

Mexico. *Mexico's Oil: A Compilation of Official Documents....* Mexico, 1940.

Meyer, Jean A. *The Cristero Rebellion: The Mexican People Between Church and State, 1926-1929.* Translated by Richard Southern. Cambridge, UK, 1976.

Meyer, Lorenzo. *Mexico and the United States in the Oil Controversy, 1917-1942.* Translated by Muriel Vasconcellos. Austin, 1977.

Meyer, Michael C. *Huerta: A Political Portrait.* Lincoln, 1972.

———. *Mexican Rebel: Pascual Orozco and the Mexican Revolution, 1910-1915.* Lincoln, 1967.

Millon, Robert P. *Vicente Lombardo Toledano; Mexican Marxist.* Chapel Hill, 1966.

Niemeyer, Eberhardt V., Jr. *Revolution at Querétaro; The Mexican Constitutional Convention of 1916-1917.* Austin, 1974.

Orozco, José Clemente. *José Clemente Orozco: An Autobiography.* Translated by Robert C. Stephenson. Austin, 1962.

Powell, T. G. *Mexico and the Spanish Civil War.* Albuquerque, 1980.

Quirk, Robert E. *An Affair of Honor: Woodrow Wilson and the Occupation of Veracruz.* New York, 1967.

———. *The Mexican Revolution and the Catholic Church, 1910-1929.* Bloomington, 1973.

———. *The Mexican Revolution, 1914-1915: The Convention of Aguascalientes.* Bloomington, 1960; reprinted, Westport, 1981.

Reed, Alma M. *The Mexican Muralists.* New York, 1960.

Richmond, Douglas W. *Venustiano Carranza's Nationalist Struggle, 1893-1920.* Lincoln, 1983.

Ross, Stanley R. *Francisco I. Madero: Apostle of Mexican Democracy.* New York, 1955.

Ruiz, Ramón E. *Mexico: The Challenge of Poverty and Illiteracy.* San Marino, 1963.

———. *The Great Rebellion: Mexico, 1905-1924.* New York, 1980.

———. *Labor and the Ambivalent Revolutionaries; Mexico, 1911-1923.* Baltimore, 1976.

Rutherford, John. *Mexican Society During the Revolution; A Literary Approach.* Oxford, 1971.

Salamini, Heather F. *Agrarian Radicalism in Veracruz, 1920-1938.* Lincoln, 1978.

Sherman, William L., and Richard E. Greenleaf. *Victoriano Huerta: A Reappraisal.* Mexico, 1960.

Simpson, Eyler N. *The Ejido: Mexico's Way Out.* Chapel Hill, 1937.

Smith, Robert F. *The United States and Revolutionary Nationalism in Mexico, 1916-1932.* Chicago, 1972.

Tannenbaum, Frank. *The Mexican Agrarian Revolution.* New York, 1929; reprinted, Hamden, 1968.

———. *Mexico: The Struggle for Peace and Bread.* New York, 1956.

Townsend, William C. *Lázaro Cárdenas: Mexican Democrat.* Ann Arbor, 1952; rev. ed. Waxhaw, S.C., 1979.

Tuck, Jim. *The Holy War in Los Altos: A Regional Analysis of Mexico's Cristero Rebellion.* Tucson, 1982.

Turner, Ethel Duffy. *Revolution in Baja California: Ricardo Flores Magon's High Noon.* Edited by Rey Davis. Detroit, 1981.

Weyl, Nathaniel, and Sylvia Weyl. *The Reconquest of Mexico: The Years of Lázaro Cárdenas.* New York, 1939.

Whetten, Nathan L. *Rural Mexico.* Chicago, 1948.

Wilkie, James W. *The Mexican Revolution: Federal Expenditure and Social Change since 1910.* Berkeley, 1967.

Wilkie, James W., and Albert L. Michaels, eds. *Revolution in Mexico: Years of Upheaval 1910-1940.* New York, 1969.

Wolfe, Bertram D. *The Fabulous Life of Diego Rivera.* New York, 1969.

Wolfskill, George, and Douglas W. Richmond, eds. *Essays on the Mexican Revolution: Revisionist Views of the Leaders.* Austin, 1980.

Womack, John, Jr. *Zapata and the Mexican Revolution.* New York, 1968.

Chapter 11. The Modern Era

Brandenburg, Frank. *The Making of Modern Mexico.* Englewood Cliffs, 1964.

Bullard, Fredda J. *Mexico's Natural Gas; The Beginning of an Industry.* Austin, 1968.

Call, Tomme C. *The Mexican Venture: From Political to Industrial Revolution in Mexico.* New York, 1953.

Castañeda, Jorge E. *Mexico and the United Nations.* New York, 1958.

Cetto, Max. *Modern Architecture in Mexico.* New York, 1961.

Cline, Howard F. *Mexico: Revolution to Evolution, 1940-1960.* New York, 1963.

Cole, William E. *Steel and Economic Growth in Mexico.* Austin, 1967.

Cole, William E., and Richard D. Sanders. *Growth and Change in Mexican Agriculture.* Knoxville, 1970.

Cornelius, Wayne A. *Politics and the Migrant Poor in Mexico City.* Stanford, 1975.

Goldman, Shifra M. *Contemporary Mexican Painting in a Time of Change.* Austin, 1981.

Goldwater, Robert J. *Rufino Tamayo.* New York, 1947.

González Casanova, Pablo. *Democracy in Mexico.* Translated by Danielle Salti. New York, 1970.

González y González, Luis. *San José de Gracia: Mexican Village in Transition.* Translated by John Upton. Austin, 1974.

Grayson, George W. *The Politics of Mexican Oil.* Pittsburgh, 1981.

Grindle, Merille S. *Bureaucrats, Politicians, and Peasants in Mexico; A Case Study in Public Policy.* Berkeley, 1977.

Hansen, Roger D. *The Politics of Mexican Development.* Baltimore, 1971.

Hellman, Judith A. *Mexico in Crisis.* New York, 1978.

Herrera-Sobek, María. *The Bracero Experience: Elitelore versus Folklore.* Los Angeles, 1979.

Hundley, Norris, Jr. *Dividing the Waters: A Century of Controversy between the United States and Mexico.* Berkeley, 1966.

Johnson, Kenneth F. *Mexican Democracy: A Critical View.* Boston, 1971.

King, Timothy. *Mexico: Industrialization and Trade Policies Since 1940.* New York, 1970.

Kirk, Betty. *Covering the Mexican Front: The Battle of Europe vs. America.* Norman, 1942.

Kneller, George F. *The Education of the Mexican Nation.* New York, 1951.

Ladman, Jerry, Deborah Baldwin, and Elihu Bergman, eds. *U.S.-Mexican Energy Relationships: Realities and Prospects.* Lexington, 1981.

Lamartine Yates, Paul. *Mexico's Agricultural Dilemma.* Tucson, 1981.

Langford, Walter M. *The Mexican Novel Comes of Age.* Notre Dame, 1971.

Lewis, Oscar. *The Children of Sánchez: Autobiography of a Mexican Family.* New York, 1961.

———. *Five Families: Mexican Case Studies in the Culture of Poverty.* New York, 1959.

———. *Pedro Martínez: A Mexican Peasant and His Family.* New York, 1967.

Levy, Daniel C. *University and Government in Mexico.* New York, 1980.

Liss, Sheldon B. *A Century of Disagreement: The Chamizal Conflict, 1864-1964.* Washington, 1965.

Mabry, Donald J. *The Mexican University and the State: Student Conflicts, 1910-1971.* College Station, 1982.

————. *Mexico's Acción Nacional; A Catholic Alternative to Revolution.* Syracuse, 1973.

Machado, Manuel A., Jr. *The North Mexican Cattle Industry, 1910-1975: Ideology, Conflict and Change.* College Station, 1981.

McWilliams, Carey. *North from Mexico: The Spanish-Speaking People of the United States.* New York, 1968.

Mancke, Richard B. *Mexican Oil and Natural Gas.* New York, 1979.

Marett, Robert. *Mexico.* New York, 1971.

Martínez, Oscar J. *Border Boom Town: Ciudad Juárez since 1848.* Austin, 1978.

Mora, Carl J. *Mexican Cinema: Reflections of a Society, 1896-1980.* Berkeley, 1982.

Morton, Ward M. *Woman Suffrage in Mexico.* Gainesville, 1962.

Mosk, Sanford A. *Industrial Revolution in Mexico.* Berkeley, 1950.

Myers, Charles N. *Education and National Development in Mexico.* Princeton, 1965.

Needler, Martin C. *Politics and Society in Mexico.* Albuquerque, 1971.

Nicholson, Irene. *The X in Mexico: Growth within Tradition.* Garden City, 1966.

Padgett, L. Vincent. *The Mexican Political System.* Boston, 1976.

Paz, Octavio. *The Labyrinth of Solitude: Life and Thought in Mexico.* Translated by Lysander Kemp. New York, 1961.

————. *The Other Mexico: Critique of the Pyramid.* Translated by Lysander Kemp. New York, 1972.

Pérez López, Enrique, et al. *Mexico's Recent Economic Growth: The Mexican View.* Translated by Marjory Urquidi. Austin, 1967.

Poleman, Thomas T. *The Papaloapan Project; Agricultural Development in the Mexican Tropics.* Stanford, 1964.

Powell, Jack R. *The Mexican Petroleum Industry, 1938-1950.* Berkeley, 1956.

Reynolds, Clark W. *The Mexican Economy: Twentieth-Century Structure and Growth.* New Haven, 1970.

Ross, Stanley R., ed. *Is the Mexican Revolution Dead?* 2nd. ed. Philadelphia, 1975.

Schmitt, Karl M. *Communism in Mexico: A Study in Political Frustration.* Austin, 1965.

Serrón, Luis A. *Scarcity, Exploitation, and Poverty; Malthus and Marx in Mexico.* Norman, 1980.

Singer, Morris. *Growth, Equality, and the Mexican Experience.* Austin, 1969.

Smith, Clive B. *Builders in the Sun: Five Mexican Architects.* New York, 1967.

Smith, Peter H. *Labyrinths of Power; Political Recruitment in Twentieth-Century Mexico.* Princeton, 1979.

Stevens, Evelyn P. *Protest and Response in Mexico.* Cambridge, Mass., 1974.

Venezian, Eduardo L., and William K. Gamble. *The Agricultural Development of Mexico: Its Structure and Growth Since 1950.* New York, 1969.

Vernon, Raymond. *The Dilemma of Mexico's Development; The Roles of the Private and Public Sectors,* Cambridge, Mass., 1963.

Von Sauer, Franz A. *The Alienated "Loyal" Opposition; Mexico's Partido Acción Nacional.* Albuquerque, 1974.

Index

Mexico: A History,

designed by Bill Cason, was set in various sizes of Baskerville by the University of Oklahoma Press and printed offset on 50-pound Glatfelter B-31, a permanized sheet, by Cushing-Malloy, Inc., with case binding by John H. Dekker & Sons.